Sheffield Football
A History
Volume II   1961–1995

Keith Farnsworth

SHEFFIELD FOOTBALL
A HISTORY

VOLUME II   1961–1995

The **Hallamshire** Press 1995

Cover: Chris Waddle and Brian Deane.
Background: Team pictures of Sheffield United from the mid-1970s and Sheffield Wednesday celebrating their Rumbelow's Cup victory in 1991;
also: Tony Currie, John Fantham, Terry Curran and Alan Woodward.

Text and Design © 1995 Interleaf Productions Limited

Published by the Hallamshire Press
The Hallamshire Press is an imprint of
Interleaf Productions Limited
Exchange Works
Sidney Street
Sheffield S1 3QF
England

Typeset by Interleaf Productions Limited
Printed by Saik Wah Press Pte. Ltd, Singapore

British Library Cataloguing in Publication Data
Farnsworth, Keith
   Sheffield Football: History. - Vol.2:
   1961–95
   I. Title
   796.3340942821

   ISBN 1-874718-14-8

Contents

This book is dedicated to my wife
Linda
without whom it would not have been possible

Introduction

IT IS DOUBTFUL whether any of the many projects I have tackled in recent times has given me more pleasure than Sheffield Football: A History—and writing this second volume has been particularly enjoyable and rewarding in that, as the period it covers, from the early 1960s to the mid-1990s, coincides almost exactly with my career as a journalist specialising in football, it has been as much an exercise in personal and professional nostalgia, as an attempt to record the highs and lows of an eventful thirty-five years on the local soccer scene.

History is not simply about statistics and facts, or dates and results, but about people, and when many of the figures featured are players, managers, administrators and others one has known (and some of them good friends), the test for the author is sticking to the essential details and remaining objective whilst also seeking to make the fullest use of the kind of background knowledge and memories which lend colour and, in some cases, significance to an episode. It is satisfying to have the opportunity to ensure that some individuals are remembered who might otherwise be forgotten, and to be able to include incidents and reflections which might not normally be placed on record, but which hopefully, will add to the reader's appreciation and enjoyment.

There have probably been more changes, not only in football but in society at large, in the last thirty-five years than in any comparable phase in the entire period covered by the one hundred and forty years of this history. This second volume starts at just about the time of the removal of the maximum wage in English football, the starting point of a revolution in the game. Many of those who were involved with the Sheffield clubs in the early 1960s could not have dreamed how different things would be by 1995; but of course, as always, sport simply mirrors society. Football has changed with the times and been influenced by remarkable developments in a wide range of fields which have re-shaped our way of life and brought new attitudes.

Most of us, as we get older and look back, tend to do so with a regret that some things have not remained as they were but, as human beings boast a remarkable talent for adapting to circumstances, there are few who don't take some pleasure in life as it is without dwelling for too long on how it was and wishing it were still as it used to be. We might not appreciate the modern tendency to tinker with the rules, and certainly some of us despair at the trend towards squad numbers (which you often cannot read) and kit patterns which resemble pyjamas (with deliberate disregard for such traditions as striped shirts, and all in the cause of commercial profit!); but we accept that, while some of it is

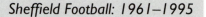

indeed, change for its own sake, there are other developments which have been inevitable and have had to come in the name of progress and survival. Certainly clubs can no longer keep going on football income alone. Someone has to pay the huge wages that even ordinary players can now command!

The merit of a detailed football history is not just in recalling matches and heroes from the past (though that in itself is invariably interesting and worthwhile), but in revealing the pattern of those key events which have created present circumstances and problems. You wonder about the turning points in the fortunes of a club: if other decisions had been made at certain moments, how different might the situation have been in late 1995?

I said that writing this book evoked many personal memories, and I remember with affection such a lot of football people who not only made important contributions to the game in Sheffield, but were generous in their dealings with the local sports writers. What a pleasure it was to work with men like Eric Taylor and John Harris, and to know such players as Joe Shaw, Don Megson, Cec Coldwell and Johnny Quinn—not just good professionals but gentlemen and good pals. In those days when it was the custom for the local writers to travel with both Wednesday and United, how good it was to spend so many hours in the company of the Blades and Owls players of the 1960s and early 1970s. To join in a quiz organised by Messrs Addison and Carlin, to share in a joke with Alan Birchenall and Len Badger, or to get involved in a debate with Messrs

Mobley, Ford and Eustace, and share a confidence with Messrs Whitham, Branfoot and Ellis was, to say the least, illuminating. To laugh along with Harold Blacow Yates (recalling how he fell in love), to spend a journey arguing with 'Dick' Wragg (about the merits of cricket at Bramall Lane!), to be invited to have a gin and tonic and participate in a wit-sharpening exercise with Eric Taylor, and to listen to the unique reminiscences of Danny Williams: ah, it was wonderful to be a part of that world.

Such fond memories, too, of matches: of delighting in the skills of Tony Currie or Alan Woodward, or the goals of Johnny Fantham; to savour the oft-unsung merits of Gerry Young or Billy Dearden; to attend post-match get-togethers and listen to the wisdom and wit of Jack Charlton, Ron Atkinson or Dave Bassett. To enjoy the friendships of people like Derek Dooley and Howard Wilkinson, and even to come to earn the respect of men with whom one didn't always see eye-to-eye, like Ken Furphy and Len Ashurst. Yes, they've been good days.

Every generation will feel its own time is the best, and as this volume has served to remind me, I have no regrets about having been around in this period of history. One might wish some of the technology which has made life easier in recent times had been available sooner, especially it would be wonderful to have had the benefits of videos of some of the matches and players of earlier years; but, whatever we may have lacked that young people of today take for granted, I wouldn't have had it any different. That is not to suggest I don't wish I were just starting out on the adventure all over again, but those beginning now will never know what fun it was twenty or thirty years ago!

If I have a regret, it is that I didn't have a better education and an earlier start in journalism, for I might have achieved so much more. Yet, all things considered, I never cease to wonder at the miracle of how the kid from the backstreets of Sheffield's East End had the opportunity to write for the old *Morning Telegraph* and, more recently, the *Daily* and *Sunday Telegraph*, and to produce a dozen or so books, despite never having gone to grammar school and being largely self-taught. My university was the editorial department of Sheffield Newspapers, when I finally got there, and my tutors were older colleagues to whom I shall forever be indebted.

Of course, the media world has changed, I hear some former colleagues suggest the job is not the fun it once was and say I'm lucky not to be a staff man in modern times. Modern technology has led to closures, staff reductions, cutbacks in spending, old pals complain there's too much to do and too little time in which to do it.

Yet there are times when I envy them their security. Since the emergence of local radio, sports journalism, especially football coverage, has been increasingly invaded by outsiders and non-professionals, it all adds up to fierce competition for the freelance, and getting work is not only about ability. However, as in other areas, it is just part of the change in attitude and philosophy that one has to learn to live with. You can only hope that merit will equate with success. Somehow we manage to survive.

So it is good to have had this opportunity to make use of knowledge and experience gained over the years, and to feel that perhaps one has made a useful contribution to the literature of the game in Sheffield, producing something which will give pleasure to supporters of all ages, enlightenment to the younger generation—and prove of value to people in football and the local media.

The list of contents highlights the main phases covered in this volume, and I hope I have been fair to those involved. The book also includes notes which feature useful statistics and match details, and it will be of interest to followers of junior football that results of some lesser competitions have been included.

Keith Farnsworth

Sheffield Football 1961-1970: A Summary

THE DECADE which has passed into social history as 'the swinging sixties' followed a familiar pattern on the Sheffield football scene in that it began with the promise of a long-awaited boom but ended in gloom. In 1960-61 Wednesday were runners-up in the League Championship and United finally climbed back to the First Division. Predictions that bright days had come to stay seemed justified in 1961-62 when both clubs finished in the top six—their highest placings as a pair for nearly sixty years. Few supporters then (perhaps other than those only too familiar with tradition) would have anticipated that Sheffield would have two Second Division clubs by the end of the 1969-70 season.

In fact, the decade saw United and Wednesday spend seven years as First Division rivals—their longest spell together in the top-grade since the 1930s and still the best sequence of the post-war era. United however, after consolidating well following promotion, suffered a sudden and unexpected slump and fell into the relegation trap in 1968; while Wednesday, having scrambled clear on that occasion, showed a similar tendency towards self-destruction when tumbling out of Division One in 1970.

Wednesday, especially, had high hopes of the 1960s, all the more so after the success of 1960-61. The loss of manager Harry Catterick to Everton in the spring of 1961 was a setback which they felt sure they would overcome. The outlook was bright, as new boss Vic Buckingham's first term in charge coincided with the Owls' European debut, which they marked by reaching the Inter-Cities Fairs Cup quarter-finals; but, finishing sixth in each of his three seasons at the helm fell somewhat short of expectations and Buckingham's contract was not renewed in the spring of 1964.

So Alan W. Brown, a former Hillsborough coach, rejoined the club from Sunderland. He arrived at a low point in the Owls' modern history, for, ironically on the weekend after Buckingham's departure, the shattering news broke that three Wednesday players had been named in allegations of involvement in a betting coup and bribes scandal which eventually led to ten professional footballers going to prison and being banned from the game. Of the Owls trio, Peter Swan and David Layne were still at the club, while Tony Kay had moved to Everton. Wednesday, of course, were the innocent victims and, as well as losing an England defender and an outstanding striker, suffered a damaging blow to their reputation.

Brown restored Wednesday's pride by guiding them to the FA Cup final in 1966, when it so happened that their Wembley opponents were Harry Catterick's Everton. The real irony was however, that the Owls lost 3-2 after leading 2-0 early in the second half, succumbing as Everton staged a dramatic recovery which made this one of the most memorable finals of modern times. Despite defeat, Wednesday were afforded a tremendous welcome on their return to Sheffield the following day. It was a homecoming which could not have been more enthusiastic had the Owls brought the Cup with them, but then it was twenty-nine years since Wednesday's last brush with glory, and many supporters wanted to believe that here was a team on the brink of sustained success. There may have been good reason for high hopes, with the emergence of such youngsters as Smith, Eustace, McCalliog and Pugh, but sadly, the promise went unfulfilled. Wednesday had paid a £37,500 record fee for a teenager in signing McCalliog from Chelsea; and, six months after Wembley, Brown broke the club's transfer record, paying £70,000 for John Ritchie from Stoke, but these investments did not prove enough.

Perhaps the best barometer of Wednesday's potential was League form: 17th place in the table put the Wembley run in a more realistic context. True, they often touched an exciting peak in the following term and, as well as making the last eight in the FA Cup, climbed into mid-table; but in 1967-68, despite claiming top spot in the early weeks, they slipped to 19th and ended up with only 2 points more than relegated Sheffield United. The Owls won only 2 of 22 League games from late December to the end of the season, and during that run, in February 1968, Alan Brown walked out and went back to Sunderland.

Wednesday's decline seemed to gather pace after Brown's sudden departure. Coach Jack Marshall stepped up but remained in charge for barely twelve months. His successor, Danny Williams, who had enjoyed notable success with Swindon, had the misfortune to take Wednesday down at the end of his first season as manager. Many have speculated on whether the pattern of events would have been different had Brown stayed, but more have pondered on what might have happened had general manager Eric Taylor not been seriously injured in a car crash barely a month before the start of the 1967-68 campaign. It is also interesting to note that Marshall's appointment on a one-year contract was confirmed just after Taylor had returned to duty following a period of convalescence in the West Indies. Taylor exerted considerable influence for many years, and indeed, it was often suggested he had too much power, but there is not much doubt that he was never the same after the accident in which he only narrowly escaped death.

The Sixties saw extensive ground improvements at Hillsborough. Buckingham's first home game as manager in August 1961 coincided with the formal opening of the new North Stand, and with Wednesday chosen to host some World Cup matches in 1966, a new West Stand was built at the Leppings Lane end, and seats were installed on the South Stand terracing in time for the event. Taylor's dream of making Hillsborough a venue fit for the best came true, but he was never to see the Owls boast a team to match the splendour of the setting. They had their

Hillsborough in 1961 after completion of the new North Stand. A few years later the Leppings Lane end was redeveloped and a West Stand built as part of further ground improvements ahead of the 1966 World Cup matches.

moments, and it would be wrong to suggest they did not provide some triumphs to treasure; but it didn't happen often enough, and the tragedy for Eric Taylor, as we shall see in discussing the 1970s, was that the last years of his life (he died in 1974) were among the gloomiest in Wednesday's history.

United's aspirations had, traditionally, always been more modest, but there was growing evidence of greater ambitions in the second half of the Sixties—though ironically, it was just when they were seeking to change their image and reach for higher goals that they suffered relegation. Indeed, the fall of 1968 probably did more to fire their determination to succeed than any other experience in the entire decade. That was also the point at which the eventual removal of cricket and the conversion of Bramall Lane into a four-sided football ground

became more certain than ever, even though the formal decision was not taken until 1971 and Yorkshire CCC played on until 1973.

United followed promotion in 1961 by finishing fifth in 1962, when they also reached the last eight of both the League Cup and FA Cup competitions. They never did quite so well again in the following years, but they only finished in the bottom half of the table twice in the next five seasons. John Harris was hailed as one of the best managers in the game for the way he kept the Blades in a respectable position in the top-grade despite limited resources—all the more so considering the effect the removal of the maximum wage in 1961 was having on the game. It was always going to be a struggle for clubs like United to keep up with wealthier rivals, and that they did so was a credit to a manager whose ability to spot a bargain was summed up in the journalistic description of him as a man who shopped at Woolworth's rather than Harrod's.

The secret of United's ability to survive was in Harris's talent for astute buys, with the acquisition of Gil Reece from Newport for £10,000 and Tony Currie from Watford for £26,500, two notable examples among many; and also in the success of the club's youth scheme. It was, perhaps, significant that the Blades won the Northern Intermediate League Cup in 1962 and followed up with a League triumph in 1963 and a League and Cup double in 1964. Products of the NIL side included Mick Jones, Len Badger, Alan Birchenall, Alan Woodward, the Wagstaff brothers and Ken Mallender. In April 1967 United actually turned out a First Division side comprising ten players who had graduated from the juniors.

In the final analysis, the success of the club's youth policy was not considered sufficient to enable the Blades to compete on equal terms in the top-grade. The departure from the side of so many experienced campaigners, epitomised in the gradual break up of that famous back-six of Hodgkinson, Coldwell, Graham Shaw, Richardson, Joe Shaw and Summers, and the loss of key figures left gaps which were never completely filled—though, in many respects, the margin between success and failure was often very narrow. Moreover, it has to be said that when one looks for explanations of why things suddenly went wrong for United in 1968, it is impossible not to wonder how different the story might have been had John Harris not lost his pal Archie Clark. The death of chief scout Clark

in January 1967 was one of the most significant events in this phase of United's history. He was one of the game's great characters, an extrovert whose apparently happy-go-lucky manner (he always answered the telephone at Bramall Lane with the words 'Best club in England!') was misleading, for there was not a harder taskmaster nor a more determined man. The fact that he was so intensely loyal to Harris, even though the Scot had beaten him to the manager's job, spoke volumes for his character and nobody was better at handling young players or at sorting out awkward older ones. He was too, the ideal man to have around in a crisis. Harris was far from being alone in regretting Clark's passing: many noted that some of the laughter was missing

United's Alan Birchenall (10) and Wednesday's Gerry Young in an aeriel duel in a Hillsborough derby match in the mid-1960s.

behind the scenes for a long time. Clark was a great competitor, but he had always had that knack of never seeming to take life too seriously, he could always lighten the load.

In 1962-63 United finished tenth, but while they had an early spell on top of the table in 1963-64, they ended up in 12th place. A dismal run of results in the later stages of the 1964-65 campaign saw them slip to 19th, though in fact it was not a position which reflected their merits. In the next two seasons they were ninth and tenth and their unexpected fall in 1968, was the consequence of an incredible decline in form, notably at home, in the last two months of a season in which they had seemed quite capable of getting out of trouble, until a home defeat against Fulham in late April set the alarm bells ringing. However, United actually won only one of their last 9 matches at Bramall Lane, and didn't win at home again after the 3-2 victory over Tottenham when Tony Currie marked his First Division debut with a headed goal.

That 1967-68 campaign was probably the most significant of the Sixties for United, in that it coincided with a dramatic change in emphasis and policy, though initially, the development was not entirely inspired by concern for team matters. In January 1966 work began on the erection at the Bramall Lane end of a new stand, which was brought into use the following October. It was the pressure to maintain the payments on this which prompted the decisions to sell Mick Jones to Leeds and Alan Birchenall to Chelsea for £100,000 each.

Jones went in September 1967 and Birchenall in November 1967, and it will serve as a reminder of financial levels then to note that United became the first club to collect two six-figure fees. However, three days before the sale of Jones, the Blades paid £40,000 to Carlisle for Willie Carlin, a pint-sized midfielder who had played nearly 200 League games with Halifax and Carlisle after starting his career at Liverpool. It was the most they had ever spent on one player, Football Section chairman Dick Wragg said it signalled a change of policy at Bramall Lane: they would buy and sell, and not depend so much on home-grown talent in future. Even so, the decision to sell Jones, a great favourite with the fans, provoked great controversy and almost prompted John Harris to resign. There was probably never a time when he missed Archie Clark more, and it was probably significant that he invited Andy Beattie, a fellow Scot and a managerial veteran known as football's 'flying doctor', to join him. The partnership did not last long, but in this spell Harris went out and spent another £40,000 on the Arsenal forward Colin Addison, who had scored 98 goals in some 280 games with York, Nottingham Forest and the Gunners, but then, on the following day, Birchenall was sold. There were other deals in and out, but the most notable capture was Tony Currie, the teenager from Watford, whose arrival at the end of January was instantly recognised as among the most astute Harris had made in his entire career. It was a contrast with the £30,000 deal completed by Beattie for Wolves winger Paddy Buckley around the same time —the Scot played only 15 League games for United after making 29 appearances for Wolves in four years.

Blades' chairman Harold Blacow Yates.

After United's fall into the Second Division, Wragg persuaded Harris to 'move upstairs' to become general manager, and Arthur Rowley, who boasted a League record haul of 434 goals with West Brom, Fulham, Leicester and Shrewsbury, was named as the new team-boss. A development which had more significant impli-cations came in August 1968 when Harold Blacow Yates, who had been a director for thirty-nine years and club chairman since October 1960, announced his retirement. Yates was

something of a character, a surgeon and a distinguished man of ready wit but great wisdom. He was another friend whose departure was a blow to Harris, and his common-sense and steadying influence was missed in the club's boardroom. Moreover, his death in November 1969 meant he did not live to see the Blades return to the top-grade (though he would not have been surprised that this didn't happen until Harris returned to team-management). Wragg was chosen to succeed Blacow Yates, and the new chairman's first important act was to persuade his fellow directors to sanction the amalgamation of the separate cricket and football committees. It was a step which marked the beginning of the end for cricket, though Wragg knew his plans to turn Bramall Lane into a four-sided soccer ground would have to wait until United were back in the top grade.

Any hopes they might have had of an immediate return in Rowley's first season, were dashed by a dismal away record which saw them register only 2 wins and suffer 12 defeats on their travels. They finished in ninth place, and Rowley was criticised for having sold Carlin to Derby for £60,000 early in the campaign—criticism all the more severe considering Derby won the Second Division title that season under the management of a certain Brian Clough. The sale of Carlin, plus Ken Mallender and David Munks, enabled Rowley to invest around £130,000 in Ted Hemsley, David Powell, John Tudor, Eddie Colquhoun and Graeme Crawford. It is relevant to note that the record £65,000 paid to Coventry for John Tudor was only just short of the £70,000 Wednesday paid for John Ritchie (Stoke). However, in 1969 Wednesday became the first Sheffield club to pay £100,000 for a player when they signed teenager Tommy Craig from Aberdeen—a purchase made while they were without a manager.

Rowley did not survive to lead a second promotion bid, for remarkably, United dismissed him three days before the start of the 1969-70 campaign. The reasons were never explained, but his enthusiasm for horse-racing did not endear him to certain people of influence. When he took the players on a pre-season tour to Holland and Germany, it happened to coincide with a pay dispute involving the players, and while they were abroad John Harris and Dick Wragg flew out to discuss the problem. On the evening of their arrival, Rowley took his men to a race meeting at Hilversum. The general manager and chairman were not impressed. However, it is impossible to say whether this had any influence on the board's subsequent decision to relieve Rowley of his duties.

With Harris back at the helm in that 1969-70 campaign, United collected 49 points, 6 more than in the previous season, and finished sixth. Their record of home and away wins improved, but they still lost 12 times on their travels and that was why they failed to match Huddersfield and Blackpool in the promotion race.

Alan Hodgkinson, United's long-serving goalkeeper.

With Wednesday losing their final game, and with it their top-grade status, it meant the Sheffield clubs began the first full campaign of the 1970s in Division Two.

It will be of interest to note that United's Alan Hodgkinson (406) and Wednesday's Don Megson (374) clocked up the most League appearances for the Sheffield clubs in the 1960s, while John Fantham (125) of the Owls and Derek Pace (90) of the Blades claimed the most League goals. Pace's record is all the more remarkable when you note that he left the club in December 1964.

Sheffield United 1961-62.

Back row: John Brewster, Barry Wagstaff, Mick Jones, Bob Widdowson, Reg Matthewson, Tony Wagstaff, Harry Orr, Dennis Shiels, Billy Hodgson, Des Thompson, Tommy Hoyland, Roy Ridge, Ken Mallender:

Middle row: Barry Hartle, Jack Parks, Len Badger, Clark, Michael Ash, Brian Richardson, Gerry Summers, Alan Hodgkinson, Keith Ketleborough, Cliff Mason, Bob Rooney, Graham Shaw.

Front row: Lee, John Docherty, Gray, Len Allchurch, Billy Russell, Cec Coldwell, Joe Shaw, Derek Pace, Ronnie Simpson.

United, 1961–1967

IF UNITED'S PRIORITY following promotion in 1961 was to consolidate their top-grade status, they made an excellent job of it by finishing fifth in their first season back in Division One—one place and a single point above Wednesday. In fact, but for a disappointing conclusion to their League programme, when they managed only two victories in the final seven games, they might easily have ended the campaign in the top three. It was a rewarding term for the promoted clubs, with Ipswich, who had pipped the Blades to the Second Division title a year earlier, lifting the Championship with 56 points.

Ahead of their return to the First Division, the only major change came with the appointment of a new coach. Shortly before the end of the previous season, George Smith had left to become manager of Portsmouth, and John Harris recruited John Short, the former Leeds United and Millwall wing-half. Short, then aged forty, had turned to coaching late in a long playing career at The Den, he spent a year at Huddersfield before moving to Bramall Lane. A product of Gateshead, he was to remain with the Blades throughout the Harris era and was one of the manager's most loyal and dependable lieutenants.

After starting the season with a home win over Wolves, United endured a testing September in which they crashed 6-1 at Chelsea and lost 4-1 when West Ham came to

Sheffield. They fell to next-to-bottom of the table, and it was not until early December that they launched a 16-match unbeaten run which transformed their fortunes and, as well as pushing them up the table, took them to the quarter-finals of both the FA Cup and League Cup. Alas, the bubble burst in March, when they won only one and lost four out of seven games. Ipswich ended United's unbeaten run and home defeats against Burnley and Blackpool dashed their dreams of a taste of cup glory on two fronts.

The FA Cup sixth-round tie with Burnley, who at the time were in with a chance of a League and Cup double, started to go wrong for the Blades within two minutes of the kick-off, for wing-half Gerry Summers was injured and spent the rest of the game a passenger—the visitors snatched victory with a Ray Pointer header after 57 minutes. United did not get revenge until seven weeks later when the teams met in a League game and goals from Billy Hodgson and Ron Simpson (penalty) sealed a 2-0 home victory which punctured the Lancashire side's Championship challenge.

In the meantime however, Blackpool—then a First Division side—had dumped the Blades out of the League Cup in a quarter-final replay, in which United's domination counted for nothing when they failed to score, and Parry and Charnley found the net for the Seasiders. The League Cup was then in its infancy, with no European incentive or even the prospect of a trip to Wembley. That it was a competition which had yet to capture the public's imagination was evident from an attendance of only 12,895 at the Blackpool replay compared with 57,000 at the Burnley FA Cup tie. Cec Coldwell, Derek Pace and Brian Richardson were the only ever-presents, while once again Pace, with 28 goals in League and Cup was far and away the top marksman. Reg Matthewson and Ken Mallender were the most notable of the Blades' newcomers, and it is perhaps worthy of note that Matthewson—destined to notch only five goals in a career

spanning 388 League games with United, Fulham and Chester—was on target when making his First Division debut at Craven Cottage in mid-March. Sadly, United lost 5-2!

The 1962-63 campaign, in which United finished in tenth place, coincided with one of the worst winters of the post-war era. Conditions were such that the Football League did not manage a full Saturday programme for twelve weeks at the height of the Big Freeze. From just before Christmas to mid-February, United played only one League game, at Wolverhampton, and when they met West Ham at Bramall Lane on 16th February it was the first match staged in Sheffield for nearly two months.

Action during United's 4-1 defeat of Bolton at Bramall Lane in October 1963, with Len Allchurch scoring. Pace and Hodgson(2) were also on target.

Joe Shaw . . . more milestones were reached by the Blades' defender in the first half of the 1960s.

Once things got back to normal, the Blades played three FA Cup ties in 11 days before falling at Southampton, but the following week they began a run in which they lost only one of 12 League matches. It was in this spell that three of the club's brightest young prospects—Mick Jones (v Manchester United) and Len Badger and Bernard Shaw (v Leyton Orient) made their First Division debuts. In March incidentally, Billy Russell's career ended after 145 League games and 55 goals when he was sold to Bolton for £20,000.

The campaign marked a milestone in the career of Joe Shaw, who played his 500th League game in late August

1962 and two weeks later 'celebrated' with a goal which goalkeeper Alan Hodgkinson described as one of the best he had ever seen. Unfortunately, Joe's header, at Villa Park, was into his own net! But, in the event, it wasn't costly, for a Barry Hartle double sealed victory for the Blades. A goal of which Shaw was much more proud, came at Arsenal late in the following season, for it set the Blades on course for a notable 3-1 victory and came at the end of an astonishing individual run which had begun deep in United's half. The veteran defender was surely harking back to his early days as an inside-forward as he carried the ball right into the heart of the Gunners' goalmouth before lobbing it over goalkeeper Jim Furnell!

United ended that 1963-64 season in 12th place, but it was a campaign which began brightly and produced many highlights. They lost only one of their first 12 matches and just two of the opening 17, and after going to the top of the table in October, spent a month in pole position. However, four successive defeats started a slide and a spell in which they managed only 2 victories in 15 games. Yet it was one of those campaigns which produced an abundance of happy memories. There were two games, a home fixture with Spurs and a visit to Nottingham Forest, which typified their ability to bounce back. They trailed 2-0 in the first game and 3-0 in the second, but emerged with a 3-3 draw on both occasions. Incidentally, when the Blades beat Wolves 4-3 in a thrilling home game at the end of March, the two goals that 'Doc' Pace scored were the last of his 163 for the club. In fact, he remained at Bramall

Lane until the following December and took his tally of appearances for United to 294 before moving to Notts County.

1963-64 however, brought the end of the line for two other favourites, Billy Hodgson and Gerry Summers. Hodgson, having scored 32 goals in

his playing days at Walsall and subsequently had spells as manager of Oxford United and Gillingham.

A feature of 1964-65 was the promotion of more products from the Northern Intermediate League side, with Alan Birchenall, Alan Woodward and Barry Wagstaff taking their bow in

Cec Coldwell took a few knocks in his United career, and here colleagues Joe Shaw, Alan Hodgkinson and Len Badger inspect a cut eye suffered by the Blades' skipper.

152 League games since his move from St Johnstone in 1957, joined Leicester for £15,000 in September; while Summers, with 260 League games to his name in seven years, went to Hull City in April—the first of that famous 'back six' to depart. Hodgson was later to play with Derby, Rotherham and York; Summers ended

a season which also saw Bernard Shaw partnering brother Graham at full-back in a game at Arsenal in March. However, while the youngsters took the spotlight, Joe Shaw reached another milestone with his 600th League outing in February, and in the following month 29,000 turned up for his testimonial match.

It is relevant too, to note that while the long-serving Cec Coldwell was no longer first-choice at right back, his three outings in 1964-65 enabled him to pass the 400 mark in the League. Coldwell, who had arrived at the Lane in 1951 and made his debut in 1953, was already turning towards coaching, a field in which he was destined to have a successful run. At this stage however, he was just starting to do a very useful job with the reserves— indeed, within a year he had captained them to the Central League title, and the club's decision to give him a testimonial match in October 1966 was greeted with approval by supporters. In truth, there was a sense of anti-climax in the later stages of the 1964-65 season, for United collected just one point from their last eight matches; and won just one of the final 12. It meant they ended up in 19th place, which left them five points above Wolves, who were relegated with Birmingham, but many agreed the position did not reflect the Blades' true potential. Moreover, Lane regulars had found a new hero in Mick Jones, who topped the scoring charts with 14 goals before gaining his first England caps, against West Germany and Sweden, in May 1965.

United did much better in 1965-66 when they lost only one of their first 13 games and led the table in October, though they paid for spells of erratic form and some disappointing away results as the season progressed, finishing in ninth place. Jones was again the leading scorer, in a term which saw Joe Shaw finally

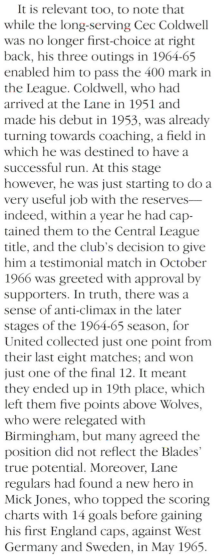

SOUVENIR **6**D. PROGRAMME

CEC COLDWELL
TESTIMONIAL MATCH

SHEFFIELD UNITED
VERSUS
ALL STAR XI

ON MONDAY, 31st OCTOBER, 1966. KICK-OFF 7.30 p.m.

BRAMALL LANE GROUND, SHEFFIELD

Souvenir **6**D. *Programme*

GRAHAM SHAW
TESTIMONIAL MATCH

SHEFFIELD UNITED
versus
SHEFFIELD WEDNESDAY

ON WEDNESDAY 26th APRIL 1967
KICK-OFF 7.30 p.m.

BRAMALL LANE GROUND, SHEFFIELD

Welsh international Gil Reece going for a high ball in United's match at Fulham in September 1966, when an Alan Birchenall goal clinched victory.

bow from the senior scene and Keith Kettleborough (Newcastle), Brian Richardson (Swindon), John Docherty (Brentford), Barry Hartle (Carlisle) and Len Allchurch (Stockport) move out, while youngsters David Munks and Frank Barlow stepped into the League side. However, Munks, a Sheffield Boys product, had the misfortune to break a leg at Arsenal a few weeks after his debut and, with substitutes permitted for the first time that year, Barlow was given his initial taste of top-grade football in rather sad circumstances, compounded by the fact that the Blades were losing 5-1 at the time of his introduction and

ended up being beaten 6-2. Happily, both Munks and Barlow enjoyed better days in their careers! For the record, the distinction of being the first substitute United used under the new ruling was bestowed on Tony Wagstaff when he replaced Birchenall in the game at Fulham in early September 1965.

United again finished in mid-table in 1966-67, which was the season when they turned out one of the youngest senior teams in the club's history, and in twenty-one year-old Len Badger they had the youngest captain in the First Division. There was one game, against West Ham late

United 1964–65.
Back row: Reg Matthewson, Brian Richardson, Alan Hodgkinson, Joe Shaw, Len Badger, Graham Shaw.
Front row: Tony Wagstaff, Keith Kettleborough, Mick Jones, Alan Birchenall, Barry Hartle.

in this campaign, when it was noted that goalkeeper Hodgkinson, a comparative veteran at twenty-nine, was the only man in the side who had not come through the Northern Intermediate League team. Phil Cliff was making his debut in the following line-up: Hodgkinson; Badger, Bernard Shaw; Munks, Matthewson, B. Wagstaff; Woodward, Mallender, Jones, Barlow, Cliff. They won 2-0 with goals from Jones and Munks.

Evidence of change was apparent as much off the field as on it, for in October 1966, United's new Bramall Lane stand, built at a cost of around £100,000, was brought into use for the home game with Sunderland—a fixture which those who were present will always remember for a marvellous solo scoring run by winger Gil Reece. The slightly-built Welshman was the latest of the many John Harris bargain buys, having cost United £10,000 in April 1965 when he was twenty-two and had made only 32 League appearances for Newport County. The wisdom of this signing is evident when one notes that Reece went on to collect 29 caps and he scored 58 goals in 210 League outings for the Blades.

By the early part of 1966-67 Reece was well established and a big

favourite with the fans, but, exactly four weeks after the Sunderland game, he suffered a broken leg in the home match with Blackpool. It was a cruel blow for the player and United. In a desperate bid to plug the gap left by the loss of the Welshman, Harris went out and paid Norwich City £5,000 for a thirty-two year-old winger, Bill Punton. The balding Punton, who had been at Carrow Road since 1959, had not played in the First Division since leaving Newcastle for Southend nine years earlier, and it was a signing which provoked a few raised eyebrows. Not surprisingly perhaps, he was limited to just 16 League appearances, but his consolation was that he earned a niche in club records because the

only Blades goal he ever scored sealed a 1-0 victory in the Sheffield derby watched by a 43,490 crowd at Bramall Lane in February 1967. It hardly mattered that the strike was a scrambled affair which arrived after 59 minutes, Punton finding the net at the second attempt after his first effort had spun out of the hands of Wednesday goalkeeper Peter Wicks. Some wins are more precious than others, and, at the end of the season, those two points helped ensure United finished just above their local rivals in the First Division table! At that moment, few could have imagined that United would slip to relegation within a year—and lose two of the most popular young Blades in the bargain.

Rise & Fall of the Young Blades

MICK JONES and Alan Birchenall made only around 100 Football League appearances together for Sheffield United in a brief three-year span in the mid-1960s, but it was enough to place them among the most popular strike partnerships in the club's modern history. They are remembered not only as classic examples of United's remarkably successful youth scheme in that era, but as symbols of a dramatic change in emphasis at Bramall Lane, when they were both sold for £100,000 in the autumn of 1967. In selling Jones (73 goals in 167 games) to Leeds, and Birchenall (30 goals in 120 games) to Chelsea, the Blades became the first English club to collect two six-figure fees.

It is fair to suggest that the best-known products of United's 'home grown' policy in this phase, were full-back Len Badger and winger Alan Woodward, both of whom gave outstanding service to the club. Indeed, Badger, once of Sheffield Boys, and at twenty-one in 1966 the youngest captain in the old First Division, made over 500 League and Cup appearances between 1963 and 1976. While Woodward, who came to the fore with Barnsley boys, not only chalked up almost 600 games between 1964 and 1978 but scored a record 175 goals. Badger collected 13 England Under-23 caps, and it was always a source of dismay to Bramall Lane regulars that he never gained

senior international honours. By the same token, when Woodward, who boasted one of the hardest shots in the game, was at his peak in the early 1970s, many believed one outing in the Football League's representative XI hardly reflected his talents.

Bernard Shaw.

United won the Northern Intermediate League Cup in 1962 and claimed a League and Cup double in 1964, and this period in the club's history coincided with the emergence of a string of youngsters who made it to the top. They included Reg Matthewson and Ken Mallender, defenders who both made their senior debut in 1962, Bernard Shaw (1963) and the Wagstaff brothers, Tony and Barry. Matthewson and the versatile Mallender (they both left in 1968) were very dependable performers. Shaw, brother of ex-

he played against Middlesbrough in April 1961. Sadly, like Gary Hamson and Julian Broddle—lads who later claimed the same honour—the slightly-built inside-forward never quite fulfilled his early promise. He will always be remembered for a

Eddie Edwards (right) was one of the great "characters" of Bramall Lane. Here the man who looked after United's juniors is pictured with David Munks.

England man Graham (who joined Doncaster in August 1967), was an excellent back who gained two Under-23 caps and might have achieved more but for an untimely spell of ill-health; while the Wagstaffs, products of the famous Don and Dearne district where United subsequently discovered Frank Barlow, Geoff Salmons, Micky Speight and others, should both have gone further than they did. Tony Wagstaff had the distinction of being United's youngest Football League debutant when, aged seventeen years and sixty-nine days,

superb goal he volleyed against Arsenal in November 1963 and for a dramatic last-gasp winner in a famous fight back against Newcastle in November 1965; but, though he had his moments and his talents were invariably appreciated by his fellow professionals, he was limited to 150 League games over nine years. Barry, who captained that notable 1964 Northern Intermediate League side, ultimately faced heavy competition in the half-back positions, but made 125 League appearances. The pair probably enjoyed the best years of

Mick Jones challenging for a high cross in a game with Aston Villa in August 1965. His pal Alan Birchenall got the winner that day.

their careers after Jack Mansell took them to Reading for a modest joint fee in 1969.

The key to the success of United's youth scheme in this phase was provided by chief scout Archie Clark, a recruit from the Joe Mercer era, plus veteran Eddie Edwards, who had been with the club since the days of Reg Freeman and was in his element looking after the juniors, and John Short, the coach John Harris brought to Bramall Lane after the 1961 promotion. Former goalkeeper Fred White was among others who made a contribution. Between them they had a remarkable knack for spotting and encouraging young talent. Naturally, many of the brightest boys were discovered in schools football, where the Blades boasted some excellent contacts, but Jones and Birchenall were notable examples of lads who

were rescued from oblivion after success at this level had failed to bring recognition.

By coincidence, they had played together in the same Nottinghamshire Boys team, though apart from that and hair which led to them being dubbed 'the blond twins', they did not have a lot in common. Jones, who came from the Worksop area, never lacked confidence or ability but was always the quieter lad, resilient but reserved. Birchenall, London-born but Nottingham-raised, was the happy-go-lucky extrovert who played his football with flamboyance and a smile. (It is intriguing to note that though Don Revie, the Leeds manager, finally plumped for Jones, his initial target was Birchenall, and it was a former professional, journalist Tom Holley, who persuaded him that Jones was the player who would be the better buy.)

The pair arrived at the club by different routes. Jones, twice rejected by West Brom and playing amateur football with Dinnington, was recommended for evening training sessions at Bramall Lane in 1961. He turned up with his boots wrapped in a paper carrier bag and, despite literally hundreds seeking to catch the eye of the coaches, did enough to earn a job on the ground staff. A couple of years later, Birchenall, then an apprentice mechanic at a Nottingham bus garage, was spotted playing with Thorney-wood Athletic. He used a week of his summer holidays to accept an invitation to train with United, and subsequently took three months' unpaid leave from his job to pursue an extended trial which led to the offer of a contract.

Jones was the only product of United's youth scheme to play for England at senior level, collecting two caps within two years of his Football League debut for the Blades, which came in April 1963, four days before his eighteenth birthday. He also collected nine Under-23 caps, his

rapid early progress ensured United did not miss the prolific 'Doc' Pace as much as they might, though the veteran, who joined Notts County in late 1964, remained long enough to help in the initial development of a youngster whose strength was not only his marksmanship, but courage, persistence and an unselfishness which made him an instant favourite with the fans.

Birchenall, too, was an immediate hit with supporters once he got his chance, and being big and given to tank-like charges at opposing defenders, he was soon nicknamed 'Sherman'. However, as he admitted, his early months with United were not the most rewarding. He needed time to adapt to and profit from the discipline of full-time training, but when he hit some 60 goals for the juniors in 1963-64 the management knew they had found another star.

Jones was already established in the senior side by that September evening in 1964, when Birchenall arrived on the Football League scene and went on to enjoy a start which was the stuff of storybooks as he claimed 10 goals in his first 12 games, assuring himself of a place in the folklore of Sheffield derby matches by scoring twice when he faced Wednesday for the first time in only the second senior game of his career.

In later years, Birchenall never forgot the thrill of the few days which turned him from an unknown, who boasted only eight Central League appearances, into a local hero, and he still smiles when reflecting on the circumstances in which he made his United debut in a midweek First Division game at Stoke. This is how

Alan Birchenall.

he recalled the episode:

'On the Wednesday morning, the gaffer, John Harris, asked me, quite casually, if I was doing anything that evening, and if not, would I like to travel with the first team to Stoke. Naturally, I jumped at the chance, and thought I was just being given an opportunity to sample the big-time atmosphere as a privileged spectator. Because I believed I was only going along for the ride, I was determined to savour every moment of the experience. I'd never sat in at a pre-match meal before, and because of the novelty, when we got to the hotel I not only tucked into my own steak, but helped Joe Shaw and Cec Coldwell finish theirs! Then, before we boarded the team-bus, I bought pounds of sweets and chocolates, and no kidding, I gorged myself silly on the journey to the Potteries.

'When we reached the Victoria Ground, I tried to make myself as useful as possible. I helped unload the skip and volunteered for the job of putting the complimentary tickets on the gate for the other players. I was lounging by the main entrance, lapping up the glamour of it all, when John Short came along and said he thought I'd better get back to the dressing room. I asked him why the hurry, and when he said "Because you're playing" I thought he was joking. But, sure enough, I found someone had brought my boots and put them beneath the peg on which the No. 10 shirt hung. I didn't have time to be nervous. I'd only just put my kit on when we got the call to go out for the game.

'Happily, I started with a win, for Mick Jones scored the only goal of the match. But if that was a thrill, it was nothing compared with what happened the following weekend. I stayed in the side when we went to Hillsborough and played Wednesday—and scored both goals in a 2-0 win. Mick hit the bar and when I managed to get my foot to the rebound, the ball somehow spun over the line and into the net; and then I headed in from a corner. I felt like a hero from the *Boy's Own* magazine.'

Birchenall scored six goals in his first four Sheffield derby fixtures, which put him into a select band of local heroes. He soon collected the first of his four England Under-23 caps, and naturally, revelled in the sudden fame. In all his time in Sheffield, he lodged with his pal, Len Badger, and they marked their elevated status with the acquisition of a Triumph sports car apiece. 'We had a lot of fun,' recalled Birchenall, 'but Mrs B., Len's mum, made sure we didn't get too big for our boots. She was as tough a disciplinarian as dear old Archie Clark!'

In that 1964-65 campaign, Jones and Birchenall shared 29 League and Cup goals, and the season saw Woodward and Barry Wagstaff make their League debuts, while John Harris also made another of his inspired signings with the purchase of Gil Reece from Newport for £10,000. Jones was named in the England squad and played against West Germany and Sweden in the end-of-season tour. The following term he enjoyed his best scoring run for the Blades with 21 goals.

It was around this time that changes were beginning to happen behind the scenes which were to have long-term implications for the club, and would indirectly influence the careers of Jones and Birchenall in a way they could hardly have anticipated. As has been explained elsewhere, the key figure in these developments was Dick Wragg, chairman of the Football Committee. Wragg, a builders' merchant, was tired of United being regarded as Sheffield football's 'poor relation' and dreamed of creating a ground to match the developments which staging the World Cup matches in 1966 had enabled Wednesday to complete at Hillsborough. Moreover, he had high personal ambitions which were fired by the news, announced in January 1967, that his Wednesday rival, Dr Andrew Stephen, had been elected chairman of the Football Association.

John Harris: a great Blades' servant who almost resigned over the sale of Mick Jones to Leeds.

It was in late 1966 that United opened the new £100,000 Bramall Lane stand, but Wragg knew further ground developments would be impossible until cricket had been removed form the place which had been the home of the summer game since 1855. He took heart when, at the club's next annual meeting, shareholders voted 37-26 in favour of abandoning cricket; though his enthusiasm was tempered by a subsequent postal vote, which confirmed the majority wanted the ground to remain a dual sports arena.

Naturally, a key to eventually persuading the shareholders and boardroom colleagues that a four-sided football ground had to be the ultimate goal, depended on United being in the top-grade, and there was some alarm when the Blades began the 1967-68 season badly. There were echoes of a similar phase in 1933-34 when United had sold their biggest asset, Jimmy Dunne, to Arsenal to raise funds to strengthen the team in a desperate bid to avoid relegation. This time the pattern was slightly different in that United signed Willie Carlin, a 5ft 4ins midfield general and a great little Scouse character, from Carlisle on 19th September, before selling Jones to Leeds three days later. There was talk at the time of United seeking to create 'a new image'. They wanted to stop being seen as a 'home grown' club and it was suggested they would forthwith compete in the transfer market and stop being so dependent upon talent they bred themselves. The £40,000 spent on Carlin was a club record (and ironically, he was to make only 36 League appearances for the Blades), but it paled against the £100,000 they

Colin Addison (left), a £40,000 buy from Arsenal, with Don & Dearne product Frank Barlow. Later in his career, Barlow was on Wednesday's training staff.

received for Jones. Many were conscious that the profit was needed to help pay off the debt on the Bramall Lane stand.

When rumours began to circulate about the imminent sale of Jones, supporters were staggered, and John Harris argued it was a step the club would regret. However, after a midweek board meeting, Wragg confirmed to waiting reporters that Leeds and Leicester would be told that Jones was available, and hundreds of young fans assembled in the pavilion carpark chanted, 'If Mick Jones goes, so do we!' as the chairman left the ground. Poor Mick Jones, bemused by the speculation about his future, sought talks with Wragg, but he was even more confused when the chairman later told the press the player had asked for a transfer. Looking back on the incident many years later, Jones said: 'There is no way I ever regretted going to Leeds, but at the time, I was content at United, did not really want to leave, and certainly I never asked for a transfer'.

Heads I win . . . Mick Jones scoring one of his two goals in a 6-1 defeat of Doncaster in a County Cup tie in 1967.

Wragg always insisted the sale of Jones was essential to his plans to re-shape the club's fortunes, but rumours persisted that he had made a pact with Sam Bolton, the vice-chairman at Leeds, and if Jones went to Elland Road then Wragg would get Bolton's crucial vote in his bid to advance his ambitions of a place in the FA hierarchy. Wragg did, indeed, eventually join the International Committee and later became its chairman; in the meantime, the Jones transfer was seen as the first indication of Wragg's growing authority at Bramall Lane.

It did look possible that John Harris might quit over the sale of Jones, but he stayed. The manager, missing the support of Archie Clark, since the chief scout's death in January 1967, recruited the services of Andy Beattie, a former manager of wide experience, in October. In late November he was given another £40,000 with which he bought Colin Addison, an inside or centre-forward, from Arsenal; but the following day Birchenall joined Chelsea. Birchenall admitted he had been unsettled by the sale of Jones, but, when he submitted written transfer requests, Harris tore them up, commenting: 'The supporters would lynch me if I sold you as well as Mick.' However, the day came when Harris took Birchenall across the pitch to the cricket pavilion, where he left him alone in an office. 'After a minute or two,' recalled Birchenall, 'the door opened and in walked Dave Sexton.' He was the new Chelsea manager's first major signing.

Neither Jones nor Birchenall had cause to regret moving on. Jones enjoyed great success with Leeds, where he was immensely popular and shared in some memorable years while scoring 111 goals in 309 appearances, before a knee injury ended his career in 1976. Birchenall raised his tally of League games to over 450 with Chelsea, Crystal Palace and Leicester, and, unlike Jones, he stayed in the game after hanging up his boots, working as a public relations man at Filbert Street.

Harris felt the loss of Jones and Birchenall as a personal blow, but, as he admitted later, coming to terms with developments he did not find agreeable was something he had little choice but to accept. At the time he kept his true feelings private, his only public comment was to suggest he still believed United had the players to get the club out of trouble. He turned his thoughts to further means of strengthening his team, and knew the ideal would be to find another youngster who might help the fans forget the departed heroes. It so happened that a teenager in his first season in Watford's first team was making a big impression, and everyone said the lad had a great future. Harris took a look and decided this was a boy he wanted to sign, and to his delight, Watford said United could have him once they were out of the FA Cup. By one of those coincidences football is always throwing up, it was the Blades who delivered the knock-out in the third round. So they got their man. His name, of course, was Anthony William Currie.

If the 1967-68 campaign is remembered for the departures of Jones and Birchenall and the arrival of Currie, it will also not be forgotten that relegation came largely as a consequence of a dreadful record in the last stages of the season, when the Blades won only one of their last nine home games and picked up just one point from the final six matches at Bramall Lane. It was a staggering collapse, right to the end their fate was in their own hands, and their fall was all the more frustrating as Coventry escaped by one point and Wednesday by two.

They had started the season with one win in the opening eight games and only two victories in the first 14. Their third success in November was a triumph all the more notable, as it came despite the loss of Alan

United's David Munks and Willie Carlin going for a high ball with West Ham's Geoff Hirst, while Ken Mallender looks on.

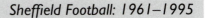

Hodgkinson with a dislocated finger after 11 minutes, and emergency goalkeeper Alan Woodward defying Leeds with an heroic display. When Currie marked his debut with a headed goal as United came from behind to beat Tottenham 3-2 in late February, the Blades had every cause to believe they could haul themselves out of trouble. It served to confirm they were better than their League position suggested when they reached the FA Cup quarter-finals before losing 1-0 at Leeds. Another of the club's bright youngsters, Phil Cliff, had scored twice in an impressive fifth-round victory at West Ham. Even after their Wembley hopes had been ended, they registered a notable League victory at Liverpool at Easter, to follow away wins at Fulham and Wolves.

The turning point in United's bid to beat the drop probably came in the midweek home game with fellow strugglers Fulham—managed, incidentally, by former Wednesday boss, Vic Buckingham. With twenty minutes left, the Blades led 2-0 with goals from Tom Fenoughty and Woodward, but Fulham then scored three times in eleven minutes; and, though they won their final away game, at Burnley, United's fate was sealed with defeats in their remaining home fixtures, against West Ham and Chelsea. United went into the last game of the season needing a win and facing a Chelsea side captained by Alan Birchenall. When Mick Hill scored 18 seconds before half-time the outlook appeared bright, but goals by Osgood and Baldwin sent them down, with relegation confirmed the same evening when Stoke drew at Leicester.

THE DEPARTURE of Harry Catterick, who walked out to rejoin Everton in the spring of 1961, was a source of considerable dismay to Wednesday supporters, and remained so in the light of what Catterick subsequently achieved, albeit with greater resources, at Goodison Park. However, the arrival of Vic Buckingham, then aged forty-five, as his successor was widely regarded as a positive appointment, and one which would see the Owls maintain the excellent progress of the previous three years. In the event, having finished runners-up in the title race in Catterick's final campaign, they failed to get that close again; and though finishing sixth in three successive seasons and playing in Europe, they did not take the anticipated step forward and seemed plagued by a tendency towards inconsistency.

Buckingham's 234 League and Cup games as an elegant Tottenham back or wing-half between 1935 and 1949 did not include any in the old First Division, but he subsequently proved his credentials as a top-class coach and manager. He coached Oxford University and the FA Amateur Cup winners Pegasus, and, after a spell at Bradford (Park Avenue), had led West Brom to an FA Cup triumph and second place in the top-grade in 1954. He was always a man with a continental view of football. Immediately before joining Wednesday, Buckingham spent two years as coach to Dutch champions Ajax (Amsterdam), but, in fact, was preparing to return to England and poised to become manager of Plymouth Argyle, with whom he had made a verbal agreement, when his old RAF pal from Rotherham, Stan Ashton (later an Owls director), alerted him to the vacancy at Hillsborough. Happily for him, the Devon club did not stand in his way.

Buckingham was very different in personality from his predecessor: he was a colourful character, elegant, debonair, flamboyant and somewhat theatrical in his manner, and there was less iron and more flexibility and wit in his make-up. He was seen as a coach with flair, a man who believed in giving players responsibility and

Vic Buckingham.

encouraging them to express themselves; but this faith was not always repaid, and the impression he gave of being somewhat laid back and happy-go-lucky in his approach to his work was regarded by some as the reason his sides tended to lack consistency. At Hillsborough his teams could attain outstanding peaks, but there were also many troughs.

Of the signings Buckingham made, the best was undoubtedly centre-forward David Layne. He cost £22,500 from Bradford City in the summer of 1962 and went on to score 58 goals in 81 games before his Wednesday career was halted in sensational circumstances in 1964. Other major buys were Eddie Holliday (Middlesbrough) and Sheffield-born Mark Pearson (Manchester United); he will also be remembered for introducing such youngsters as Colin Dobson, the South Bank product (who remained an amateur until finishing his ship-building apprenticeship on Teeside), Stocksbridge discovery Peter Eustace, Chesterfield lad John Hickton and Vic Mobley (who arrived via Oxford City) into the senior side. One of his successes which is often forgotten was the conversion of the ever-dependable Gerry Young into a wing-half following the sale of Tony Kay to Everton.

Kay was the most notable departure in Buckingham's era: after 203 games for the Owls he rejoined Catterick for a £55,000 fee (then a record for a wing-half) in December 1962, and went on to win an England cap, though circumstances limited him to 50 League games for his new club. Bobby Craig (Blackburn), Keith Ellis (Scunthorpe) and Billy Griffin (Bury) also moved on in this spell. Craig,

who had made 84 appearances for the Owls and was at times such an influence, was destined to play in just ten games for Blackburn, and after a spell with Oldham he subsequently returned to Scotland and joined St Johnstone.

Buckingham also recruited a new right-hand man in Gordon Clark, the old Aldershot manager and his former assistant and successor at West Brom. Later he brought in Jack Mansell, the former Cardiff, Portsmouth and England 'B' full-back, as coach. Mansell, who was to spend many years working abroad in his coaching career as well as managing Rotherham and Reading for a time, arrived in 1962 after a spell with Blau-Wit in Holland.

The 1961-62 campaign which launched the new era was notable on several counts: not least that Buckingham's first home game in charge, a 4-2 defeat of Bolton on the evening of 23rd August, coincided with the opening by Sir Stanley Rous, secretary of the Football Association, of the new North Stand. Built at a cost of £150,000 and paid for by debenture shares, its 10,008 capacity raised the ground's total seating to 16,000.

This was also the season in which Wednesday made their debut in the Inter-Cities Fairs Cup reaching the quarter-finals before falling to Barcelona, who went through thanks to a 2-0 victory in Spain after Wednesday had won the home leg 3-2. Wednesday had begun their European venture with a dramatic 7-6 aggregate defeat of Olympique Lyonnais. At one stage in the first leg in Lyon, the Owls trailed 3-0 but recovered to emerge with a 4-2 deficit. The French side came to

Work in progress on Wednesday's cantilever stand in 1961.

Hillsborough and promptly increased their lead to 5-2, but Johnny Fantham, playing at centre-forward for the first time, sparked another famous revival with one header, then after goals from Griffin, Dobson and Tom McAnearney (penalty), he sealed a memorable victory with another. In this period, flying headers were a Fantham speciality, and his form brought him his only England cap, against Luxembourg at Highbury, plus appearances for the Football League against the Irish and Italian Leagues.

In Division One, the Owls finished ten points behind champions Ipswich, and their inconsistency is evident when one notes they won four of their first five games, then went five without victory, claimed maximum points in four of the next five, and, after a spell of one success in seven in February and March, they ended the season with four straight wins. One of their most satisfying triumphs came early in the campaign, at Everton, where they won 4-0 and Ellis Rimmer, a Wednesday idol of the 1930s, commented: 'I haven't seen football like that from an English team for years.' They also reached the FA Cup fifth round, losing at home to Manchester United after a goalless draw at Old Trafford; and it is worth recording that the novelty of the season came in the 75th League derby with Sheffield United in September at Bramall Lane, where they played the first half in black shorts and the second in white ones at the request of referee Kevin Howley.

Wednesday 1962-63.
Back row: Robin Hardy, Peter Johnson, J.J. Roy McLaren, Brian Hill, Billy Griffin, Gerry Young.
Middle row: Ralph O'Donnell, Derek Wilkinson, Peter Swan, Ron Springett, Tom McAnearney,
Keith Ellis, David Layne.
Front row: Alan Finney, Eddie Holliday, Tony Kay, Colin Dobson, John Fantham, Don Megson.

Features of the 1962-63 campaign were the success of newcomer David Layne, who was top marksman with 29 League goals, and in October, the staging of an England-France European Championship match, and an unforgettable friendly between Wednesday and Brazilian champions Santos. The same month also saw Ajax (Amsterdam) visit Hillsborough and attract a 21,810 crowd for Redfern Froggatt's benefit match. Froggatt, who at that time held the club's aggregate post-war League scoring record with 140 goals, had not played in the senior side since April 1960.

Remarkably, Layne, who had gone to the same Tinsley school as England World Cup goalkeeper Gordon Banks and played alongside Fantham and Freddie Hill (Bolton and Manchester City) with Sheffield Boys, had doubts about his ability to make the grade in the First Division. Yet, after Rotherham had sold him for £500 in 1959, he had excelled at Swindon (where one stunning free-kick prompted a description as 'the hardest shot in the west' and inspired the nickname 'Bronco' after a television cowboy hero of the day) and went on to claim 46 goals in 69 games, including a record 34 in the League in 1961-62, for Bradford City. Once back in his native Sheffield, Layne owed a lot to the

Redfern Froggatt.

(his goals came after 2, 28 and 40 minutes) claim a hat-trick for the Brazilians, with Griffin (30 min) and Layne (33) on target for Wednesday.

From the outset, there was a sense of anti-climax about what proved to be Buckingham's last season in charge in 1963-64, for Wednesday made their poorest start for six years, collecting only six points from the first eight games. It was mid-October before they launched a decent unbeaten run, which spanned nine matches. Alas, they also went out of the FA Cup at the first hurdle, losing 3-2 at Fourth Division Newport; and hopes of some Fairs Cup glory were ended with second-round defeat by FC Cologne. High points included a 5-0 home victory over Wolves, which came a week after Wednesday had come from 3-0 down at Stoke to draw 4-4. In the light of later events there was some irony that Layne, who finished the season with 28 goals, scored the last hat-trick of his Owls career in a 4-1 win at Ipswich in January.

encouragement of Mansell, but Buckingham always said his emergence as one of the best centre-forwards in the game was entirely down to the player's determination to improve his skills.

When England met France at Hillsborough in early October 1962, Blackpool's Jimmy Armfield was the national captain for the first time and the side included four new caps—Ray Charnley (Blackpool), Mike Hellawell (Birmingham) and Chris Crowe and Alan Hinton (both Wolves). Alas, England's display was well below expectations, and it took a dubious penalty, converted by Ron Flowers, to salvage a 1-1 draw. The only Wednesday man on duty that evening was Ron Springett. The Owls goalkeeper, incidentally, was the 'victim' of a much more notable penalty a couple of weeks later when the legendary Pele produced a piece of intricate spot-kick 'magic' almost on half-time to complete a 4-2 win for Santos on a memorable floodlit Hillsborough occasion which thrilled 49,058 spectators who saw Coutinho

Ron Springett . . . Wednesday's most-capped England player.

David Layne . . . made an instant impact and was one of Wednesday's best post-war centre-forwards until he was banned, along with Peter Swan and Tony Kay.

The decision not to renew Buckingham's contract was probably inevitable, for there had been considerable speculation about his future for some weeks ahead of the formal announcement in the second week of April. If he was dismayed by the news, Buckingham remained philosophical, and returning to Holland soon afterwards, he laughed when he discovered his old track suit was still on the same peg in the Ajax dressing room where he had left it three years earlier! However, the manager had barely departed the Sheffield scene when, the following weekend, Wednesday were thrown into turmoil by sensational developments as traumatic as they were unexpected.

It was the weekend of the Scotland-England game, and the club's chairman and vice-chairman, Dr Andrew Stephen and Harold Jessop, had travelled north to be at Hampden Park. Jessop often recalled that it was during their return train journey on the Sunday that he casually picked up *The People* newspaper and could barely believe his eyes when he spotted allegations that three Wednesday players—Tony Kay (by now at Everton), Peter Swan and David Layne—had been involved in a fixed-odds betting coup. Stephen and Jessop did not imagine there could be any truth in the story, nor did anyone at Hillsborough or any of the club's supporters; but the players subsequently admitted having placed £50 bets on Wednesday's match at Ipswich in December 1962 when the Owls lost 2-0—it led to bans from football and prison sentences.

The immediate upshot was that Swan (capped 19 times by England between 1955 and 1962 and boasting 285 League and Cup games) and Layne were initially suspended by Wednesday on full pay. In the meantime, the club tried to come to terms with a situation in which they were the innocent victims, while completing the two remaining games

Peter Swan.

of their 1963-64 programme. It so happened that, on the day after the allegations became public knowledge, the Owls had a home match with Tottenham. That they won 2-0 with goals from deputy centre-forward Derek Wilkinson was almost incidental to an emotional evening remembered for a half-time message which general-manager Eric Taylor broadcast to the 31,377 spectators, asking supporters to 'bear with the club in this most tragic affair'.

It was a cruel development for a club which had always prided itself on doing everything by the book and they were a long time recovering from a blow which was much greater than simply the loss of an England centre-half and an outstanding centre-forward. It is worthy of emphasis that other players and clubs (but none so famous) were involved in this dark episode, for it is not without irony that it is invariably remembered as a scandal synonymous with Wednesday

and Swan, Layne and Kay. The Sheffield men's misfortune was that they were the best-known of the dozen or more footballers exposed by *The People*.

It is often forgotten that the so-called bribes, match fixing or betting coup scandal (as it was variously called) involved many players caught up in a syndicate backed by professional gamblers, with the key football figure a former Charlton and Plymouth player called Jimmy Gauld, a Scot whose link with Layne was that they had been colleagues at Swindon. Layne, his team-mates and his club might have been spared had he not bumped into Gauld again quite by accident when attending a match at Mansfield, where the Scot's playing days had been ended by a broken leg, as a spectator. Gauld's punishment as ringleader (it was he who sold his story and identified the other players

Tony Kay.

in *The People*) was four years in jail; that the Wednesday men had been drawn into something they didn't fully understand until it was too late was evident from the fact that, of the ten players sent to prison, they received the smallest sentences—four months. There were others who escaped prosecution. The Wednesday men's 'crime' was having a bet, and they always claimed they did not realise they were doing anything wrong.

'We certainly didn't think we were committing a criminal act,' said Layne. 'We were innocents really, and what we did was more bravado than anything. If anyone had pointed out the implications we would never have done it. It seemed such a small thing at the time, a bit of foolishness. There was never any question of fixing or throwing a match. In fact, the game in question, at Ipswich, was one in which, on the day, we were never in a position to win. It was only when the full story emerged that we saw we'd been bit players implicated in some-

thing which was very serious. We knew we'd done wrong and been silly, but even so, we were shattered to be charged with conspiracy to defraud.'

All three players were horrified at having tarnished the game and the name of their club, and let down supporters, but knew it was too late for regrets; yet prison, a life ban from football and having to face the stigma for the rest of their lives added up to a very heavy punishment. The bans were lifted after eight years, but though Swan and Layne returned to Wednesday in 1972, Swan made only 17 more senior appearances while Layne, dogged by fitness problems he had never experienced in the old days, managed none. Their best days were behind them: Swan had a spell at Bury, and Layne had four games with Hereford United before knee trouble forced him to retire. For both the only consolation was they had been forgiven by the club and the fans, and they still maintain regular contact with old colleagues.

Flying Fantham . . . Wednesday's post-war record marksman beating Gordon Banks in an early 1960s duel with Leicester City.

OFFICIAL PROGRAMME PRICE FOURPENCE

FOOTBALL LEAGUE DIVISION 1

SATURDAY, 26th AUGUST, 1961
KICK-OFF 3.0 P.M.

CONSILIO ET ANIMIS

SHEFFIELD WEDNESDAY

VERSUS

BIRMINGHAM CITY

Football at Hillsborough

What difference the presence of Swan and Layne might have made to Wednesday in those 'lost' years is something we can only speculate upon. However, we do know that when Wednesday looked for a successor to Vic Buckingham, they felt circumstances demanded the appointment of a disciplinarian, and preferably, someone known to them and familiar with the club and its traditions—which is why they chose to bring Alan Brown back to Hillsborough.

Wednesday players, in Scarborough for special training, ahead of the March 1963 FA Cup replay with Arthur Rowley's Shrewsbury. In the picture are Eddie Holliday, John Hickton, Alan Finney, David Layne, Peter Swan, Gerry Young, Tom McAnearney, Derek Wilkinson, Ron Springett, Brian Hill, Roy McLaren and John Fantham.

Alan W. Brown, 1964–1968

ALAN BROWN'S appointment, as the new Wednesday team-boss, in the summer of 1964 was not unexpected, though some people were probably surprised by his decision to quit Sunderland so soon after finally leading them back into the top grade. There was a predictable logic in his selection by general-manager Eric Taylor and the Hillsborough directors. The tall North Easterner was almost certainly the first name the Owls put on their wanted list after that dreadful weekend when Vic Buckingham's departure was followed by the Betting Coup scandal revelations which shook the club to its foundations. Brown, then almost fifty, looked the ideal candidate—if he could be persuaded to come. It was in his favour that he was familiar with the club and had worked with Taylor before; but more than that, he had a reputation as a tough disciplinarian, and was the kind of man who would relish the challenge of restoring the dignity and pride tarnished by recent unfortunate events. Moreover, since his earlier spell in Sheffield, he had spent ten years in management at Burnley and Sunderland and achieved reasonable success while enhancing a reputation as an astute tactician.

As a player Brown, a product of Corbridge, had been an uncompromising centre-half who made some 170 peacetime appearances with Huddersfield, Burnley and Notts County between 1933 and 1948. He

really came to the fore as captain of Burnley's Second Division side which reached the FA Cup final and gained promotion in 1946-47. His playing days ended in anti-climax in a brief and unhappy spell at Meadow Lane, after which he returned to Burnley and ran a cafe until Eric Taylor persuaded him back into football, in January 1951, as Wednesday's trainer-coach, following the sudden death of Billy Knox.

Alan Brown.

Brown is often remembered as the man who helped 'make' Derek Dooley in that memorable promotion campaign of 1951-52 when the Owls bounced straight back to the First Division. It is of interest to note that when Brown looked back on his own career in later life, Dooley was one of the two 'old boys' he recalled with

Wednesday in 1965.
Back row: Don Megson, Wilf Smith, Brian Hill, Ron Springett, Peter Eustace, John Hickton, Vic Mobley.
Front row: Howard Wilkinson, John Fantham, John Quinn, Colin Dobson.

the most affection. The other was also a centre-forward, whose career was prematurely ended by injury—Brian Clough, the player he took from Middlesbrough to Sunderland for a £40,000 fee in 1961. What these players had in common was courage in the face of misfortune, which was something Brown admired. He also appreciated them because, as players, they responded to his authority and ideas. It is worthy of note that when Clough became a manager he used Brown as his model.

Brown's first spell at Hillsborough lasted until August 1954 when he was appointed manager of Burnley, who twice finished in the top seven in his three years in charge. In 1957, after Sunderland had been rocked by allegations of illegal payments to players, he was attracted to Roker Park; but he was unable to prevent them losing their top-grade status for the first time in their history in 1958 (they went down with Wednesday). The battle to guide them back proved tougher than anticipated, but, after being pipped to promotion on goal-average in 1963, they finally made it in comfort in 1964. Somehow, it was typical of the man that, just when he might have been expected to savour his success, he elected to walk out and accept a different challenge at Hillsborough. He was a man full of surprises, though it is fair to suggest that when he eventually returned to Sunderland in February 1968, those who knew him well did not find the decision entirely unexpected.

Dubbed 'the Iron Man', Brown was a complex, sometimes difficult and often cold and inflexible character, but he had a capacity for great warmth and had a talent for inspiring tremendous loyalty in his players, many of whom achieved far more under his influence than they might in the charge of someone else. He was a great man to have on your side in a crisis, and his loyalty to those who responded to his ideals of discipline and dedication knew no bounds. He did however have a tendency for making snap judgements which, even if proved wrong, he stubbornly refused to reverse; and he could be ruthless with those who failed him, so that some of his sudden and unexpected decisions dramatically changed the careers of others. You were not advised to get on the wrong side of Alan Brown.

Dave Smith, who spent a couple of years as coach at Hillsborough, was a typical example of someone who saw both sides of Brown. As a young full-back with Burnley, Smith was given his senior debut by Brown in 1955, but a succession of serious injuries limited the young Scot to around 100 appearances, and though he later had spells with Brighton and Bristol City, he was forced into premature retirement around 1962. It was no surprise that, even at a distance, Brown kept tabs on Smith's progress, and impressed by his determination to overcome adversity, he brought him back from a coaching spell in Libya to a job with the Owls. Smith, who later enjoyed some success in management in the lower grades with Mansfield, Southend and Plymouth, was an extrovert and very confident fellow, and by early 1967 his forthright style had begun to irk Brown. So, when the manager chose to reshape his training staff, Smith was dismissed,

and at the same time, the long-serving Tommy Walker and Johnny Logan departed the scene.

In fact, that was the moment when Brown chose to give another 'unknown', Lawrie McMenemy, a local government worker from Gateshead, his first job in League football, alongside another newcomer Ian McFarlane; former coach Jack Marshall returned to Sheffield at the same time. This trio of appointments probably said as much about the Wednesday boss as his decision to dispense with the services of those they replaced. McMenemy, of course, went on to earn fame as a manager, enjoying great success at

Don Megson . . . Wednesday captain from 1964–1970.

Southampton after spells with Doncaster and Grimsby; and, though he had a less happy time at Sunderland, he later became No. 2 to England manager Graham Taylor before returning to Southampton.

An incident which typified Brown's penchant for bold, spur-of-the-moment decisions, came when the club's captaincy changed hands at half-time, during a friendly match in Denmark, early in his first season as Wednesday's manager. When Wednesday lost 4-1 to Aarhus FG that September day in 1964, veteran wing-half Tommy McAnearney was given the run-around by a youthful opponent, and during the interval, the Owls skipper felt the full force of Brown's anger. He made the mistake of arguing with the manager, the upshot of which was that Brown suddenly picked up the match ball and threw it to Don Megson, telling the full-back to lead the side out for the second half. McAnearney's senior career was all but over: he played only four more times, and, in the club's next First Division game, at Everton, the Scot's No. 4 shirt passed to Peter Eustace. Megson, who had joined the club as an amateur in 1952 and made his League debut in 1959, began a run as captain which lasted until 1970, by which time he had chalked up over 440 appearances for the club.

Brown's first term, in which the Owls finished eighth in the table, also marked the end of the line as a regular for another veteran, Alan Finney, and it saw the introduction onto the League scene of youngsters Howard Wilkinson, Wilf Smith and Peter Wicks. Finney, who had made his League debut as a teenager early

in Brown's spell as the club's coach fourteen years before, remained long enough to take his tally of appearances for the club to over 500 (he scored 90 goals) before his 1966 move to Doncaster.

It was in November of that 1964-65 campaign, incidentally, that Brown made one of his most interesting conversions when he switched John Hickton to centre-forward: the lad from Brimington (Chesterfield) claimed 10 goals in 26 games. Hickton had made his senior debut as a full-back in the Buckingham area, but then developed into a very useful centre-half. In fact, he hit 21 goals before reverting to central defence in the reserves; yet was never given the chance to stake a claim for the same job in the first team after regular centre-half Vic Mobley was injured in the 1966 FA Cup semi-final. Typically, Brown ignored the advice of his coaching staff and gave the job to teenager Sam Ellis.

An intriguing tailpiece to the Hickton story came when Brown sold him to Middlesbrough for a bargain £20,000 in September 1966, then went out and paid a club record £70,000 fee, for centre-forward John Ritchie. It was, admittedly, true that Brown was helping out his old Sunderland captain, Stan Anderson, by selling him a defender; but it was not without irony that Hickton was subsequently switched into Boro's attack and, indeed, claimed 185 goals for the Teesside club. For many years, the Owls wished they had held on to Hickton.

The high point of Brown's stay at Hillsborough was, of course, the run to the FA Cup final in 1966, when remarkably, they reached Wembley without playing a single tie at home, in a campaign which saw them manage only three away victories in their First Division programme. Indeed, a haul of just eight away points explains why they finished 17th in the table, a mere three points above Northampton, who were relegated with Blackburn. (It is, incidentally, intriguing to note that Wednesday won only 21 of 86 away games in the Brown era). Somehow, on the road to Wembley, everything 'clicked' and, on a succession of heavy pitches, a significant factor no doubt, the youngsters whom Brown introduced touched unexpectedly high performance levels. Hickton, Dobson and close-season signing (from Sunderland) Brian Usher, who all missed out on the ultimate glory, were there at the outset, and while it

was Johnny Fantham's last-minute strike which sealed the 3-2 third-round victory at Third Division Reading, Dobson was on target in the 2-1 win at Newcastle in the fourth round, and Usher snapped up the winner as the Owls came from behind to triumph at Huddersfield at the next stage. Johnny Quinn made his first Cup appearance of the season in the quarter-final at rain swept Blackburn, where goals from Fantham and young David Ford sealed a 2-1 win on an appalling Ewood Park pitch.

The most memorable triumph of the season came in the semi-final, when the Owls defeated the highly-rated Chelsea 2-0 on a black, treacle pudding of a pitch, at Villa Park. Nobody gave Wednesday a chance, but heavy rain fell for hours before the game and, once again, the conditions suited Brown's youngsters,

Fantham (No.8) celebrates David Ford's winner in the 1966 FA Cup quarter-final with Blackburn at Ewood Park.

Gerry Young in a duel with Chelsea's Peter Osgood in the 1966 FA Cup semi-final at Villa Park.

while denying Tommy Docherty's side the chance to show their normal fluency and flair. Yet nothing should detract from the merit of a victory achieved despite having centre-half Vic Mobley reduced to a passenger for an hour, after suffering damaged ankle ligaments in a clash with Chelsea's George Graham. Substitutes were not then permitted in the FA Cup.

Gerry Young, on whose shoulders the chief central defensive duties were thrust by Mobley's injury, produced one of his finest displays; while midfielder Graham Pugh, only six weeks past his eighteenth birthday and on his FA Cup debut, typified the sheer exuberance of the younger members of the Owls team. Pugh's golden moment came eleven minutes into the second half when Ford headed a Fantham cross back into the Chelsea goalmouth and the teenager

nipped in to break the deadlock. Jim McCalliog, who by coincidence had joined Wednesday that season from Chelsea for a £37,500 fee (making him English football's most expensive teenager), headed the second goal a minute before the final whistle.

The 1966 final is remembered as one of the most exciting in Wembley history, with Wednesday's inexperience finally exposed as they surrendered a two-goal lead and Everton recovered to claim a famous victory. The team Don Megson led out on that May day included six players aged twenty-one or under, with Sam Ellis (making his FA Cup debut) and Pugh each boasting only nine senior appearances, while Ford and McCalliog had played in fewer than 30 games. Ironically, Everton's hero just happened to be the man making only his ninth appearance and playing in

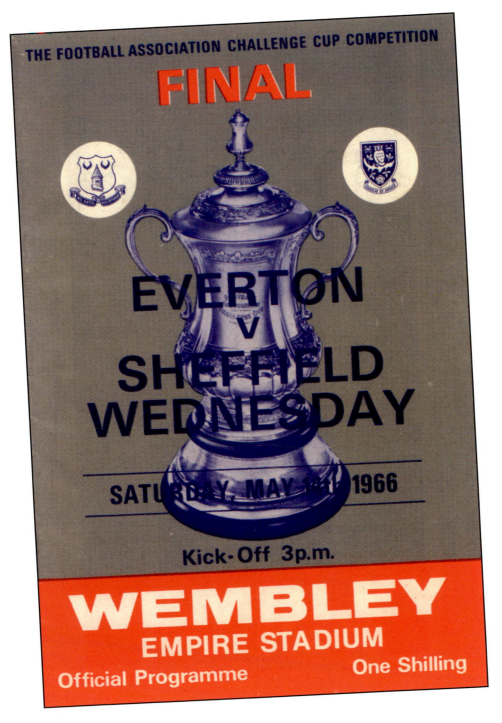

1966 FA Cup final programme cover.

his second and last Cup tie for the Merseysiders—Mike Trebilcock.

Everton, the first team to reach Wembley without conceding a goal, were firm favourites, but Wednesday stunned them with a goal after only four minutes. Ford collected a Eustace throw-in and turned the ball inside for McCalliog to hit a shot which was deflected off defender Wilson's leg and past goalkeeper West into the net. When, eleven minutes into the second half, Ford made it 2-0 after West had stopped but not held Fantham's shot, few could have imagined that the FA Cup was not bound for Sheffield. Everton's Colin Harvey, who was destined to have a spell at Hillsborough later in his

1966 Cup Final ticket.

The men who went to Wembley 1966.
Back row: Peter Eustace, Sam Ellis, Ron Springett, Wilf Smith, Gerry Young, Jim McCalliog.
Front row: Graham Pugh, Johnny Fantham, Don Megson, David Ford, Johnny Quinn.

Wednesday still came home to a tremendous welcome despite losing to Everton in the 1966 FA Cup final.

Cover of Wednesday's first FA Cup tie programme after Wembley, the home duel with Queens Park Rangers in which the Springett brothers were the opposing goalkeepers and the Hillsborough club launched 'Ozzie Owl'.

career, once told me: 'People talk of that final as a classic Everton win, but forget that Wednesday had us on the ropes for an hour, and we were grateful to get back into it. Sheffield started with four men in midfield to our two, and we were over-run until we scored our first goal two minutes after going 2-0 down'.

The strike which turned the game came when Harris flighted the ball into Wednesday's penalty area and Temple headed it into the path of Trebilcock, who scored from 12 yards.

Six minutes later, Megson was harshly alleged to have obstructed Scott on the right, and when the winger's free-kick, aimed at the head of Brian Labone, eluded the Everton skipper at the back post, the ball caught the challenging Gerry Young's neck and fell perfectly for Trebilcock to hit it past Springett on the half-volley. The cruellest blow of all came after 73 minutes, and the victim was Young, normally the most dependable of players. An Owls attack broke down, and goalkeeper West gathered the ball and threw it to Harvey, who, from just outside the Everton penalty area, hit a hopeful long clearance which fell a yard beyond the centre-circle in Wednesday's half of the field. Young appeared to have the ball covered, but incredibly, it spun under his right foot and straight into the path of Temple, running behind the defender. Temple sped to the edge of the penalty area before delivering his shot inside Springett's right-hand post. The Wembley line-up was:

Wednesday—Springett; Smith, Ellis, G. Young, Megson: Pugh, Eustace, McCalliog, Quinn; Fantham, Ford.

Everton—West, Wright, Labone, Harris, Wilson, Scott, Gabriel, Harvey, Temple, A. Young, Trebilcock.
Referee: Jack Taylor (Wolverhampton).

There were many times in the 1966-67 season when Wednesday touched the heights and suggested that those who had predicted a bright future after Wembley might be right, but in the event, this proved to be Alan Brown's last full campaign at the helm and, ultimately, the promise proved an illusion as an air of disenchantment gradually developed. It was a boom year in terms of season ticket sales and a big increase in attendances, partly due to the interest stimulated by Wednesday's Wembley run but also stemming from England's World Cup triumph on home soil. Taylor had revelled in the use of Hillsborough as one of the World Cup venues, and there were many occasions in the years immediately after the summer of 1966 when the ground was packed for big domestic fixtures involving the Owls.

The FA Cup campaign for 1967 produced two such 'special' days, with a 40,000 crowd watching Wednesday beat Queens Park Rangers 3-0 (Ritchie hit a hat-trick) in the third round; and a staggering 49,000 present for the 4-0 fourth-round defeat of another Third Division side, Mansfield. Evidence that the club was seeking to exploit their increased popularity came when the QPR tie coincided with the launch of a new Ozzie Owl mascot and the opening of a new restaurant bearing the same name; though, in fact, the day is more readily remembered for the appearance of the goalkeeping Springett brothers, Ron and Peter, on opposing sides. In the summer of 1967, the pair swopped clubs, with Wednesday making a £35,000 cash adjustment.

Wednesday's dreams of a prompt return to Wembley were shattered in the quarter-final when Tommy Baldwin's last-minute strike enabled Chelsea to avenge the semi-final defeat of the previous season. The Owls had, incidentally, elected to enter the League Cup for the first time in 1966-67, encouraged by the knowledge that success offered the promise of a Wembley final and a place in Europe; but sadly, their debut in the competition coincided with a

John Ritchie . . . £70,000 record signing.

humbling, if narrow, home defeat against South Yorkshire neighbours Rotherham. So the only Owl who went back to Wembley in 1967 was Jim McCalliog, for when he was chosen to face England in April, he became the first Wednesday player for forty-seven years to be capped by Scotland.

The Owls began 1966-67 with a seven-match unbeaten run, but then managed just two wins in seventeen games. However, they finished 1966 on a high note with a 6-1 defeat of Chelsea on New Year's Eve. Their nine victories in the second half of the campaign, included a 7-0 crushing of Burnley on a May day when new England Under-23 cap David Ford grabbed a treble, and Jack Whitham started his habit of scoring as a sub-stitute, when he celebrated his League debut with a double strike. By losing only two of their last seven matches, Wednesday finished eleventh in the table.

Wednesday, of course, reached their centenary in 1967, but overall, it was a year of extremes in fortune when circumstances conspired to prevent the kind of celebration they might have wanted. Club chairman Dr Andrew Stephen became Football Association chairman; but in July, general-manager Eric Taylor was badly injured and narrowly escaped death in a car crash, and in September young David Ford was also injured in a fatal crash.

Wednesday won five of their first six games in 1967-68, including a 1-0 victory at Sheffield United, and led the First Division at one stage. However, they were subsequently hampered by injuries to Ford, Pugh (he was dogged by knee trouble for a long time) and Smith. A run which saw them collect just 10 points from 22 games from mid-December pushed them desperately close to the relegation precipice. In truth, they were one of several clubs grateful for Sheffield United's astonishing late slump that year.

It is sometimes forgotten that in this season, the versatile Johnny Quinn was told he could not be guaranteed a first-team place and joined Tommy Docherty's Rotherham for a give-away £27,000; and John

Fantham finally topped Redfern Froggatt's post-war aggregate record of 140 League goals. But it is invariably remembered as the term when Alan Brown quit and returned to Roker. The Owls won only one of the last 12 League games under Brown, and his final match, on 3rd February, just happened to be against Sunderland, who came to Sheffield and claimed their first win for three months. Sunderland axed their manager, Ian McColl, within a few days, and though Brown insisted his resignation from the Wednesday post was just coincidence, nobody was surprised when he was installed at Roker barely 24 hours later. Brown succeeded in keeping Sunderland in Division One, but they were destined to fall within a couple of years, going down in 1970—with Wednesday!

At the time of Brown's departure, there was every danger of the Owls getting caught in the relegation trap that season, for they were already in the middle of a miserable sequence. Under Brown's assistant, Jack Marshall, who took over, they man-aged only two wins in their remaining 15 matches, losing 8, and it was just enough to avoid disaster. However, with Sheffield United failing to beat the drop, the spring of 1968 was hardly a vintage phase in local football history; and, at Hillsborough, there were already fears that things might get a lot worse before they started to get better again.

Marshall & Rowley, 1968–1969

WEDNESDAY'S Jack Marshall and United's Arthur Rowley did not have a lot in common other than that their managerial careers briefly coincided when they were in Sheffield at the same time towards the end of the 1960s, with neither enjoying much success. Both, no doubt, considered themselves victims of circumstance, though, significantly perhaps, they did not go on to greater things after leaving. One might fairly suggest their best days as managers were already behind them: Marshall having reached a pinnacle in seven seasons at Blackburn Rovers, Rowley touching a peak in ten years (seven as player-boss) with Shrewsbury Town.

Marshall was a likeable Lancastrian whose playing days as a Burnley full-back had been blighted by injury and shortened by the war, limiting him to a mere 27 Football League and FA Cup games in peacetime, the first in September 1938 and the last in November 1946. However, he compensated with success as a coach, first with Bury and later at Stoke City; then, in 1954, his old Turf Moor pal, Alan Brown, recommended him as his successor for the job of Eric Taylor's trainer-coach at Hillsborough. When Taylor relinquished the team-manager's duties and Harry Catterick was recruited from Rochdale in 1958, Marshall was chosen to fill the vacancy created at Spotland. In September 1960 he moved into the old First Division at Blackburn, where he built a reputation as a boss who liked his teams to play attacking football. Alas, his time at Ewood turned sour following Blackburn's relegation to Division Two in 1966 (the same year as the Owls beat them en route to the FA Cup final); and following the board's installation of Eddie Quigley, an old Rovers favourite and an ex-Wednesday man, as assistant manager with total control, Marshall put up with it briefly before taking the hint and resigning in February 1967. He did not need much persuading to accept Alan Brown's offer of a return to Hillsborough in a far less demanding role soon afterwards.

Rowley, a product of the Black Country and a big, lethal-footed forward, had enjoyed more fame than Marshall in his playing days, and indeed, had assured himself of a place in soccer history with a record haul of 434 Football League goals in 619 games spanning nineteen years and four clubs. (His older brother, Jack, scored 208 League and Cup goals for Manchester United between 1937 and 1955). Arthur began with West Brom towards the end of the war, and, after a later spell at Fulham, really made his mark with 251 goals in 303 games for Leicester City, with whom he had collected two Second Division championship medals between 1950 and 1958. As player-manager at Shrewsbury he led them into the

Third Division in his first season, and to within one point of the Second Division in his last. After hanging up his boots in 1965, he had looked almost a permanent fixture at Gay Meadow, until being recruited by Sheffield United in July 1968. The Blades' relegation prompted chairman Dick Wragg to persuade John Harris to vacate the team-boss' chair and become general manager; both agreed that Rowley appeared to have the credentials which would ensure he and Harris could form a successful partnership.

Across the city at Hillsborough, it was always felt by those close to Marshall that, after Alan Brown walked out in February 1968, the man they called 'Jolly Jack' accepted the step back into front-line management at the age of fifty with considerable reluctance, and would have preferred to remain in a supporting role. It said much that he was happy to accept the unpromising one-year contract offered by the club. Initially, he inherited coaches Lawrie McMenemy and Ian McFarlane; but later, in October 1968, former captain and wing-half, Tom McAnearney resigned the manger's job at Aldershot to return to Sheffield as Marshall's assistant, and in November, McMenemy—who had fancied succeeding Brown but didn't get the chance because he lacked the managerial experience to match his high ambitions—left to succeed George Raynor as manager of Doncaster Rovers. McFarlane, the former Chelsea and Leicester defender, also began to believe his future lay elsewhere, although he remained until June 1969, by which time Marshall had long departed the scene.

Initially, Marshall was unlucky with injuries, later he was troubled by a spell of ill-health, and, one way or another, his dreams of creating a side to fulfil attacking philosophy never got started. He was, perhaps, unfortunate in having to follow Brown when the players were glad of release from the former manager's iron discipline. Somehow, there was a readily perceptive switch to a more relaxed operation, and many felt Marshall never gained the full backing or respect of all his players. His period coincided with a spell of mounting dressing room disenchantment, with several key men, including Mobley, McCalliog, Ellis, Ritchie and Eustace, submitting transfer requests.

Wednesday's results had been in decline for some time before Brown left, and, in the remaining weeks of the 1967-68 campaign after his departure, they won only 2 of 15 First Division matches. Their slide gathered pace in 1968-69 when they won only ten games, failed to claim a single League double for the first time in eleven seasons, and did not score in 18 matches. Moreover, starting with

Jack Marshall (right) talking to Peter Eustace.

Marshall's last match at the helm, a 3-0 defeat at Coventry in early March, they were without a single victory in their final 12 games. They finished 15th in the table. It was, perhaps, typical of their extremes of form and fortune in this term that at the end of August they came from behind to defeat Manchester United, the European champions, 5-4 in an unforgettable Hillsborough duel in which Jack Whitham claimed a hat-trick; yet five days later they suffered the indignity of losing 3-1 at Fourth Division Exeter City in the Football League Cup. Marshall, it should be noted, missed both games, being

in hospital recovering after an operation; and, by the way, the woe of the trip to Devon was compounded when record signing John Ritchie suffered knee damage in the tie and was forced to miss the next 13 games.

Other than the Manchester United triumph, the highlight of Wednesday's season was a memorable FA Cup victory in a third-round replay at Leeds in January. When the teams shared a 1-1 draw at Hillsborough, few would have backed the Owls to succeed at Elland Road, where they were without the injured David Ford. However, teenager Brian Woodall enjoyed his one moment of glory, in

Alan Warboys (left) in action against Burnley in September 1968.

an otherwise disappointing career, by celebrating his Cup debut with a famous double strike; and, with Ritchie also on target, Wednesday came from behind to win 3-1.

That triumph will always be synonymous with Peter Eustace, who produced perhaps his finest display in a Wednesday shirt. It was no surprise when, in the same month, the elegant midfielder was called into the England squad ahead of the Wembley international with Rumania. He didn't make the final eleven, but it emphasised the opportunities which beckoned a man recognised as a very gifted footballer. The Stocksbridge lad never went as far as he might. Within less than a month of his England call he found himself suspended when he broke club rules by going skiing on the local moors, suffering a gashed leg in the process. Many believed he suffered more than most from the loss of Brown's influence, though others, notably Woodall and Pugh, might have especially benefited from the old manager's discipline.

Marshall felt a key to a revival in Wednesday's fortunes lay in restoring wing play to the side, but all his attempts to find the right man failed. Ironically, in the summer of 1968 he had parted with one natural winger, Brian Usher, who went to Doncaster in the exchange deal which brought big young striker Alan Warboys to Sheffield. Of course, the truth was that Usher had seldom managed to repeat the form he had shown at Sunderland and became the target of cruel criticism from supporters. The man Marshall wanted for the No. 7 shirt was Barry Lyons, the former Rotherham man then with Nottingham Forest. When that didn't happen,

he spent £20,000 on an unknown Scot, Archie Irvine, from Airdrie, but in the event, the little man never quite managed to fit the bill.

When Marshall played five first-teamers in the reserves—including skipper Don Megson, whose testimonial year it was—it served to confirm the depth of the problems facing the manager; and a 5-0 home defeat, at the hands of Arsenal on the first Saturday in March, signalled the beginning of the end for him. There was a certain irony in that, two weeks after this game, Arsenal were themselves humbled in the League Cup final when they fell in extra-time to Third Division Swindon—managed by Danny Williams, the man destined to succeed Marshall. The chop came for 'Jolly Jack' a few days after this historic Wembley occasion, which had no direct Hillsborough links other than that it almost certainly prompted

Tommy Craig, Wednesday's first £100,000 signing.

Arthur Rowley (centre), with John Harris (left) and Dick Wragg, after Rowley's appointment as United's manager.

Messrs Taylor, Stephen and others in the Owls' boardroom to identify Williams as the man they wanted. However, with Swindon still chasing promotion and Williams not immediately available, the decision was taken to put coach Tom McAnearney in temporary charge. The Scot was away with the players at the Lilleshall national training centre in Shropshire when he learned the news.

There was a major footnote to the season, and one Marshall no doubt smiled about as he considered his future. Several times during the season he had joined Eric Taylor and Andrew Stephen on 'secret' trips to Scotland, where most people knew they were watching eighteen-year-old Aberdeen player Tommy Craig. Aston Villa were supposed to be favourites to sign him, but, early in May,

Wednesday learned their £100,000 offer had been accepted; and though still without a manager, they made the lad the club's first six-figure signing and the most expensive teenager in British football. He made his debut in the last game of the season, against Tottenham at Hillsborough.

When Wednesday went into the close season of 1969 looking to appoint a team-boss, few could have predicated there would also be a managerial change at Bramall Lane before the start of the new campaign. After relegation, United had disappointingly finished only ninth in the Second Division, despite heavy spending which contributed to a £98,670 loss on the year, but the odds on Arthur Rowley at least seeing out his three-year contract looked good. It was known Rowley had fancied the

Leicester job after the axing of Matt Gillies in late 1968, but he was never a serious candidate and most people considered he had made a fair start with United and was destined to remain. The man himself would have put money on it.

United suffered only three home defeats in 1968–1969, but a paltry two away victories was the reason they failed to make a serious impression in the promotion race. It just added insult to injury that their record included a shock FA Cup third-round defeat at Third Division Mansfield. They boasted only one double, which came against relegated Bury, and two five-match sequences constituted their best undefeated runs. They won four of the opening five matches, but then claimed only one victory in the next ten; and though they had a couple of reasonable spells, three successes in their final eleven fixtures killed off any hopes of a late challenge. Such was the disappointment among supporters, that when the Blades met Blackburn in their last home game, the 9,654 attendance was the lowest in the League at Bramall Lane for twelve years—since the 7,710 at the West Ham game (also in Division Two) in September 1957.

Rowley's first signing was his old Shrewsbury captain and wing-half, Ted Hemsley, who cost £25,000, in August; but five days later he stunned Blades' followers by selling the popular and influential Willie Carlin to Derby for £63,000. Subsequently, with the

Tony Currie on target in the October 1968 match with Middlesbrough.

United's record signing, John Tudor, meets coach John Short.

Eddie Colquhoun.

benefit of hindsight (and after Carlin had helped Brian Clough's side win the Second Division title) Rowley admitted the sale of the little midfield general was a major error of judgement. In September, the manager followed up a tip from his brother, Jack, and paid Wrexham £28,00 for their new Welsh international defender Dave Powell; and in October the influence of John Harris was apparent when West Brom's Scottish Under-23 centre-half, Eddie Colquhoun, was bought for around £30,000. In mid November the Blades broke their transfer record with the capture of striker John Tudor from Coventry for £65,000.

All four men might fairly be described as excellent buys. Powell, who went on to take his tally of Welsh caps to eleven while with United, was the unluckiest in that injuries limited him to 89 League games, but nobody ever doubted his quality. Hemsley and Colquhoun were outstanding signings. Hemsley, a Worcestershire county cricketer, already boasted 235 League outings for Shrewsbury (he made his debut at sixteen), and added 247 with United; but the 'making' of him as a Blades favourite was John Harris' decision to switch him from wing-half, where he was not effective, to left-back in the 1969-70 campaign. Colquhoun, who had started his career with Bury, took over the captaincy from Badger almost as soon as he arrived, and he not only went on to make over 360 League appearances, before leaving in 1977 to try his luck in America, but collected nine Scottish caps between 1971 and 1973.

Tudor, a product of Ilkeston, was the initial surprise package, in that he arrived without much of a reputation, though to be fair, some of the 77 games in which he had scored 15 goals for Coventry had been in defence. Something of a latecomer to the professional scene, he had had to battle to get his chance and prove himself, and he boasted an instinctive self-belief which proved invaluable. He hit 11 goals in 19 League matches in his first term (only Alan Woodward with 12 in 42 games scored more), including two on his debut at Bury and three in the home return with the same opponents in February—when he claimed United's first League hat-trick since 1963. In all, Tudor managed 31 goals in 71 League outings

before going on to enjoy a successful spell at Newcastle after Harris used him in the 1971 deal which brought goalkeeper John Hope and ex-Wednesday man David Ford to Sheffield and significantly influenced United's belated but successful push towards the top-grade. Reference to Hope prompts one to note that in 1968-69 Alan Hodgkinson was still very much the No. 1 choice in the green jersey; and as one of only two ever-presents in the side, he celebrated his testimonial season by taking his tally of League games past 500.

As well as parting with Carlin, Rowley's lone season with United saw him sell local lads Ken Mallender, who went to Norwich for £38,000, and David Munks, for whom Portsmouth paid £20,000. After the end of the season, he let Jack Mansell's Reading have the Wagstaff brothers, Tony and Barry, and Bernard Shaw was sold to Wolves. Such youngsters as Mick Harmston, Ian Mackenzie and Dave Staniforth had been given their first taste of senior football, but it was the end of the line for such home-grown players as Mick Heaton, Tom Fenoughty and Phil Cliff. Full-back Heaton went on to enjoy a successful run with Blackburn and began a link with Howard Kendall which lasted many years after the end of his playing days; while Fenoughty and Cliff both concluded their League careers at Chesterfield. Incidentally, Rowley's last signing came a month before his sacking, when he brought John Flynn from Workington for £5,000—a profitable capture in that the defender was to make some 200 appearances.

The end of the line for Rowley came suddenly just three days before the start of the 1969-70 campaign and soon after the first-team squad returned from a pre-season trip, which saw them based at Bemmel in Holland, facing three Dutch clubs and one German side. The events of that short tour probably contributed to the board's unexpected decision. At the time the players sailed to Holland they were in a dispute with the club over an incentive scheme, and, in an attempt to resolve the problem, chairman Wragg and general-manager Harris flew out for a special meeting at which they made a new offer. If they were dismayed when the players again rejected the deal, Wragg and Harris were not impressed when, almost as soon as the meeting ended, Rowley whisked his men away to attend an evening pony trotting race meeting at Hilversum. Everyone was familiar with the manager's passion for horse-racing, but some of those present at the team's Golden Apple tour headquarters that day were astonished that he went ahead with this particular trip.

It was a costly gamble, for the United party had not been long back home from their trip when Rowley's dismissal was announced. The reasons were never made public. John Harris, having been told only twelve months earlier that the job was too much for him, resumed his old role as team-manager, all the more determined to prove he still had the ability to repeat his 1961 achievement and guide the club back to the top-grade. Meanwhile, Rowley, who soon returned to management with Sunderland, no doubt consoled himself with the knowledge that several of the men he had recruited were destined to play prominent parts when the Blades did finally make it back to Division One.

LEN'S LINE UP

Len Badger Testimonial Match Magazine 8p

Sheffield United v Sheffield Wednesday
Tuesday March 20th 1973 kick off 7-30pm

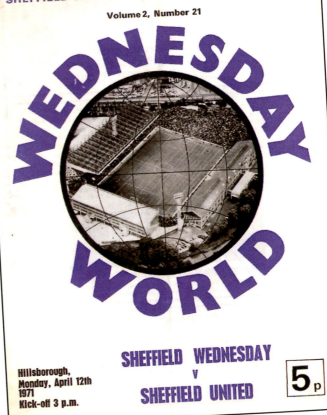

SHEFFIELD WEDNESDAY F.C. OFFICIAL MAGAZINE

Volume 2, Number 21

WEDNESDAY WORLD

Hillsborough,
Monday, April 12th
1971
Kick-off 3 p.m.

SHEFFIELD WEDNESDAY
v
SHEFFIELD UNITED

5p

The Seventies: A Summary

THE SEVENTIES proved to be one of the most dismal decades in Sheffield football history: a period short on glory and long on gloom, with both city clubs on the slide— though it should be noted that United enjoyed a memorable return to the top-grade in 1971 and had a UEFA Cup place in their sights right up to the last match of the 1974-75 campaign ahead of a dramatic decline which matched that of their city rivals.

Wednesday dropped out of the First Division at the end of 1969-70, when, despite having looked favourites for the drop all season, they went into their final game, at home to Manchester City, with a golden opportunity of scrambling to safety. Alas they failed to take it. In 1974-75 they did manage to retain their Second Division status with a last-day victory, but it proved only a brief stay of execution and they crashed into Division Three in spectacular and sorrowful fashion a year later in 1975. United's fall began in 1976, three years after cricket got the boot from Bramall Lane, ironically, the drop coming at the end of a season which had coincided with the opening of their new 7,992-seater South Stand. Like Wednesday, United were destined for a long wait to return to the top grade and indeed, by 1979, they and the Owls were both in the Third Division.

That Sheffield's passion for football was not diminished by so much despair was evident when a crowd of 49,309 packed into Hillsborough on Boxing Day 1979 to witness the first-ever Third Division meeting of the city clubs. At the time, the Blades looked the more likely promotion contenders, but a 4-0 Wednesday victory on the day inspired a dramatic Owls revival and induced a sudden dip in United's fortunes. The upshot was that while Wednesday ended that season with a return to the Second Division, within a year United found themselves in Division Four and at the lowest ebb in their history.

Not surprisingly, the 1970s was a phase which saw the arrival and departure of a succession of managers in both city camps. When Wednesday sacked Danny Williams in January 1971, after hopes of a prompt promotion were dashed by a dismal first half of the 1970-71 Second Division campaign, the under-fire chairman, Sir Andrew Stephen and general-manager Eric Taylor thought they had pulled a masterstroke by whisking old idol Derek Dooley from the club's development office and into the Hillsborough hot-seat. However, though he seemed at one stage to be pointing the side in the right direction, Dooley did not enjoy the best of luck, and it ran out in 1973-74. A mystery virus contributed to a drop into the bottom places, and

Eric Taylor pictured with new chairman Matt Sheppard in January 1974 when the long-serving secretary and general manager announced his plans to retire at the end of the season. Sadly, Taylor was already ill, and he died in the following September.

when, in early December, Stephen and his vice-chairman Keith Gardiner resigned, Dooley's days were numbered. However, it was still a shock (and remains one of the most insensitively-timed sackings in the club's history) when new chairman, Matt Shepherd, chose Christmas Eve as the moment to tell the manager his services were no longer required.

Sadly, Wednesday's slide gathered pace after Steve Burtenshaw, a former Arsenal and Queens Park Rangers coach, was given his first taste of front-line management. He only succeeded in guiding the Owls into Division Three and was sacked, in October 1975, following a poor start to the new campaign. Bert McGee, who had switched roles with chairman Sheppard in September, recruited the old Sunderland back, Len Ashurst. Having served a tough managerial apprenticeship with Hartlepool and Gillingham, Ashurst relished the challenge of waking what he described as a sleeping giant, but he faced a daunting task in financial circumstances which left him with severely limited resources. His initial term saw the Owls clinch a last-match victory over Arthur Rowley's Southend to avoid falling into the Fourth Division. While Ashurst achieved some progress in a period of desperate cash restraint, it was largely by way of clearing the dead wood and rebuilding the foundations on which someone else would create a side capable of promotion, that his success had to be measured.

The long-awaited turning point came following the appointment of Jack Charlton, who was persuaded to come out of retirement in early October 1977. A hero of England's 1966 World Cup winning side, 'Big Jack' had proved at Middlesbrough that he was the 'winner' McGee was seeking, and, though success did not come overnight, he took the Owls up to Division Two within three years. Moreover, by the time this was achieved, the club's financial stability had been firmly re-established.

When Sheffield United, having put John Harris back in charge of team affairs in 1969, clinched promotion in 1971 and made a sensational start with an unbeaten 10-match run on their return to the top, few could have anticipated the gloom which

Alan Woodward on target for United in the 4-0 defeat of Blackburn in November 1969.

descended on Bramall Lane later in the 1970s. Early in the decade Tony Currie and Alan Woodward starred in a team which had the capacity to entertain and delight the fans, and with some of the manager's astute investments producing dividends and much to savour, the outlook appeared bright. In truth, of course, things were not always as promising as they sometimes appeared on the surface, but United's followers, though enduring some painfully unsuccessful sequences, always seemed to have more to cheer— before the inevitable fall.

The cricket era ended in 1973, which was also when the club installed a new secretary, ex-Football League referee Keith Walker, as the long-serving Arnold Newton's

replacement in January, and a new manager, former Watford boss Ken Furphy, who came from Blackburn in December. Newton bowed from the scene after more than twenty years; while, once again, Harris was pushed aside, but he was to make another comeback before being returned to the background for the last time. In the summer of 1977 the man so long synonymous with the Blades elected to transfer his affections across the city by joining Len Ashurst as Wednesday's chief scout. Earlier, in November 1974, Derek Dooley, after a spell with a sports equipment firm, following his departure from Hillsborough, moved in the opposite direction and joined United as commercial manager—the start of a climb which led to the old Owls'

When United's long-serving goalkeeper Alan Hodgkinson celebrated his testimonial, he was presented with a painting by Peter Cooper and other South Yorkshire journalists.

favourite becoming Sheffield's first paid football director and later managing director.

Dick Wragg's shock decision in mid-1974 to stand down as chairman and hand over to John Hassall because he preferred to concentrate on his Football Association interests, and especially his duties as chairman of the International Committee, took many by surprise, particularly those who believed United's cause was more important. All the more so as the club had embarked on the building of a costly new stand which threatened to be a financial millstone unless they enjoyed outstanding success on the field. Moreover, it was abundantly clear that money for strengthening the team would be severely restricted. Though, despite evidence that paying for the new

stand was the top priority, with the unexpected £160,000 sale of Geoff Salmons compensating for a £170,000 loss reported to the annual meeting of 1974, the Blades contrived to finish sixth in Division One in Furphy's first full season—and just missed out on a place in Europe. The irony, of course, was that Stoke the club which had pipped United in the chase for European qualification, were themselves denied because UEFA officials decided the Potteries side hadn't finished high enough up the table and accepting them would devalue the competition!

Even so, this proved the high point of United's modern history. Some might suggest it was always an illusion considering the sudden, dramatic and sustained decline which followed—with three experiences of relegation

Farewell to cricket at Bramall Lane...action in Yorkshire's final county match at the ground in August 1973.

For some time after the building of the new football stand, the old pavilion survived.

between 1976 and 1981 in a traumatic spell summed up by statistics which show the Blades won 19 of 130 away matches in this phase and had an overall League record which read:

Played 260, won 79, drawn 64, lost 117.

The slide had started before Furphy was sacked in October 1975, and a new manager Jimmy Sirrel, despite an impressive record at Notts County, was unable to halt it. Indeed, the veteran Scot was so dismayed by the circumstances which denied him the chance of strengthening an ailing side, that he considered his task virtually impossible almost from the outset. The inevitable relegation in 1976 was followed by the departure of the

Blades' most precious playing asset, Tony Currie, who went to Leeds for £240,000. He had been unsettled throughout a nightmare campaign.

Sirrel struggled on until late September 1977, when, with the Blades 21st in the table, he beat Len Ashurst to the bullet by eight days as Sheffield football faced its second double managerial change in two years. However, while Charlton's arrival at Hillsborough was to signal the start of better things for Wednesday, Harry Haslam's appointment brought an eventful interlude in United's history but failed to halt their slide. The former Luton boss, known as 'Happy Harry' and one of the game's great wheeler-

Action during Sheffield FC's FA Vase final with Billericay at Wembley in April 1977. Sheffield players are Strutt and Pugh.

dealers, profited from stand-in Cec Coldwell's efforts in keeping the Blades out of the danger zone in his first term, when they finished 12th in Division Two; but, though some of his excursions into the transfer market were, to say the least, adventurous, especially bringing Alex Sabella from Argentina, and a few of his sales excellent business, he took United down in 1979 and Sheffield went into the 1980s in the unenviable position of having both clubs in the Third Division.

As has been noted, it was just a few days before the end of the decade that the clubs met for the first time at this level, and it turned out to be a clash which ensured the blue half of Sheffield began the 1980s with more cause for optimism. Wednesday climbed into the Second Division at the end of that season to confirm their years of strife were just about over; within a year, alas, United crashed into the Football League's bottom grade—doomed by a missed penalty in the last minute of the final match of the 1980-81 campaign.

A positive note on the local scene was provided by Sheffield FC, who went all the way to the final of the FA Vase competition in 1976-77. They took their place at Wembley with pride, but drew 1-1 with holders Billericay in a duel which went to extra time; and, unfortunately, they lost 2-1 in the replay at the City Ground, Nottingham.

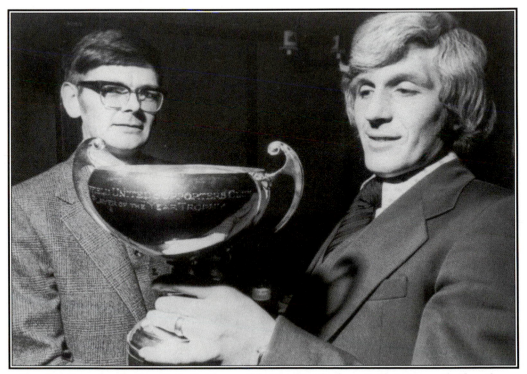

Alan Woodward collecting United's Player of the Year Trophy from Keith Farnsworth (then the Morning Telegraph's sports editor) in 1976.

Wednesday team group, 1970.
Back row: Peter Grummitt, Harold Wilcockson, Colin Prophett, Sam Ellis, Alan Warboys, Kenny Burton, Jack Whitham, Peter Springett.
Front row: Don Megson, Steve Downes, Wilf Smith, Gerry Young, Jackie Sinclair, Tommy Craig, Tony Coleman.

Danny Williams, 1969–1971

Danny Williams

ON PAPER the appointment of Danny Williams as Wednesday's new team-manager in the summer of 1969 looked an inspired choice. His achievement in leading Third Division Swindon to promotion and a famous League Cup final triumph over Arsenal the previous spring, plus the fact that he was recognised as one of the most popular figures in football (moreover, one with an apparent winning touch), all suggested an ideal candidate for the big Hillsborough challenge. Sadly, the old Rotherham United favourite did not enjoy a happy return to his native South Yorkshire. He survived only eighteen months, and during his stay Wednesday's slide was hastened rather than halted. Indeed, his only full campaign in charge coincided with relegation from the top flight as the Owls suffered their worst season for fifty years with a paltry 8 victories and 25 defeats.

Thrybergh-born Williams, who started his working life on the pit top at Silverwood Colliery and spent the first eight years of his professional football career, from 1943 to 1951, as a part-timer, made his name as an attacking wing-half in 620 games for Rotherham over a span of nearly twenty years. As a youngster he rejected overtures from Arsenal, Leicester and Sheffield United and preferred to join his home-town club, where he typified the happy band of local heroes, most of them miners, whom Reg Freeman and Andy Smailes

fashioned into a colourful side which climbed from the old Third Division (North) to the brink of the First Division. There were many who felt Williams at his best was good enough to play for England, but the nearest he got to a cap was when Wales, thinking him a Welshman, called on him only to find he was a true-born Tyke!

Happy-go-lucky Danny loved a joke, but there was no more dedicated footballer, and while he belonged to that breed who played more for pleasure than for the modest pay packets of those days, long before he hung up his boots he was canny enough to invest in a sports outfitter's business. This gave him financial independence but did not prevent him seeking to stay in the game, and he savoured his first taste of management with Rotherham between 1962 and 1965. Then when he did decide to pack up, and proposed to retire to Bournemouth, he was persuaded to make a quick comeback with Swindon, whom he kept in the top half of the Third Division for three seasons before hitting the jackpot in 1969 with promotion and that epic extra-time Wembley triumph. (By coincidence, one of his most memorable successes as a player had also been against Arsenal, when Rotherham won a famous FA Cup third-round second replay in 1960—at Hillsborough.)

Williams was unique, very much a one-off in style and character, but he always said that as a manager he modelled himself on his old Millmoor boss, Reg Freeman—one of the game's real gentlemen and such a quiet and kindly fellow that you couldn't imagine him shouting at anyone. Freeman, who later joined Sheffield United, could be tough but had an easy manner which, combined with his great knowledge of the game, inspired respect and loyalty. Said Williams: 'Reg produced a team of captains. Everyone took responsibility and pulled his weight, and the players had a terrific feeling for each other but didn't hesitate to sort out anyone guilty of letting the side down'.

This was an atmosphere he sought to create at Swindon, and he succeeded. He made several astute signings, but none more significant than the capture of Stan Harland from Carlisle. The defender cost a modest fee, was promptly installed as skipper, and led by example as he typified the dedication and spirit which enabled

the Wiltshire club to prove they could, on their day, match the best. Their keynote was a work rate and dedication which amply compensated for any lack of outstanding talent. Williams had players who made his own job easy. 'I never had to worry about the dressing room and was left to concentrate on studying the opposition and plotting how to beat them,' he said.

When the opportunity to join Wednesday came, it arrived out of the blue in the form of a telephone call from Wednesday general-manager Eric Taylor. Williams recalled he was flattered but initially reluctant: 'I was more than content living in

Tommy Craig.

Bournemouth and working at Swindon, but Eric was very insistent and said I was the man they wanted, and after 'Doc' Stephen and his vice-chairman, Keith Gardiner, came to see me, I accepted'.

He soon discovered that circumstances in Sheffield were very different from those at Swindon. He always said he was not troubled by the higher expectations, and stepping up into the top-grade did not scare him; but he was dismayed by the low morale in the dressing room, and it was a blow to discover the depth of the unrest amongst the players—many of whom wanted to leave. Long after his Hillsborough days were over, he remembered: 'I told the directors

it had taken me four years to turn things round at Swindon, and it would take as long to do it at Wednesday. This was even more evident after our first match, at Manchester City, and I think they recognised there was a hell of a lot to do. Unfortunately, they ended my stay after eighteen months, and it wasn't long enough.'

Williams arrived to find he had inherited the club's newly-signed first £100,000 player, Tommy Craig; while striker John Ritchie had been sold back to Stoke City for a give-away £25,000 and Scottish forward Jim McCalliog was all set to join Wolves for £70,000—a deal Eric Taylor was keen to complete in order to pay Aberdeen for Craig. Williams was not

Goalkeeping rivals: Peter Springett(left) and Peter Grummitt.

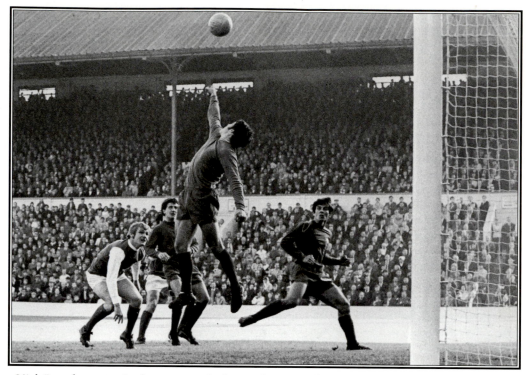

Mick Prendergast poised to pounce, Owls v Derby, September 1969.

particularly impressed with Craig, mainly because he had been told to expect a midfield ball-winner in the Billy Bremner mould and found he had what he regarded as a replica of Peter Eustace. In Craig's defence, he ultimately did well enough in a difficult phase, but Williams, who was sometimes to be heard describing the Scot as 'a tanner ball player', considered him an expensive luxury— and it did not go down well with the board when he talked of dropping the expensive teenager.

It was after the opening game at Maine Road, where the Owls lost 4-1, that Williams, speaking on television, said 'I've only got six good players'— hardly a statement designed to boost morale in the dressing rooms. He later explained he had not meant this

as a criticism of the others but to emphasise how badly the team needed strengthening. 'I was shocked at how poor we were against City and felt we needed five new players before we could seriously expect to progress,' he said. 'I wanted the supporters to know I couldn't work miracles with a team that wasn't good enough as it stood.'

Ironically, Williams subsequently sold most of the men he identified as his best players, while certain others, for various reasons, never played to their full capacity in that dreadful 1969-70 campaign. Those who departed in this phase included Eustace, who joined West Ham for £90,000, centre-half Vic Mobley (QPR, £55,000), and David Ford, who went to Newcastle in the swop deal which brought Scottish winger Jackie Sinclair to Sheffield.

It was often said that Williams sold better players than he bought, though he, naturally, disputed this and insisted he was told he had to make a profit in his transfer dealings. 'You can't do that and build a team,' he argued. Among the players he recruited were full-back Harold Wilcockson (Doncaster), exchanged for Ian Branfoot and Archie Irvine; former Doncaster winger Tony Coleman (Manchester City, £15,000); goalkeeper Peter Grummitt (Nottingham Forest, £30,000); and winger Willie Lawson (Brechin, £4,000). A deal which illustrated the ineffectiveness of some of Danny's deals in that first term was the purchase of Steve Downes, a young striker from Rotherham, for £38,000. The twenty-year-old scored a memorable goal against Sunderland on his Boxing Day debut, but managed only 3 more goals and 29 appearances and proved an expensive flop. Ironically, the Owls had sold John Fantham to Jim McAnearney's Rotherham for a bargain £5,000, and while it is true the club's post-war record marksman was past his peak there were those who felt he could still have been more useful than those who replaced him.

Wednesday won only 2 of their first 11 League games and went 12 without a victory between early October and late December. It simply compounded their woe when, having been dumped out of the League Cup at Third Division Bournemouth in September, they completed an embarrassing double by losing at home to Forth Division Scunthorpe United in the FA Cup fourth-round—a tie, incidentally, which marked the last senior appearance of skipper Don Megson, who left to join Bristol Rovers as player-coach before stepping up to player-manager.

Three wins on the trot in February were followed by another poor spell which brought only one victory in eight, yet they went into their final match, at home to Manchester City, still in with a chance of avoiding relegation and sending Crystal Palace down instead. The 45,258 spectators who were present on that wet April evening could hardly believe their eyes as Wednesday threw it all away with a display lacking in spirit and character. Somehow, the early departure of defender Wilf Smith, who had been doubtful ahead of the game and retired injured, epitomised the sense of inevitable doom. Eric Taylor said afterwards: 'We didn't play like a team that wanted to win. City played with their hands in their pockets, and we still couldn't beat them'. The manager, meanwhile, was left musing: 'What kills my pig is we would never have lost this game if we'd had eleven players called Danny Williams in the team. There's no wonder people say it's a different game these days!'

Manchester City, preoccupied with a Cup-Winners' Cup final date the following week, soon indicated they would be content to get through the game without injuries and wouldn't be too troubled if Wednesday took the points. Early on, there was an astonishing incident when the visitors were awarded a penalty. Tony Book, their skipper, ran the length of the field to speak to Mike Doyle, and while what he said was never re-vealed, Doyle's spot-kick was so tame the ball rolled gently to goalkeeper Grummitt. Then City took the lead with a remarkable goal from Ian Bowyer. The 21st minute substitute looked to be aiming his speculative shot for the far corner flag, but, incredibly, the ball swerved and dipped between the goal posts. Home hopes were revived when Coleman, one of the few Wednesday men who consistently displayed the required spirit, hit a superb equaliser, but, as Williams said later, when Smith walked off 'the bottom fell out of the team'. Yet the turning point was induced by a misunderstanding which prompted City manager Joe Mercer to rush to the touch line and urge his side to go for victory. Bowyer again obliged, hitting the goal which sent the Owls to a 2-1 defeat.

There is not much doubt that, until City winger Mike Summerbee was injured in a clash with Owls' defender Colin Prophett, Mercer, the former Sheffield United boss and a good friend of Eric Taylor's, had hoped his side would not be responsible for sending Wednesday down. However, when he saw the extent of Summerbee's injury, Mercer was beside himself with rage and convinced Colin Prophett was to blame. He failed to notice that the City man had committed the foul and, in effect, had injured himself. The referee awarded the free-kick to Wednesday, and it was not until after the game that Mercer appreciated this. He was quick to apologise to Prophett, but it was too late to alter the result!

Wednesday's relegation prompted angry scenes at the club's annual meeting, but retiring directors Keith Gardiner and Dick Gunstone were re-elected despite a strong challenge from Shareholders Association 'rebels' Harry Allen and Roy Whitehead. Allen,

John Sissons.

who owned a chain of chemists shops, never sought election again, but Whitehead did gain a place on the board within a few years.

Almost as soon as the season ended, Wednesday sold Jack Whitham to Liverpool for £55,000, which looked a fair deal considering the striker had been limited to 21 games through injuries; and Coleman moved to Blackpool for a small fee. Williams intended using the money to acquire the midfield ball-winner he felt his side lacked. He wanted Burnley's Brian O'Neill, but when he and Eric Taylor drove over to Turf Moor, they discovered their target had just signed for Southampton. Remarkably, Burnley boss Harry Potts talked them into taking Northern Ireland international Sammy Todd instead. Todd, who cost £40,000, had already gained 8 of his 11 caps, but most of his 116 games for Burnley had been as a defender. Proof that he was hardly the man Williams had been seeking came when he was limited to a mere 26 senior outings in three years at Hillsborough.

The only other close-season buy of note was at least a man who went on to play 126 games and score 15 goals—former England Under-23 winger John Sissons. He cost £65,000 from West Ham and arrived with the experience of over 260 League and Cup appearances. Six years earlier, at the age of seventeen, he had been the youngest player to score in an FA Cup final and in 1965 had helped West Ham win the Cup-Winner's Cup.

The record books showed Wednesday had a habit of bouncing straight back after relegation, but in 1970-71 they never remotely resembled promotion candidates. In truth, there were times when they looked more likely to suffer another fall. They won only one of their first eleven matches, and alarm bells were ringing loudly after they lost 5-1 to Luton in October—their heaviest Second Division defeat at home for twenty-five years.

Almost as soon as the season began they parted with Wilf Smith, who finally got his wish to leave when he joined Coventry for £100,000, then a record for a full-back. It left a gap which Williams was not able to fill until after the Luton setback, when he recruited the experienced Welsh International Peter Rodrigues from Leicester for £55,000. Wednesday won six and lost four of the next 14 games, but it was not enough to persuade the club's directors to persist with Williams, whose destiny was probably shaped by three results over

Christmas and the New Year. On Boxing Day at Hull (where teenage defender Jimmy Mullen made his debut) the Owls had to settle for a draw after leading 4-1; a week later they went out of the FA Cup at Tottenham; and this was followed by a 4-0 defeat at Cardiff, where City's hero was two-goal Alan Warboys, the striker acquired from the Owls a month earlier for £42,000.

Williams was dismissed after being in charge of 69 League matches, 17 of which had been won and 35 lost. At the time of his departure Wednesday supporters were left reflecting that the club's League record since Alan Brown had walked out in February 1968 read: Played 125, won 29, drawn 37, lost 59. It added up to an alarming decline, and, desperately seeking a saviour, preferably one who would have the immediate affection and support of the fans, chairman

Peter Rodrigues.

Stephen (due to stand for re-election at the next annual meeting) and general-manager Eric Taylor decided the answer was to invite the club's greatest modern day idol, Derek Dooley, to leave the security of the Hillsborough development office and put his unique status and reputation on the line by taking over as team-boss.

David Sunley (left) and Jimmy Mullen, who got their big chance in 1970-71 before the end of the brief Danny Williams era.

The Blades Bounce Back, 1970–1971

WHEN JOHN HARRIS resumed control of team-affairs at Bramall Lane in August 1969, there were few who doubted that, with John Short as his assistant and former long-serving defender Cec Coldwell as his chief coach, the quiet fifty-two year-old Scot with the promotion knack would guide the Blades back into the top grade sooner rather than later. In fact, he managed it within two seasons; though he might well have succeeded at the first attempt had United shown a bit more consistency in a 1969-70

campaign in which they finished sixth but only four points adrift of second-placed Blackpool. Remarkably, the Blades won more games in the year they failed to go up than in the promotion campaign which followed; but the difference was 15 defeats in the first term compared with 7 in the second.

There was one spell midway through 1969-70 when United led the Second Division; and notable triumphs over Newcastle (who finished seventh in Division One) in

Gil Reece (right) scoring the equaliser in the memorable FA Cup triumph over Everton in January 1970.

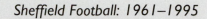

Alan Woodward (left, behind Dearden) just fails to score with a shot against Sunderland in February 1971. One of the Sunderland men in the picture is Ian Porterfield, later a Blades' manager.

Ted Hemsley . . . converted to full-back.

the League Cup, and Everton, the League Champions-elect, in the FA Cup confirmed their capacity to match the best. All the more so as the defeat of Newcastle was achieved despite having striker Alan Woodward as emergency goalkeeper for the final 15 minutes; while the success against Everton stemmed from a splendid display in which the Blades came from behind to win 2-1 with headed goals from Gil Reece and Colin Addison.

United started 1969-70 with six wins and only one loss in their first eight matches, which included their biggest away victory for over eight years—a 5-1 thrashing of Portsmouth. However, four defeats in six games followed (in October Blackpool were the first visitors to win at Bramall Lane in 23 League and Cup matches) before another unbeaten run of five fixtures saw them again hit peak form, notably in emphatic home wins against Aston Villa (5-0) and Birmingham (6-0).

This was a phase during which Harris made the astute decision which gave Ted Hemsley's career a shot in the arm, converting the former Shrewsbury wing-half into a left-back, where he became one of the ever-dependable Len Badger's most consistent partners; and John Flynn was given his first experience of Division Two. It was also when Woodward and Tony Currie began to capture the imagination of supporters as a duo poised for big things; while Scottish skipper Eddie Colquhoun, Welsh winger Gil Reece, the experienced Colin Addison, and Dave Powell were amongst the team's key performers. There were useful contributions, too, from Don & Dearne products Frank Barlow and the maturing Geoff Salmons, with the big and speedy Salmons looking a very useful prospect on the left side of midfield.

In the end, the Blades' 1970 promotion hopes were dashed by four successive defeats in March. It was in the wake of this unhappy sequence that manager Harris, already planning for the next campaign, elected to invest the £30,000 he had received from Ipswich for lanky reserve striker Mick Hill. The £20,000 he spent on the experienced Nottingham Forest inside-forward John Barnwell failed to pay a dividend because the ex-Arsenal man suffered untimely illness and injury; but a deal which proved an outstanding bargain was the £10,000 he paid to Fourth Division Chester for Billy Dearden.

Former gas-fitter Dearden had begun his career in 1963 with his home-town club, Oldham, moved to Crewe on a free transfer in 1966, and then scored 22 goals in 85 League games in two years with Chester. He was already twenty-six and largely unknown outside the lower grades;

but he emerged a key figure in the Blades' 1971 promotion side—and there have been few more dependable or popular players in the club's modern history. He hit 61 goals in 175 games for United before re-joining Chester in 1976, but statistics alone fail to reflect the full measure of a man whose commitment and courage (he often played when dogged with knee trouble and deferred an operation at one stage at the request of manager Harris) made him as much a favourite with his colleagues as with supporters.

The Blades made a gloomy start to a 1970-71 campaign which ultimately turned out so well, winning only one of their first five matches. However, an unbeaten run of 16 League games

Billy Dearden . . . ever-dependable striker.

United 1970-71.
Back row: Ian MacKenzie, Len Badger, Billy Dearden, Tony Currie, Geoff Salmons, John Tudor.
Middle row: John Flynn, Dave Powell, Graeme Crawford, Alan Hodgkinson, Frank Barlow, Colin Addison.
Front row: Paddy Buckley, Alan Woodward, Eddie Colquhoun, Gil Reece, John Barnwell.

between early September and the end of November confirmed their credentials. While it was touch-and-go right through to the final ninety minutes of the season, they combined quality and a reputation as one of the most entertaining teams in the Second Division with grit and character when it mattered—and were good value for their promotion prize.

That excellent autumn sequence included another 5-1 triumph at Portsmouth (Woodward got the Blades' only hat-trick of the season) and an exciting 3-2 defeat of Wednesday, with substitute John Tudor claiming the winner, in Sheffield's 89th Football League derby. It was however a 1-0 defeat of Leeds in the League Cup early in this spell which emphasised United's potential and boosted the team's self-belief. The tie was settled with a memorable goal from Currie, who outpaced defender Terry Cooper and scored with a superb 25-yard strike.

Tudor missed only two games before his shock departure in late January, and his value to the side was emphasised on a couple of occasions when he was switched to centre-half. His nine goals in 1970-71 included one in each of the two instances when he was used as a substitute. The Wednesday winner has been mentioned, but, earlier, in the home game with Bristol City in September, he stepped from the bench to contribute to a dramatic recovery which many considered the turning point in United's season. The Blades trailed 3-0, but Woodward (with the kind of stunning strike fast becoming his hallmark) and Dearden reduced arrears before Tudor grabbed the equaliser in injury-time.

Tudor's transfer to Newcastle came suddenly and unexpectedly, but a defeat at Bolton had persuaded Harris that drastic action was required. As had been the case when plotting the promotion success of ten years earlier, the manager decided his side needed the impetus of a few new faces. The long-serving Alan Hodgkinson, veteran of over 600 games and an automatic choice for seventeen years, was starting to struggle in coping with high crosses, and it was affecting his confidence. Harris had little choice but to use Tudor in an exchange deal to get 6ft. 1in. goalkeeper John Hope, and former Wednesday forward, David Ford, returned from Tyneside to his home city as part of the deal. The Blades also lacked steel and fire in midfield, and this prompted the signing of the aggressive and experienced ball-winner Trevor Hockey, who arrived from Birmingham for £40,000.

Hope initially excelled because his height enabled him to look good dealing with situations which had begun to trouble Hodgkinson, but long term he never matched the

Tony Currie attacks the Bolton goal, October 1970.

Trevor Hockey (right) arrived to boost the 1971 promotion run, and in his second season with • *United he won the Player of the Year trophy, which he is seen here collecting from former Blades' favourite Jack Smith.*

consistency of his predecessor. Many considered the big North Easterner, limited to 63 League games over four years, fortunate to share in a promotion triumph after only 17 outings. However, he did what was expected of him when it mattered in those final months of 1970-71. Hockey, who had made his debut with Bradford City more than ten years earlier at the age of sixteen, numbered Nottingham Forest and Newcastle among his former clubs. He already boasted some 420 League and Cup appearances, and, long-haired and bearded, he sometimes resembled an Indian 'extra' in a Wild West film, but the tough little Tyke was a great favourite and exactly the battling extrovert the team needed to boost morale off as well as on the field. He spent two years at Bramall Lane, making only 68 League appearances; but in that time had such an impact that, despite being an Englishman, he established

himself as a Welsh international. He went on to collect nine caps, being the first of a new breed of footballer who qualified to play for the country of their father's birth rather than their own. He was a wonderful character who later served Norwich and Aston Villa before concluding his League career back at Valley Parade. Sadly, his life ended in tragic circumstances in 1987 when he collapsed and died playing in a charity match at the age of forty-six.

Hodgkinson, soon to join the backroom staff as coach to the reserves, watched from the sidelines at Oxford as Hope and Hockey made their Blades debut in a 2-1 victory sealed with a Dearden double. (Ron Atkinson, who many years later managed Wednesday, played for the home side in that match and wasn't very pleased when he was substituted!). Ford was introduced the following week in a home game with Luton which saw Woodward score both goals in another 2-1 win; and a further success at Charlton in mid-February saw United enjoy a brief spell on top of the Second Division.

However, as is invariably the case with two places at stake and half-a-dozen serious contenders, the promotion race remained desperately tight, and United suffered two painful setbacks in quick succession against close rivals Carlisle and Hull. It was a particularly hard blow when Hull became the first side to win at Bramall Lane all season, in a bruising floodlit duel watched by a 40,227 crowd early in March. Ken Knighton, later to play with Wednesday, was making his debut for Hull that evening after signing from Blackburn, and it would be an understatement to say the tough-tackling midfielder made his physical presence felt throughout the 90 minutes. Many a home fan would willingly have lynched him that night!

Gil Reece.

As it happened, that fall was United's last defeat of the campaign, for they concluded their programme with an unbeaten run of 11 matches, six of which were won—though it will not be forgotten that the sequence nearly didn't get started. Just four days after Hull had dented their pride, the Blades went to Queens Park Rangers and, with two minutes left, found themselves trailing 2-0. Their followers were in despair. Then Woodward reduced arrears, and, when Dearden was brought down, Hemsley stepped up to level the scores from the penalty spot in the nick of time. It was another psychological boost which could not have been better timed. The only disappointment was that Powell suffered damaged knee ligaments, and missed the last ten matches of the campaign.

Hemsley wasted a spot-kick in the next game, at home to struggling Blackburn, but it didn't prevent United from romping to a 5-0 victory, and

The third goal in United's memorable defeat of Cardiff, April 1971.

though they failed to score in three of their next four matches (including a goalless draw at Hillsborough, where the attendance topped 47,500), the Blades climbed back into second place with home wins against Millwall and Birmingham—Reece scoring one of his most memorable goals and following up with another, a diving header, in the 3-0 defeat of the Midlanders.

The crunch match, and the one which produced an unforgettable occasion for Blades supporters, came in the season's penultimate fixture, at home to promotion rivals Cardiff, on Tuesday April 27th. The 42,963 spectators packed into Bramall Lane knew it was United's night from the sixth minute, when Dearden put them ahead, and though the visitors pulled one back after Flynn had added a second, goals from Currie, Reece and Dearden (with his 14th of the season) clinched an emphatic 5-1 victory. It meant United needed one point from their last match, at home to Watford, to go up with Leicester.

On a gloriously sunny first day of May, there was only one moment when Watford seriously threatened to spoil the party: eight minutes after kick-off, winger Stewart Scullion thundered a volley against United's bar at the Shoreham Street end. Then,

Currie sees the ball go the wrong side of a post during the Watford game in which United clinched promotion in May 1971.

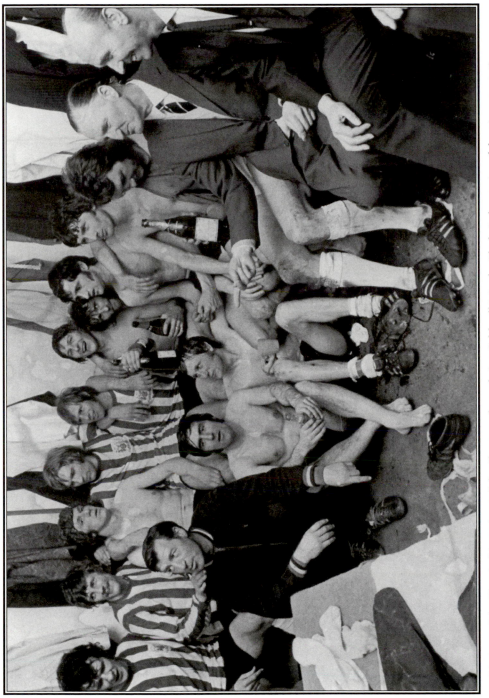

Manager John Harris, his assistant John Short, and coach Cec Coldwell join the Blades' players in celebrating promotion after the last-day defeat of Ken Furphy's Watford, May 1971.

in the 21st minute, Reece was brought down by Keith Eddy, and leading marksman Woodward calmed home nerves by shooting the Blades in front from the penalty spot for his 15th goal of the season. Reece made it 2-0 soon afterwards and scored again in the second half. So promotion was sealed in style, United's line-up on the final day was:

Hope, Badger, Hemsley, Flynn, Colquhoun, Hockey, Woodward, Salmons, Dearden, Currie, Reece. Sub: Ford.

Incidentally, within a week, Scullion was snapped up by Harris for £30,000.

The two Second Division seasons under Harris saw Badger, Currie and Woodward play in every League game, while Colquhoun missed only three. Woodward (33), Currie (21) and Reece (22) shared half the goals the Blades scored in this spell; and United's home record added up to 30 wins and just four defeats, with 99 goals scored and a mere 28 conceded.

There was good reason to believe they could more than hold their own in the top-grade. If Harris had a regret it was that his old chairman Harold Blacow Yates had not lived to see promotion clinched. As for present chairman, Dick Wragg, he insisted United's return to the top meant full steam ahead for his plans to turn Bramall Lane into a four-sided soccer ground.

⚽10 *Derek Dooley, Manager*

DEREK DOOLEY had hit 63 goals in 63 senior games for Sheffield Wednesday when his short but remarkable Football League career was ended in February 1953 by the injury which almost cost him his life. His scoring feats and the circumstances in which he was finished at the age of twenty-three when he had so much left to give ensured him a special place in Sheffield football folklore. However, though his playing days were over, Dooley was determined to remain in the game, and as he lay in a Preston hospital recovering from the amputation of his right leg, he said: 'They can stick me in the ground and use me as a corner flag, so long as I can stay in football.'

Dooley, despite his misfortune, could always appreciate the humour as well as the realism in Eric Taylor's comment that the Owls idol would have to 'go out into the world and learn to stand on his own two feet' before he could look for another role in football. The Sheffield *Star* launched a shilling fund which enabled Dooley and his wife, Sylvia, to buy a house at Norton, and he was granted a testimonial match (Hillsborough's first game under floodlights: attendance 55,000) in March 1955. So there was no immediate financial stress, the initial challenge was adjusting to a life in which football would not be the main focus, at least for the present. His first job was as a telephonist at Owls director Dick Gunstone's bakery, and he was for a time in demand as a newspaper pundit. One way or another, he was never far from the game. His formal return to the Hillsborough scene as a full-time employee came in 1962 as organiser of the club's new development fund.

It was a position which suited him, and he could have spent the rest of his working life in a comfortable and secure job, close to the heart of the club (he did have a spell looking after the Owls juniors) but without pressure or risk. Almost eighteen years on, in January 1971, he was still a legend, idolised by the fans and the

Derek Dooley.

popular choice as president of the supporters club. When the offer of the team-managers job came out of the blue, he found it impossible to resist, even though he knew that if he failed it could shatter the legend and would almost certainly lead to a break with the club. There could be no going back to the development office (where he was succeeded by another old favourite, Dennis Woodhead). It is now history that, in fact, what began as a dream opportunity ended in trauma, with his sacking on Christmas Eve 1973; but Dooley always insisted he never regretted taking the job. He never agreed with those who suggested he was 'used' by Sir Andrew Stephen and Eric Taylor to ensure the chairman's re-election at the annual meeting in the summer of 1971. Dooley did not lack faith in his ability to succeed as a manager. Indeed, when he looked back in later years, he always believed he did a decent job, but was defeated by circumstances which conspired against him; he ran out of luck at the very moment when he needed it most.

Dooley was team-boss for just a few weeks under three years. In that time the Owls played 135 League and Cup games, wining 43 and losing 57. His League record of 38 wins and 52 defeats in 121 matches was at least an improvement on the previous three years, but sadly, it was never quite sufficient and, apart from a brief spell in his second full season, promotion from the Second Division remained a distant dream. In truth, the statistics do Dooley less than justice. He helped restore some pride and discipline, and at another time, he might have survived longer and

ultimately succeeded. However as Wednesday, hit by a mysterious virus, struggled desperately in Dooley's last months at the helm, he paid the price because his own apparent failure to turn the tide was compounded by an

John Holsgrove.

Brian Joicey.

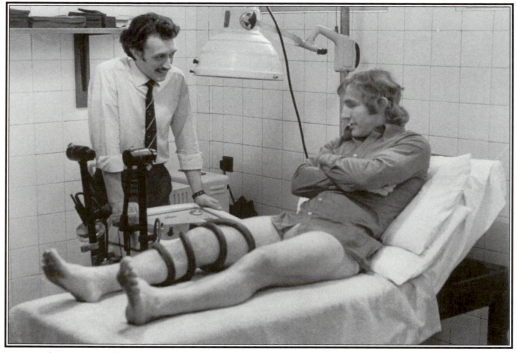

Dave Clements, on the treatment table, discussing matters with physio Geoff Eggington.

aura of decline which spanned six rather than three years.

The old hero did not have an easy start in management. When he took over, Wednesday had 16 games left and they won only three; but, despite finishing without a win in the last seven matches, 11 from a possible 32 points proved enough for them to finish in 15th place, well clear of the danger mark.

Unfortunately, they collected only one point from the first six games in 1971-72, and though this was followed with a sequence in which they lost just one in 15, they then won only two of the next 15. Three wins in the final five fixtures saw them finish in 14th place.

Dooley tended to bank on experience in his excursions into the transfer market. Ahead of the 1971-72

season, he paid £50,000 for centre-half John Holsgrove, who had made his League debut with Crystal Palace in August 1964 and figured in over 200 games for Wolves. Early in the campaign the manager acquired Coventry's versatile Irish international midfielder Dave Clements, a veteran of over 250 League games, in a £100,000 double deal which also brought former North Shields amateur centre-forward Brian Joicey to Sheffield. Holsgrove, who was installed as skipper, went on to make 115 appearances. Clements had 87 outings, he left in 1973 mainly because he was unhappy about being permanently switched to left-back. Clements collected 13 of his 48 caps while at Hillsborough, and his obvious quality was appreciated by supporters, but once he had decided

Derek Dooley welcomes Peter Swan (left) and Bronco Layne (right) back to Hillsborough following the lifting of the ban inflicted after the 1964 scandal.

he wanted to go Dooley knew he couldn't keep him. It is fair to say that Joicey, though the least-known of the newcomers, probably proved the best buy in scoring 53 goals in 164 games —including 16 which made him top scorer in his first term.

The 1972-73 campaign was the one when Dooley came closest to turning the tide, for the Owls led the Second Division in the early weeks before finishing tenth, and a run to the FA Cup fifth round hinted that the potential was there to bridge the gap which separated them from the front runners in the promotion chase. However, they finished 17 points adrift of second-placed Queens Park Rangers, and a mere two wins in their last eight matches ensured they were never a threat to the leaders.

The season was noteworthy on several counts: not least that the directors finally chose to restore the traditional striped shirts, they also welcomed back Peter Swan and David Layne when their life bans were lifted after eight years. In the event, only centre-half Swan played in the senior side, making 15 appearances following an emotional return on the opening day of the campaign. Centre-forward Layne was unable to recapture the resistance to injury which had been a hallmark in the old days and he had to move on to Hereford before enjoying a brief taste of League football. Dooley also recruited another 'old boy' in Peter Eustace. West Ham had paid £90,000 for him in 1970, but he had made only 43 League appearances, and it was

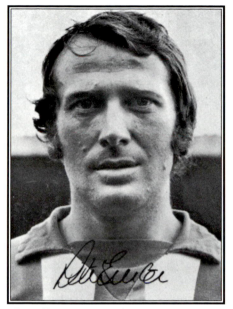

Peter Eustace.

sighted that he had to keep his eye on the touch line to be sure of where he was as he tricked and trundled his way down the wing, but his dribbles delighted the fans, confounded the opposition and lent abundant colour and excitement to many a grey afternoon.

After beginning the season with five wins in the first seven games, Wednesday remained in the top two places until mid-October, but thereafter fell to mid-table and were never

following a loan spell at Rotherham that Wednesday paid £12,000 to bring him home.

There is not much doubt that the best signing Dooley made in that summer of 1972 was the one which many people considered the least likely to pay off. Willie Henderson, a twenty-eight year-old former Scottish international winger, who had won every domestic honour north of the border by the time he was nineteen, but had left Glasgow Rangers with a reputation as a rebel. Many predicted he would prove more than a handful for Dooley, but in the event, he was a model professional and never an ounce of trouble, and, though he was limited to 56 games and five goals in his short stay, the only people hurt by his arrival were opponents. Few players can ever have given Hillsborough regulars so much pleasure in such a short space of time. It was said he was so short-

Willie Henderson.

A memorable winning goal from Willie Henderson, against Sunderland in February 1973.

able to sustain a serious challenge for a promotion place. The FA Cup brought a dash of excitement, and a peak was reached in the fourth-round when they beat Crystal Palace at the third attempt in a memorable second replay at Villa Park, where Joicey, who finished the season with 20 goals, notched a hat-trick in a famous 3-2 victory sealed in extra time.

This was the season in which young David Sunley came to the fore as a striker with a bright future, scoring 12 goals; Tommy Craig, who finished with 11, had one of his most consistent spells; and Roy Coyle, a signing from Glentoran in early 1972, collected his first Irish cap after only seven League outings. In mid-March, incidentally, Eustace had the novelty of acting as emergency goalkeeper when Peter Springett was injured in the home 1-1 draw with Brighton; and at the end of the same month Peter Fox, then aged fifteen years and eight months, became the youngest Owls'

player to make his League debut when he played in goal against Orient. The Scunthorpe product was destined to make his name in over 400 appearances for Stoke City, but on that afternoon at Hillsborough he showed great pluck in playing most of the game with a broken toe after colliding with an Orient forward—and he started with a clean sheet, too.

It was not without irony that Dooley went into what proved a traumatic 1973-74 campaign, confident that Wednesday were set to make a serious promotion bid. Disappointed that Clements was determined to leave, the manager recruited the former Sheffield United back, Bernard Shaw, from Wolves for £40,000; and he paid Hull City £60,000 for Ken Knighton, the tough tackling midfielder who had started his career at Molineux and also served Oldham, Preston and Blackburn. Again Dooley had gone for experience, though it is relevant to note that this was a season

Dooley's men . . . the Owls' manager with Henderson, Rodrigues, Prophett, Craig, Grummitt, Sissons and Coyle.

Mick Prendergast

in which youngsters Eric Potts and Allan Thompson established themselves.

Alas, Wednesday's start was well below what they had anticipated: they won only two of their first seven games. In late September Mick Prendergast, the Don & Dearne product and a brave centre-forward of the kind Dooley most appreciated, hit a hat-trick in a 4-0 defeat of struggling Crystal Palace, and when this was followed with another home victory, over Millwall, it raised hopes of a sustained revival. Sadly, the Owls recorded only two wins in their next 16 League and Cup games, and in this spell tumbled to an 8-2 defeat at Queens Park Rangers in the League Cup.

It was in early September that Wednesday were first troubled by a virus which was to seriously affect no

Tense moment in the dug-out for manager Dooley in the early weeks of the 1973-74 season.

fewer than 16 players over a span of two months. Henderson was the first to go down with it on September 5th and Shaw and Joicey were the last victims of the epidemic at the end of October. At the peak of the crisis, Wednesday struggled to turn out a team, but when they asked the Football League for a postponement of the home game with Notts County in late October their plea was rejected.

Had such a situation occurred in either of the previous two seasons, it might have been received with more sympathy than it was by the supporters, but, with the calls for the heads of Stephen, Taylor and Dooley increasing at matches at which enthusiasm and attendances were

declining, many had become impatient and regarded it as just another excuse. It was only in retrospect that the full extent of the circumstances were appreciated.

Wednesday's slide into the bottom places of the Second Division set the alarm bells ringing, and by mid November, with 12 points from 17 games, the situation was clearly heading towards a climax. Moreover, Dooley's job was plainly not the only one under threat. The first hint of dramatic developments came in early December when Sir Andrew Stephen and his vice-chairman Keith Gardiner resigned, with Matt Sheppard, a forty-nine-year-old chartered accountant, installed as the new chairman.

Sheppard, who had been the club's accountant for many years, had been invited onto the board two years earlier—by the man he now replaced.

Within a week the vacancies were filled by local businessmen, H.E. (Bert) McGee, aged fifty-six, and Roy Whitehead, forty, and, by an ironic twist, the new-look board met for the first time on Dooley's forty-fourth birthday. Two days later Wednesday lost 3-0 at home to Fulham before a crowd of 7,925—an attendance which spoke volumes for the decline in the Owls' fortunes.

When Wednesday went to Crystal Palace a week later and emerged with a 0-0 draw, it left them with 14 points from 21 games and a mere five victories; but Dooley had been heartened by a display which he believed confirmed the worst was behind them. As he drove to Hillsborough on the following Monday morning (which happened to be Christmas Eve) he was anticipating a happier holiday than he had thought likely a couple of weeks earlier.

What Dooley didn't know was that the board had met on the previous day, barely 24 hours after the Palace game, and decided to dispense with his services. When he arrived at the ground and was called in to see chairman Sheppard, the last thing he expected was to be told he was sacked. It was a Christmas present he never forgot. He had joined Wednesday in June 1947, and for over twenty-six years the club had been his life. 'It wasn't the sack that hurt, but the timing.' he said many times afterwards. 'I knew when I took the job that I might one day be dismissed if I didn't get the results. I never considered myself a special case

because of who I was, and, though I had lost a leg playing for the club, I didn't expect to be treated any differently from any other manager. But to be sacked on Christmas Eve was the most shattering experience of my life.'

With the benefit of hindsight, there is little doubt Matt Sheppard and his colleagues would have withheld their decision until after the holiday period. As it was, they did something which remains perhaps the most insensitive action taken by a Wednesday board in the entire history of the club. To sack a manager, even an idol like Dooley, had to be accepted as part and parcel of the game; but doing it so close to Christmas was an inexcusable blunder. Remarkably, those responsible were taken aback at the critical reaction to the timing of their announcement.

A heartbroken Dooley drove away from the ground so overwhelmed by emotion that he could hardly concentrate on negotiating the road to his Norton home on that December day. Not surprisingly, he vowed he would never go back to Hillsborough. In fact, it was twenty years before he returned to watch a Wednesday game, and ironically, when he finally went there again it was with Sheffield United on an evening when the Blades completed a memorable double over their city rivals in a game which will be discussed in a later chapter.

Dooley initially found employment as a sales representative with a firm manufacturing sports goods, but in November 1974 was appointed Sheffield United's commercial manager. He was quickly accepted at Bramall Lane, and became as

Caps on display . . . Dooley's 'full' and Under-23 internationals on parade in 1973: Sammy Todd, Dave Clements, Peter Swan, Gerry Young, Jim Craig, Peter Grummitt, Peter Springett, Jackie Sinclair, Willie Henderson, John Sissons, Ron Staniforth, Peter Rodrigues and Roy Coyle.

dedicated to United's cause as he had once been to Wednesday's. He admitted that, deep down, Wednesday would always have a special place in his heart, but it was a Wednesday that had gone. It was not long after Dooley's sensational departure that Eric Taylor, still stunned by the way his colleagues dismissal had been handled, announced his retirement. He would have wished to bow from the scene after nearly forty-five years in happier circumstances, but it was not to be. Taylor intended to formally retire in June, but he had been in poor health for some time through the after-effects of his 1967 car crash. He spent the remaining months of his life fighting a desperate battle with cancer, before his death at the age of sixty-two in September 1974. In the meantime he was succeeded as secretary by the loyal and ever-dependable Eric England.

Unfortunately, neither Eric Taylor nor Sir Andrew Stephen lived to see Dooley re-establish himself as a leading figure in Sheffield football circles. Taylor especially would have appreciated the irony of it happening through a link-up with the Blades, who made him Sheffield soccer's first paid director in April 1983. By January 1986 he had become managing director, and in late 1995 he was still with the Blades, recalled from retirement and within sight of a unique fifty years' service to pro-fessional football in his home city.

JOHN HARRIS produced a string of bargain buys in his time as Sheffield United's manager, but few proved more satisfying or rewarding than the acquisition of Tony Currie for £26,500 from Watford in late January 1968. Although many Harris signings became big favourites, none was more popular than the blond inside-forward who arrived at the age of 18 and went on to earn a permanent place alongside such post-war idols as Jimmy Hagan and Joe Shaw in the club's Hall of Fame.

It was Currie's misfortune that his eight years as a United player, while featuring some memorable days, coincided with a phase in which the club experienced more trials than triumphs. There was a spell following promotion in 1971 when the Blades played some of the best football seen at Bramall Lane for many years, but the opportunity to progress was never taken because circumstances meant very limited resources were available for strengthening the team.

United returned to the top-grade in 1971 with a bang, winning eight games in an unbeaten 10-match run ended by the brilliance of George Best at Manchester United in early October. However in winning only four of 19 League fixtures between January 1st and the end of the season and slipping to tenth in the table, they exposed a tendency for tempering a capacity for brilliance with an inhibiting inconsistency. This

Tony Currie . . . he could do magic!

was especially evident when they finished 14th in 1973 and 13th in 1974; and, even as they climbed into sixth place and aspired to qualify for the UEFA Cup in 1975, there was a suspicion of shortcomings which demanded urgent and substantial team-strengthening. Alas, with the financial implications of the new South Stand to consider, buying new players good enough for the First Division was not the top priority. So the fall of 1976 was perhaps inevitable, and only the suddenness with which it came unexpected.

Currie's consolation was that, before relegation prompted a £245,000 move to Leeds in the summer of 1976, he had lent lustre and colour to the Bramall Lane scene and produced many magical moments which would always have a treasured

A memorable goal from Currie against Liverpool, 1971.

place in the memories of supporters of that era. United followers from the early 1970s have only to hear *Limmie and the Family Cookins* 'You Can Do Magic' and the memories flood back. That was the 'pop' hit played at Blades' matches by way of tribute to the man the fans called 'TC' (like the cartoon character Top Cat), and it still evokes the image of the essential Currie: long blond locks touching his shoulders, the red-and-white striped shirt outside his shorts, the ball at his feet, and his arms in the air waving to fans who delighted in his skills. He saw himself as an entertainer and it was not unknown for him to salute supporters with both arms raised as he dribbled down the wing.

He often blew kisses to the crowd, though, reflecting on those days some twenty years later, he insisted he didn't do it as often as some memories suggest. He also reflected that, though many fans still recall the day he stopped proceedings by sitting on the ball during a match at Bramall Lane in September 1973, most forget why he did so. It was like this. In January of the previous year, Arsenal came to Sheffield and crushed the Blades 5-0, thus avenging in some style a famous victory United had achieved with a Stewart Scullion goal at Highbury during that memorable start to the 1971-72 campaign. The Gunners were not satisfied simply to win: Alan Ball, their new signing from Everton, sat on the ball in a gesture of disdain for the flimsiness of Uniteds challenge. Now the boot was on the other foot, the Blades had scored four times in the first 17 minutes and were heading for a 5-0 victory—'TC' could not resist showing Ball he had not forgotten the earlier insult.

Currie's flamboyant rapport with the crowd was sometimes highlighted at the expense of his skills, but few players have been more readily appreciated, and the fans savoured sharing his sheer delight in an ability to express his talents with such style. In terms of personality, he was not as much a 'character' as the man he replaced in the No. 10 shirt, Alan

Alan Woodward.

Birchenall, but a similar sense of fun was evident when the pair were involved in the famous 'kissing' incident during the last home match of 1974-75. Birchenall (then with Leicester) and Currie tumbled to the ground together in a challenge, and, before helping each other up, shared a mock kiss in a moment of zany humour typical of both—but misunderstood by those who didn't know the pair!

Currie scored 59 goals for United, and many were strikes of exceptional quality. One of the best sealed a 1-0 League Cup defeat of Leeds in September 1970; and another, against Liverpool in October 1971, earned the only point the Blades gained in the month when they struggled to regain the winning touch after their 10-

match unbeaten start to the season had been shattered. However, the strike which brought 'TC' national fame was one which BBC-TV commentator John Motson called 'a quality goal from a quality player' when Match of the Day cameras featured United's 3-2 defeat of West Ham in March 1975. The nonchalant manner in which Currie feinted one way, went the other, and then threaded a low shot into the net when there seemed little space in which to score, was truly memorable. It was his second goal of the game and his 51st in the League for the Blades; all this on his 300th appearance for the club, and a fitting way to top what was perhaps his most outstanding United display.

It was often said in those days that it was worth the admission price just

Woodward's superb goal against Everton, 1974.

Eddie Colquhoun makes an aeriel challenge in the 1972 game with Everton, with Currie and Warboys looking on.

to see Currie pass the ball. This was probably an injustice to his colleagues, for United had other players who were good to watch. However, it was true that, passing long or short, Currie put the ball 'on a plate' for the man at the receiving end; and nobody benefited more than Alan Woodward. The winger had speed and power, and to see him burst through onto a Currie pass was a thrilling sight; as was the ploy they worked whereby Currie would take a corner-kick, and Woodward, lying deep and leaving his run until the last possible moment, contrived to meet the ball and volley it first-time into the net.

Woodward, of course, produced many moments of magic which were essentially of his own making, and, considering he ended up claiming a post-war record haul of 175 goals in 595 games, it is hardly necessary to emphasise his place in the Blades' Hall of Fame. In fact, the former Barnsley Boys forward had been in United's team four years before Currie arrived, and he remained three years after his colleague; but they are invariably remembered as a pair. In a sense, it was his link with Currie which inspired Woodward's progress from a very good player into an outstanding one. Like Len Badger and Keith Eddy at their best, Woodward

Colquhoun on target against Wolves, 1975.

merited wider recognition, and it was a source of disappointment to supporters that international honours were never forthcoming.

Woodward had an uncanny talent for 'bending' free-kicks; in fact he scored several goals direct from corner kicks, including two, against Leicester and Coventry, which helped maintain that famous unbeaten run in 1971. He had immense natural ability, but his secret was the time he spent working on his technique in training. There was an amusing occasion when *Morning Telegraph* photographer, David Vaughan, who was rather accident-prone, was sent to capture Woodward's skills on film, and, sitting too close to the near-post, he felt the full force of the winger's bending flag-kick as the ball smashed the camera Vaughan was holding close to his face. The photographer, who returned to

his office looking as if he had gone ten rounds with Cassius Clay, wryly admitted: 'That United player's got a hell of a shot in him!'

It is worthy of note that nobody made more appearances (204) or scored more goals (64) than Woodward in the 1971-76 period, and the contributions of Colquhoun (195 games), Len Badger (154), Ted Hemsley (160) and Billy Dearden (133, with 47 goals) are confirmed by the figures. A player who also excelled in this phase was Keith Eddy, who came from Watford for £50,000 in 1972 and proved to be another of John Harris' astute signings. Eddy had already clocked up over 350 League games, with Barrow and Watford, before reaching Bramall Lane, and the combination of experience and a touch of class saw him play some of his best football with the Blades before his departure for America in 1976.

Currie played 17 times for England, seven caps coming while with the Blades. He made his international debut against Northern Ireland at Wembley at the end of that first season back in Division One, during which there were also call-ups for Colquhoun (Scotland) and Trevor Hockey (Wales); but after six caps in eighteen months 'TC' lost his place in the national side following a knee injury and the sacking of manager Sir Alf Ramsey (Dick Wragg did the axing!) in 1974. The period during which his England career came to a temporary halt was significant for Currie in other ways. In December 1973, United again pushed John Harris 'upstairs' and appointed Ken Furphy, aged forty-two, as manager. Furphy, who had spent most of his playing career with Darlington and Workington and boasted over 520 league games, joined the Blades after two years as Blackburn's manager; but he had been in charge at Watford when Currie was discovered by scout Frank Grimes, and, indeed, gave 'TC' his League debut at seventeen.

It was around the time of Furphy's arrival that Currie, now almost twenty-four, was being sought by Manchester United, but the Blades, despite increasing financial pressures, knew selling their biggest asset would not please supporters. In fact, Currie was then quite content with his lot and savouring his role as the Blades' biggest favourite since Hagan, and he needed little persuading to accept the offer of a new contract (five years with a one-year option) aimed at keeping him at Bramall Lane until he was thirty. As Currie understood his discussions with chairman Wragg, the intention was to consolidate United's top-grade status by rebuilding the team around him—a flattering prospect.

It so happened that a knee injury caused Currie to miss the whole of February 1974. When he returned he was given the captaincy, but after only five more games, his season was brought to an abrupt halt when he returned from an England trip (on which he hadn't played) in urgent need of a cartilage operation. This, incidentally, was the first season of three-up and three-down, and the absences of Currie, who had missed only 14 games in the previous $5^{1}/_{2}$ seasons, but managed only 29 outings in 1973-74, coincided with a run which brought only 5 wins in United's final 17 games. They finished only four points clear of relegation.

Yet Currie recalled that, for all the frustration induced by his injury and his inability to contribute to the Blades' cause in the later stages of the season, he felt, in the light of Wragg's promise of investment in team-building, that he had good cause to look ahead with optimism. The truth, of course, was that United had such financial problems they could never hope to make a splash in the transfer market. The decision to proceed with the erection of the new £1-million South Stand, after the cricket era at Bramall Lane formally ended in the summer of 1973, meant the priority was cash to finance this project. Vice-chairman Maurice Board had told shareholders the club would need average gates of 31,000 to succeed; indeed, he added that annual profits

Geoff Salmons.

of £100,000 would be required for the next ten years just to pay the interest on the bank loan!

The problem for the Blades was they needed a four-sided ground to generate the kind of income to enable them to operate as a Division One club, especially in terms of buying top-class players. Everybody knew they couldn't do this while cricket remained. However, before they could reap the dividends of a 'proper' football stadium, they had to create one. This was a gamble which could only succeed if the club remained at the top and enjoyed sustained success; and doing that demanded constant investment in new players—it was the classic chicken-and-egg situation, an unenviable position.

Having said that, it should be noted that soon after Furphy arrived he spent £100,000 on bringing Tony Field and Tony Garbett from his old club Blackburn Rovers. Also, after John Connaughton, an earlier £15,000 buy from Manchester United, failed to impress following the loss of young Tom McAlister with a broken leg (suffered in a clash with Manchester City's Rodney Marsh), the new manager paid Chesterfield £65,000 for goalkeeper Jim Brown. Long term, however, United only got value for money from Brown. Moreover, a later Furphy signing, £90,000 striker Chris Guthrie, was also a disappointment.

The clearest indication of United's priorities came at the end of the 1973-74 season, when they announced a loss of £170,000 and had little option but to accept the £160,000 which Stoke offered for Geoff Salmons in July 1974. Salmons was another of the Don & Dearne products who had come through the ranks, developing into an exciting midfielder with speed and power which made him an integral part of the team. Early in his career he almost went to Blackburn for £25,000, but, after 180 League games, he was such an asset that supporters could only view his sale with dismay. Currie was especially disappointed. 'How can you build when you sell your best players?' he asked.

Insiders were well aware that the club's position was far from promising, and it was at this point, ahead of the 1974-75 campaign, that Dick Wragg stunned his colleagues by announcing that he was standing down as chairman. This, he insisted, was entirely due to increasing commitments with the Football

Association, and especially, his role as chairman of the International Committee to which he had been elected in 1971, on the eve of United's triumphant return to the

Keith Eddy.

top-grade. His fellow directors were dismayed that Wragg considered these duties more important than seeing through the job he had started at Bramall Lane. Wragg, who was later made club president, remained a director, but Maurice Board, a genuine and likeable man who had been a director for fifteen years, chose this moment to announce his retirement owing to pressure of work in his own business.

The new men at the helm were John Hassall, a forty-seven-year-old managing director of a Sheffield building firm, and Albert Jackson, the fifty-four-year-old senior partner in a local firm of chartered surveyors and estate agents. New chairman Hassall

had been a director since May 1963. All things considered, it was remarkable that United should confound the pessimists and finish sixth in Division One in 1974-75. They probably surprised themselves, and had they collected just one more point and been allowed to qualify for a UEFA Cup place, the income it would have generated might have enabled them to devise a plan to direct some funds towards gradually rebuilding a team in which half-a-dozen players were at, or nearing, the age of thirty.

United started the season with two points from three games, won four on the trot and then managed one victory in seven; but they climbed into the top six in November before another poor run; one win in eight saw them slip into the bottom half of the table by February. However, they lost only two of their last 19 League matches and concluded the campaign with a sense of achievement which inspired great optimism and high hopes for the future.

Four players—Currie, Woodward, Brown and Field—were ever-present, while Colquhoun, Badger, Hemsley and Eddy did not miss many games. Woodward (12) and Field (11) led the scoring charts, and six of Eddy's nine goals came from the penalty spot. It is worthy of note that while Currie was ignored by England and lost the captaincy to Eddy, he enjoyed a vintage campaign. There were some other notable individual successes, though one or two senior professionals could not have imagined how close they were to the end of their Bramall Lane careers.

The sudden collapse of United's fortunes so soon after finishing in the

United 1974-75.
Back row: Steve Goulding, Ted Hemsley, Steve Faulkner, Steve Conroy, Jim Brown, Tom McAlister,
Len Badger, Terry Garbett, Colin Franks, Alan Ogden.
Front row: Alan Woodward, David Bradford, Tony Field, Keith Eddy, Tony Currie, Eddie
Colquhoun, Billy Dearden, Terry Nicholl, Mick Speight, Gary France.

top six was as staggering as it was unexpected. The Blades didn't fall from the First Division in 1975-76, they crashed out with a mighty wallop, and it added up to the most traumatic campaign in the club's history. They won only six games— with four victories coming *after* their fate had been sealed.

The irony was that all this happened in the very season when Bramall Lane finally became a four-sided soccer ground, though, on the sunny August day when the new South Stand opened for the first match of the campaign, against Derby County, few of those present could have imagined what lay in store over

the coming months. After starting with a 1-1 draw, the Blades lost seven on the trot, did not win a game until late September, and accumulated a paltry five points and a staggering 18 defeats from their first 22 games. They didn't claim their second victory until their 29th match, in February.

Currie missed only nine matches and was briefly recalled to the England team, but it was not a happy season for him. Barely a fortnight after collecting his seventh cap he suffered the indignity of being substituted for the first time in his United career. This happened at West Ham in late September, and coincided with the debut of Cliff Calvert, a

defender Furphy signed from York for £40,000. It was often said it was not Furphy's decision to pull off Currie that signalled the end for the manager, so much as recruiting Calvert in a deal the board had not formally approved. Whatever the truth, Furphy was sacked within a fortnight. The full circumstances were

never spelt out, but it was evident to those close to the scene at the time, that the relationship between Furphy and new chairman Hassall suddenly turned sour. The fact that United had won only one game in eleven from the start of the season only partly explained why Furphy's contract was terminated on October 6th—two days

Len Badger, Ted Hemsley and Billy Dearden.

after United lost at Birmingham in a game in which Badger, on his 499th appearance, was sent off.

Initially, Harris was brought back and he and coach Cec Coldwell ran team affairs, but, within nine days, Jimmy Sirrel, a fifty-three-year-old Scot who had been Notts County's manager since 1969, was appointed as Furphy's successor. Sadly, though Sirrel had enjoyed success on a shoestring at Meadow Lane (and was to do so again in later years), he almost immediately regretted moving to Sheffield. He achieved only one win in his first 23 games and soon confessed that with the financial situation as it was, he felt himself in an impossible position. In other circumstances and at another time, Sirrel might have succeeded, but he knew the moment was wrong for him and the club, though he battled bravely and it would be wrong to suggest he gave up without a fight. He

stayed for just under two years, and it was always felt he returned to Meadow Lane with great relief. Meanwhile, Furphy landed himself a lucrative job as coach to the New York Cosmos.

Badger, Hemsley and Dearden were among those who departed in Sirrel's time. Sirrel's recruitment of former Scottish international Jimmy Johnstone was a gamble which failed, but £60,000 defender Paul Garner, proved an astute capture from Huddersfield; and, before the end of his first term in charge, he had given debuts to Edwards, Kenworthy, and Stainrod, youngsters who all ultimately made their mark in the Football League. Currie, the subject of speculation all season and constantly linked with Leeds, finally left in June. His farewell appearance was in veteran trainer Harry Latham's benefit match on May 10th 1976. It was the end of an era.

Relaxing on Lindrick golf course . . . Ted Hemsley, Tony Currie, Cec Coldwell and Alan Hodgkinson.

Burtenshaw & Ashurst, 1974–1977

AFTER THE HASTE with which Derek Dooley had been dismissed, it took Wednesday five weeks to appoint his successor. There was some surprise when the job of lifting the club's fortunes was entrusted to thirty-eight year-old Steve Burtenshaw, for though the man who had spent his entire playing career with Brighton & Hove Albion had made an impact as a coach with Arsenal, and in seven months as chief coach at Queens Park Rangers, he had no managerial experience. He

arrived at Hillsborough on January 29th 1974 and survived until October 1st 1975; in the meantime, Wednesday fell into the Third Division for the first time in their history.

Coach Gerry Young's spell in temporary charge of team affairs had brought only one defeat in five matches (in an FA Cup replay at Coventry), and Wednesday had 16 Second Division games left when Burtenshaw took over. They won six and a haul of 16 points was just

Celebrating a relegation escape . . . Wednesday fans carry skipper and marksman Ken Knighton shoulder high after his goal against Bolton ensured Second Division safety for the Owls in April 1974.

enough to avoid relegation. Safety was clinched thanks to a 1-0 defeat of Bolton on the last day of the campaign, when skipper Ken Knighton sealed victory with an 86th-minute goal which was greeted with as much enthusiasm by the 23,234 crowd (Hillsborough's biggest of the season) as if it had won promotion.

Burtenshaw's home debut as Wednesday's manager on February 10th, coincided with the first Football League fixture ever staged at Hillsborough on a Sunday. Some years later, of course, Sunday Football at this level became a normal part of the sporting scene, but in 1974 it was a novelty—and not entirely welcome. It came about owing to problems in the power industry which put the nation on a three-day working week because of restricted electricity supplies. The Owls, however, produced a livewire display against Bristol City, and a 15,888 crowd saw goals from Brian Joicey, Willie Henderson and Bernard Shaw, seal a 3-1 home victory.

Wednesday twice scored five in the following weeks, at Notts County and at home to Cardiff, but their short-comings were cruelly exposed in late April when they were crushed 8-0 at Middlesbrough—the Ayresome Park Club were Second Division champions-elect and their manager a certain Jack Charlton, destined one day to help reshape Hillsborough fortunes. Burtenshaw didn't need telling that this was the second time the Owls had conceded eight goals in a match in that season, for, in the previous November, he had been coach of the QPR side which had hammered Dooley's team 8-2 in a League Cup tie.

Realists in the Hillsborough camp may well have feared Wednesday's fortunes were unlikely to enjoy a major upswing in 1974-75, but even the most pessimistic could not have expected the astonishing collapse which sent the Owls plummeting to relegation in the worst season in the club's history—even worse than the dreadful campaign of 1919-20. They managed a mere five wins and collected just 21 points, finishing 15 points adrift of the safety mark. Moreover, in scoring only 29 goals, they failed to find the net in no fewer than 22 games; and, between January 11th and the end of the season they scored in only two of 17 fixtures and didn't win any. Wednesday's last victory of the season actually came as early as December 28th, when they won 1-0 at Southampton, with a goal from Eric Potts, the team's only ever-present.

Perhaps it was hardly surprising that at one stage their plight induced so much alarm that the local evening paper, *The Star* (ironically, the sports editor at the time was their former Blades' reporter Peter Howard) launched a 'Save our Owls' campaign—but abandoned it in despair when it was obvious the situation was hopeless!

It spoke volumes that the club's top scorer boasted only six goals, and the distinction belonged to the on-loan Irishman Eric McMordie, whose nine appearances between mid-October and early December coincided with a run which brought nine points and seemed such a luxury after they had managed just one victory in their opening 13 matches. McMordie's scoring debut coincided with Wednesday's first home win, against Hull, and he was again on target in a

Cheers! Rival Sheffield managers, United's Ken Furphy (left) and Wednesday's Steve Burtenshaw meet to toast a successful joint spell in the city, but their hopes went unfulfilled.

3-0 defeat of York, often remembered as the day a veteran male streaker appeared on the pitch, and a 1-0 win against Fulham on November 23rd which remarkably, was the final home success of the season. Incidentally, McMordie's last home outing before his return to Middlesbrough, came in an eventful 4-4 draw with Manchester United on the Old Trafford club's only Second Division visit to Hillsborough since 1938. The game, which attracted a 35,067 crowd, was blighted by a pitch invasion by visiting fans, and mounted police were required to restore order.

At a time when such veterans as Liverpool's Bill Shankly and Tottenham's Bill Nicholson had elected to quit the pressures of management, and even someone with the talents of Brian Clough endured trauma in a 44-day spell as new

England chief Don Revie's successor at Leeds United. The struggle Burtenshaw had in seeking to turn the tide at Hillsborough received little attention beyond Sheffield and even less sympathy from within. Many were not surprised by his inability to arrest the decline and felt he had exposed himself to a situation which clearly demanded a manager with the kind of experience and managerial skills he lacked. Moreover, the circumstances of Wednesday's slide over some five or six years had created a deepening cash crisis: in 1975 they reported a £224,000 bank overdraft and revealed that heavy weekly losses were pushing them deeper into debt. Some years later, Bert McGee was to recall: 'At that moment in our history our finances were such that we were quite literally bleeding to death.'

Burtenshaw sold Tommy Craig to Newcastle for £120,000 in December 1974; and his excursions into the transfer market as a buyer with modest resources not surprisingly failed to halt the slump. Defender Hugh Dowd, who cost £30,000 from Glenavon, at least remained five years and made 136 appearances; but, for different reasons, the money invested in midfielders Phil Henson (£45,000) and Colin Harvey (£60,000) reaped little reward. Henson, aged twenty-one and bought from Manchester City, was promising and not without skill or vision, but far from the finished product at that time; while Harvey, though a veteran of 384 games with Everton and a man with an outstanding pedigree, was denied by injuries and other circumstances from exploiting his experience with any degree of consistency. Free transfer men Fred McIver and Bobby

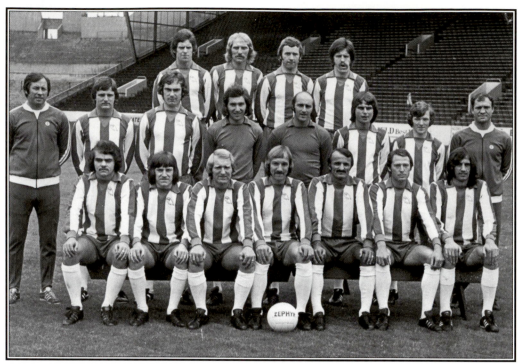

Burtenshaw's Wednesday, 1974.
Back Row: Bernard Shaw, Roy Coyle, Tommy Craig, Danny Cameron.
Middle row: Steve Burtenshaw (manager), Jimmy Mullen, Hugh Dowd, Patterson, Peter Springett,
David Sunley, Eric Potts, Gerry Young (coach).
Front row: Allan Thompson, Eddie Prudham, Ken Knighton, Brian Joicey, Peter Rodrigues, Peter
Eustace, John Holsgrove.

Brown made no impact, while ex-Celtic man Jimmy Quinn's contribution was limited; and the situation hardly aided the development of teenage forwards Ronnie Ferguson and David Herbert when they were thrown in at the deep end.

The climate was one of almost continuous despair, and the situation led to the resignations of vice-chairman Arthur Broomhead and director Stan Ashton from the board in March; and, while their replacements, Stan Speight and Cliff Woodward, were ultimately involved in reviving the club's fortunes, with relegation looking unavoidable, it was obvious things would get worse before they got better. Bert McGee took over Broomhead's role, and once the season was over, Burtenshaw was urged to cut the wage bill, which he did by giving free transfers to Springett, Eustace, Holsgrove and Rodrigues, and dispensing with the services of chief scout Fred Scott and physiotherapist Geoff Eggington. Springett, who had topped 200 games for the Owls but lost his place to Peter Fox, went on to make some 200 appearances for Barnsley; but it was Rodrigues who provided the most unexpected footnote to the clear-out, for, within a year, he had the satisfaction of captaining Southampton to a famous FA Cup triumph over Manchester United.

Even before the start of the first Third Division campaign in Wednesday's history, in 1975-76, it was evident that Burtenshaw was on borrowed time, and only likely to survive if the Owls began the season with the look of genuine promotion contenders. Unfortunately, they resumed where they had left off, and after only two wins in their opening eight games, plus an embarrassing League Cup defeat by Darlington, the inevitable dismissal came. It was confirmed by new chairman Bert McGee soon after he switched boardroom roles with Sheppard. Unfortunately, Burtenshaw's failure also meant the sack for Gerry Young after twenty years with Wednesday, and that was a misfortune the former defender did not deserve.

Len Ashurst.

Len Ashurst, a thirty-six year-old Merseyside product, who had made over 400 League appearances in Sunderland's defence, was named as the new manager, and having served a three-year apprenticeship at Hartlepool followed by a year at Gillingham, he relished the challenge of awakening what he described as 'a sleeping giant'. He was following in the footsteps of his mentor, Alan Brown, but his arrival at Hillsborough had hardly come in circumstances which compared with those Brown had enjoyed ten years before. Wednesday clung to their image as a big club, and the potential was still there; but they no longer enjoyed the status or resources of old. Ashurst knew from the outset that he would be expected to operate on a shoe-string. If his initial target was to ensure the Owls did not fall any further down the Football League, his goal in the longer term was to rebuild the club from the foundations.

Ashurst often described his first six months with Wednesday as the toughest of his life, though in fact, it was the end of April, when Wednesday beat Southend 2-1 in their final game of the season to escape relegation to Division Four, before he could begin to smile. The Owls won only 9 of 36 League games following his arrival, and it was a run which saw them collect maximum points from their last five home matches that spared them the indignity of a fall into the League's bottom grade.

It was not a happy time. Cost-cutting was a priority, and, in this context, George McCabe, John Haselden, Ron Staniforth and Jim McAnearney (acting team boss immediately before Ashurst came) were all sacked. McCabe later joined Sheffield United; and Haselden, the former Rotherham defender, was able to remain in the game by virtue of his training in physiotherapy. The most notable departure from the playing staff during the season was David Sunley, a young man who had once been rated in the £100,000 class when that was big money; but when he left for Hull in January 1976 after 145 appearances, a tribunal fixed his fee at a paltry £7,500. At the end of the season, Ashurst gave free transfers to Bernard Shaw, Allan Thompson, Colin Harvey, Fred McIver, David Herbert, Brian Joicey, Bobby Brown and Ron Ferguson.

Anyone who had any doubts about Wednesday's financial plight had only to consider, not so much that Ashurst's earliest signings included two of his old players, Neil O'Donnell (Gillingham) and Barry Watling (Hartlepool) on free transfers, so much as that they were accommodated not in one of Sheffield's leading hotels, as had been the custom with newcomers, but in rooms over Sheila's Cafe, which stood just down the road from the ground. Of course, there was nothing wrong with this residence, but using a transport cafe emphasised how far the Owls had fallen. The new manager also spent £25,000 on recruiting Richard Walden, the long-serving Aldershot defender, and centre-forward Peter Feeley, another recruit from Gillingham.

The methods of the new regime were certainly a shock to the system for many of the men Ashurst inherited, for he brought with him a former Marine commando called Tony Toms, and together they ensured that

"**I've been roughing it on these moors for years and I'm STILL no good at football!**"

How The Star's cartoonist Ralph Whitworth reflected the humorous reaction to Len Ashurst's unusual preparation methods on his arrival at Hillsborough.

the physical fitness and endurance of the players was tested to the limit. The team spent some bitterly cold nights camping on snow-covered peaks beyond Sheffield in the depths of a bleak January. It prompted cartoonist Ralph Whitworth to create a memorable drawing in the local paper: a group of sheep stood shivering on a hillside, with one saying: 'I've been roughing it on these moors for years and I'm STILL no good at football!' It didn't do a lot for the Wednesday lads either, at the time.

However, there was considerable improvement in the club's playing record in 1976-77, when they finished eighth in the table and lost only four home games, with just six points separating them from Crystal Palace,

Strikers Rodger Wylde and Tommy Tynan.

who went up with Mansfield and Brighton. They collected 10 points out of 12 from their first six matches; dropped only 3 points in an 8 game run between early November and mid-January; and finished the campaign with 7 wins in their final 8 home fixtures. That it did not add up to promotion was due to some poor displays on their travels, for though they finally ended a near two-year wait for an away win, and claimed seven victories on opponents grounds, they often lacked the consistency shown at home.

When Ashurst was sacked in October 1977, his pal Tony Toms said the Owls' boss had been 'a spit away from success', and the 1976-77 campaign was the high point of his spell in Sheffield. His consolation was that he had not only laid the foundations on which his successor could build, but he had recruited a number of people who would in some way contribute to the club's subsequent progress.

His notable signings in this spell included Jeff Johnson, a former Welsh Under-23 international, who arrived on a free transfer from Crystal Palace and was destined to make 211 appearances and emerge a big favourite with supporters. The irony was that when Ashurst ultimately took Johnson to Newport in 1981, a League tribunal set his fee at £60,000. Tommy Tynan and David Rushbury, too, proved profitable acquisitions. Tynan cost £10,000 from Liverpool and went on to score 37 goals in 107 games; and having made only six League appearances before moving to Sheffield, he boasted 629 League outings and 253 goals before hanging up his boots at the end of a career in which his clubs included Lincoln, Plymouth and Rotherham. Rushbury, whose move from West Brom was initially on loan, remained until 1979 and made over 130 appearances.

There were other moves which did not succeed long term, entirely because of circumstances, notably the purchase of former Sheffield schoolboy international, Paul Bradshaw, the Shiregreen lad who was brought home from Burnley for a £25,000 fee, but was ultimately limited to 75 senior outings because of an injury which prematurely ended his career.

It was in 1976-77, incidentally, that Ashurst promoted a young, local-born goalkeeper called Chris Turner, who missed only one match that season and would be sold to Sunderland for £90,000 after clocking up 115 appearances; later returning via Manchester United. Moreover, late in what was Ashurst's last full campaign, he paid Dover FC a nominal £1,000 for another promising goalkeeper, Bob Bolder, who, though he had to wait for his chance, eventually enjoyed a long run in which he missed only five of over 170 games; and he completed 224 appearances before being sold to Liverpool for £125,000 in 1983.

Ahead of the 1977-78 season, Ashurst sold winger Eric Potts to Brighton, and brought inside-forward Ian Porterfield from Sunderland for £20,000; but perhaps his most astute capture was ex-Blades manager, John Harris, who came as chief scout. Harris was then fifty-nine, and his great experience and knowledge, astonishingly considered surplus to requirements at Bramall Lane, proved of immense value to the Owls long after Ashurst had gone. It was no surprise that, when Jack Charlton took over, he used Harris as his right-hand man. United's loss was Wednesday's gain: much of what Charlton achieved was due to the influence of the quiet Scot in the background, and Harris was always grateful that Ashurst had kept him in football.

However, the new season did not coincide with the anticipated continuation of upward progress. A couple of successes in the League Cup offered promise, but Third Division fortunes slumped as Wednesday managed five draws and no victories from their first ten games. With the club at the foot of the table and alarm bells ringing as loud as ever, Ashurst's dismissal was as inevitable as that of Jimmy Sirrel by Sheffield United the previous week. Ashurst left without any bitterness but felt six weeks of failure had destroyed all he had achieved; though, ultimately, many looked back on his spell at Hillsborough and acknowledged that he made a significant contribution to the ultimate improvement in Wednesday's fortunes. What he lacked was results, and as McGee said, Ashurst had to be sacrificed to make way for someone with 'the winning touch'.

Within the boardroom, there was considerable debate in the quest to identify the right candidate, and Cliff

Woodward was the director who first suggested Jack Charlton fitted the bill perfectly. Woodward, whose passion for the club was such that he eventually sold a thriving business in order to retire early and devote his time totally to Wednesday's cause, was always the director most respected by the professionals, and shortly before his sudden death in 1994, he recalled it was during a chat with John Harris that the idea of trying to lure Charlton out of retirement was mooted.

Jeff Johnson . . . one of Ashurst's best signings.

United 1976.
Back row: Jimmy Sirrel (manager), Eddie Colquhoun, Jim Brown, Steve Faulkner, Colin Franks, Chris Guthrie, Cec Coldwell (coach).
Front row: John McGeadie, Paul Garner, Steve Ludlam, Tony Currie, Dave Bradford, Alan Woodward, John Flynn.

Blunt Blades, 1976–1981

THE MANNER in which Sheffield United plunged out of the old First Division in 1976 was painful enough for supporters, but, in the following five years, things went from bad to worse as the Blades endured relegation on two more occasions, in 1979 and 1981, and ended up in the Football League's bottom grade. Statistics showing they won only 79 and lost 117 of 260 League games in this period (including a mere 19 away victories in 130 matches) cannot adequately reflect the trauma of the darkest phase in the club's history.

Of course, it was not total gloom every step of the way, for the team and certain individual players provided some bright interludes, and the phase was not uneventful in other ways; but, as had already happened across the city at Hillsborough, there was an inevitability about the collapse in United's fortunes. This stemmed from attitudes and errors of judgement in boardroom and dressing room, and the speed of their sudden decline induced fears that it might be a very long time before the tide turned for the better.

In the remaining seventeen months or so he spent at the club after the 1976 relegation, Jimmy Sirrel made a number of signings, most of them modest and sadly none outstanding in terms of what they achieved for themselves or the team. His costliest buy was Ian 'Chico' Hamilton, an experienced Aston Villa forward, at £40,000, other recruits included full-back John Cutbush (Fulham) and Belfast-born striker Bobby Campbell (Huddersfield), who each cost £10,000. Cutbush at least made over 130 appearances, but Hamilton was limited to 60 League games before his contract was cancelled in January 1978 to enable him to go to America, shortly before Eddie Colquhoun; while Campbell managed only 37 outings.

The season following their fall from the top-grade saw the Blades grateful to finish in mid-table, and a mediocre campaign is best remembered for three individual milestones of special note. Inside-forward Gary Hamson, at two months past his seventeenth birthday, became United's youngest League debutant when he played at Cardiff in late October; veteran Alan Woodward, still producing some memorable strikes, passed Derek Pace's post-war scoring record with his 141st League goal in the home game with Bristol Rovers in December; and teenage striker Keith Edwards, who emerged top marksman with the first 18 of the 163 goals he was destined to claim in two spells at the club, enjoyed one run, starting in mid-March, when he scored 11 times in eight successive matches.

In 1976-77 United waited until their fifth game before registering a victory, and managed only two wins in their first 11 matches. This was followed by a spell between December and March when they collected maximum points just once in 10 fixtures. Sirrel knew something better had to be achieved at the start of 1977-78, and after they began with a single success in the first seven games it was no surprise when his contract was terminated. He soon returned to Notts County, where he started to enjoy success again—and incidentally, at Meadow Lane he subsequently contributed to the development of a future Sheffield Wednesday manager, Howard Wilkinson.

Sirrel departed on September 27th 1977 and was succeeded by Harry Haslam on January 26th 1978. In the intervening four months the ever-loyal Cec Coldwell once again emerged from the shadows to take control of team affairs; that he did not fare badly is evident considering United won 9 and lost 5 of 19 matches. One of those victories was a remarkable 6-1 success at Cardiff in December, and there was a time when Coldwell looked to have a fair chance of getting the manager's job on a permanent basis. However, Coldwell himself never felt he had much hope of getting the long-term vote of chairman Hassall and his fellow directors: indeed, he believed Haslam's appointment had been fixed almost as soon as Sirrel left, and the formalities only delayed until the new boss was free to move to Sheffield. In any event, heavy defeats at home to Arsenal (in the FA Cup) and Bolton, and at Sunderland —all in January—strengthened the board's conviction that they were right to ignore Coldwell's credentials. Coldwell had been frustrated by his role under Sirrel, and now he was unfortunate to find himself again pushed deep into the background

when Haslam brought his own chief coach, the Uruguayan Danny Bergara. In truth, he and Bergara worked well together (Haslam actually had very little to do with the day-to-day training and related activities), but the old defender can only have been dismayed at the continuing decline at the club. He cared for United with a passion many of the outsiders who came in invariably lacked, and deserved better treatment than he was accorded—especially towards the conclusion of a Bramall Lane career which finally ended in 1983.

Haslam, then fifty-six, arrived with a reputation as an astute manager, a wheeler-dealer wise in the ways of the game and something of a 'character'. As a full-back with Oldham, Brighton and Leyton, he had been a modest performer, but extensive experience in non-League football, notably with Eastbourne, Barry Town and Ton-bridge, had given him an insight into coaching and management. He had also made quite a name for himself as a coach at Fulham and later in the roles of coach, chief scout and even promotions manager at Luton Town. Elevated to manager at Luton in 1972, he led them into the First Division in 1974 and subsequently steered them through a financial crisis.

He looked an ideal candidate for the daunting task of halting United's slide, but unfortunately, 'Happy Harry' did not give Blades' supporters a lot to smile about. He lent a little colour and excitement to the scene, notably with his transfer activities, but, in truth, few of his deals really paid off, especially in terms of what was achieved on the field. He will be remembered as a man whose four terms at the club coincided with

United 1977.
Back row: Cliff Calvert, John Flynn, Dennis Longhorn, Chris Guthrie, Steve Conroy, Jim Brown, Eddie Colquhoun, Colin Franks, Tony Kenworthy.
Front row: Gary Hamson, John Cutbush, Mick Speight, Alan Woodward, Ian Hamilton, Simon Stainrod, Steve McKee, Paul Garner, Keith Edwards.

relegation from the Second to the Fourth Division—though he missed the last stages of the slide into the bottom grade in 1981 owing to illness.

After Haslam moved in, United won only 6 of their remaining 16 games, but, thanks in some degree to what had been achieved under Coldwell, it was enough to see them end the season in 12th place, albeit only three points above the danger mark. It was hardly a situation designed to inspire excessive optimism. However, the following summer brought a remarkable series of developments as the manager persuaded the board (which included newcomers Alan Laver and Albert Bramall) to forget their troubled financial circumstances and back him in a bold adventure in the transfer market: he was sure that

this course of action would ensure a promotion triumph in 1978-79 and lead to an easing of their problems!

The summer of 1978 has a special place in English football history because Argentina's triumph in the World Cup inspired Tottenham Hotspur to break new ground by acquiring two of the South American country's outstanding stars, Ossie Ardiles and Ricky Villa, for a combined fee of around £700,000. It was an exciting and innovative development widely acclaimed in the game, and it came as a major surprise to football followers in Sheffield when, within a few days, United added an unexpected tailpiece to the story by negotiating a £160,000 deal with River Plate for the Argentinian international forward Alex Sabella. Moreover, ahead of the season, Haslam invested £90,000 in Chelsea's Scottish striker Steve Finnieston, spent £80,000 on Arsenal midfielder John Matthews, and in September, paid another £80,000 to bring former Luton forward Peter Anderson back from Tampa Bay. Later in the campaign he bought Dundee defender John MacPhail for a bargain £30,000 and Ipswich back Les Tibbott for £100,000.

Unfortunately, Finnieston, plagued by injury problems which had limited him to 90 games in which he had scored 37 goals for Chelsea, made only 23 appearances for United before being forced to quit; and Anderson was to have only 30 outings. Sabella had some delightful skills but in 76 League games never had the anticipated impact; though the consolation was that Haslam later sold him to Leeds for £400,000 and so within two years the Blades picked up a big profit on a player who had really been an expensive luxury.

In the summer of 1978, Haslam's only major outgoing deal was selling striker Keith Edwards, then boasting 29 goals in 70 League games, to Hull for £50,000; but later in the season, no doubt to cover the signings he made to try to avoid the fall into Division Three, he sold Simon Stainrod to Oldham for £60,000 and Imre Varadi to Everton for £80,000. The Varadi deal was as remarkable as it was unexpected: the youngster had arrived on trial in the summer and made only ten appearances (four as a substitute), and while the success he achieved later in his career confirmed his talents, nobody at Bramall Lane had rated him anything more than a promising striker, everyone there considering his sale a fine piece of business. Only the sales of

Harry Haslam.

Gary Hamson (Leeds, £140,000) and Ian Benjamin (West Brom, £125,000) in 1979 were considered better business —the Benjamin sale, at the end of August 1979, especially staggered everyone in coming after the lad had made only five League appearances. He had scored with two penalties on his full debut, in Division Two against Leicester on May 8th 1979; and was on target from the spot when the Blades made their Third Division bow against Swindon in the following August—two weeks before he was sold.

There were other departures of note in 1978-79, with several going to America, including goalkeeper Jim Brown (Detroit), defenders Colin Franks and Cliff Calvert (both Toronto Blizzards), and Alan Woodward (Tulsa Roughnecks). Brown had been displaced by Steve Conroy, but the versatility of Franks made him an asset who would be missed; though the heaviest blow was undoubtedly the loss of Alan Woodward, especially as it happened as early as September. Secretary Keith Walker also joined the exodus after landing the top adminis-trative post in the North American Soccer League.

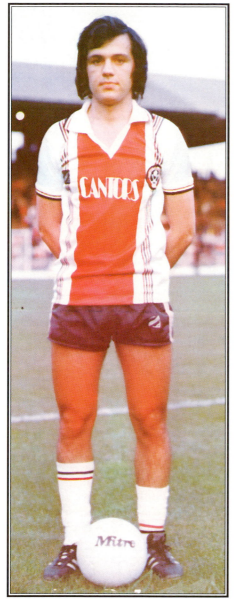

Alex Sabella.

United spent most of 1978-79 in the relegation shadow. They won only two of their first eight matches, and between late October and mid-March managed a mere two victories whilst suffering 10 defeats in 19 games. When Bruce Rioch (another of the Luton links evident in so many Haslam deals) was brought on loan from Derby in late March, his experi-ence helped the Blades enjoy their best sequence of the season, four wins in five matches. However a single success in their final seven games was not enough, and four defeats in this spell pushed them into the last relegation place (Charlton escaped by one point and Luton by two)—and, sadly, United's final home game of the campaign, against Leicester, was marred by crowd trouble.

The Blades began their first-ever season in the Third Division wearing sponsored shirts which hardly pleased Bramall Lane traditionalists in featuring a broad central red stripe which prompted one wit to say they resembled an Embassy cigarette packet! However, what mattered more than how they looked was how they played; and promotion appeared a serious proposition when United claimed eight wins from nine matches between mid-September and October 22nd and shot to top place in the table.

Unfortunately, they then suffered three straight defeats, and, after that, never quite got back into top gear, though they remained in No.1 spot until mid-January. The turning point is often identified as the 1979 Boxing Day clash with Sheffield Wednesday at Hillsborough. At the time the Blades appeared a much better promotion bet, but a 4-0 defeat, in front of the biggest crowd in Third Division history, knocked them off their stride and they managed only 4 victories in their remaining 22 games, while the fortunes of the Owls took a dramatic upturn, Wednesday ending the season with a place in the Second Division.

Once again, Haslam invested with nothing to show for it in the final analysis: Dutchman Len de Goey, a £125,000 buy from Sparta Rotterdam, made 33 appearances in 1979-80, but his contract was cancelled in October 1980. Jeff Bourne, the former Derby and Crystal Palace striker, came back from a spell in American football and led the scoring charts with 11 goals in 26 outings, but in March returned to play with Atlanta Chiefs.

A setback which almost certainly contributed to United's failure to stay in the promotion race was a problem with the goalkeeping position, for in early December Steve Conroy's run came to an end when he suffered a broken arm in an Anglo-Scottish Cup tie at St. Mirren. The much-travelled Neil Ramsbottom, whose previous clubs included Wednesday, had been signed in October, but he made only two senior outings, and, just ahead of the Sheffield derby at Christmas, the Blades paid Queens Park Rangers £50,000 for Derek Richardson. Later in the season Terry Poole had a run of seven games after arriving on loan from Bolton.

Although United had finished 12th in the table in 1980 and hardly inspired serious hopes of being promotion pacesetters in 1980-81, few people would have predicted a drop into the Fourth Division, and nobody could have dreamed up the nightmare circumstances in which that misfortune befell them in the final five dramatic minutes of a troubled campaign. Ahead of the new season they sold Sabella to Leeds and Mick Speight went to Blackburn. Haslam's penchant for experienced

and familiar players was evident as he recruited veterans Stewart Houston (Manchester United), Bob Hatton (Luton) and Martin Peters (Norwich), who between them had already clocked up over 1,300 League games! The manager also brought in mid-fielder Mike Trusson from Plymouth for £60,000. In September defender John G. Ryan, once of Luton and boasting 429 League outings, arrived from Seattle Sounders; and Exeter forward Steve Neville, a £70,000 buy, came in October.

United won five of their first seven games, but then collected one point from the next six, and though they followed that with four wins in five, another five without success made November a gloomy month: all the more so as elements which may have seemed insignificant at the time began conspiring to shape the club's destiny. At Walsall, for example, Hatton gave the Blades a 4-3 lead in injury time only for the home side to go straight downfield and equalise without a United man touching the ball.

At Christmas, United began a spell which brought one victory in ten matches, and penalty misses by Ryan in successive single-goal defeats at Portsmouth and at home to Gilling-ham in January, plus a last-minute defeat at Rotherham in February, all added up to an ominous pattern as they slipped out of the top half of the table. Moreover, when it emerged that Haslam was too ill to attend the Gillingham fixture, it not only signalled the end of his managerial career, but prompted the promotion of player-coach Martin Peters for what proved a traumatic period in charge—nothing like he had envisaged when he joined the Blades from Norwich, expecting to spend a couple of years being groomed as Haslam's successor.

Peters, capped 67 times and one of a famous trio of West Ham heroes in England's 1966 World Cup triumph, was an outstanding player at his peak. Alf Ramsey had once described him as being 'ten years ahead of his time'. However none of his 697 League games had been in the Third Division, and, for all his knowledge and ability, the trials of management were a totally new experience when he was thrown in at the deep end in late January. He was, no doubt, in an unenviable position and probably merited some sympathy, but the cold reality was that he guided United to only three victories in their remaining 16 matches, and took them down. They lost seven of those games, and it was the last defeat which haunted not only him, but players John Matthews and Don Givens, for years.

United went into their final fixture, at home on Saturday May 2nd 1980, requiring one point to retain their Third Division status, and by an accident of fate, their opponents were Walsall, who needed a victory to avoid the drop back into the bottom grade which they had left a year earlier. As Walsall had won only two of their previous 13 games and not managed an away success since October, the odds favoured the Blades.

A drab duel was drifting to what seemed an inevitable goalless draw when, with four minutes remaining, the situation took a dramatic turn which led to a sensational climax. This all started when home defender John MacPhail was adjudged to have brought down Walsall player-manager, Alan Buckley, and referee George

Flint awarded a penalty. As Buckley had scored from the spot against United earlier in the season, he was expected to take this one, but, surprisingly, it was Don Penn who stepped up and, in beating Conroy to convert his first penalty of the campaign, he appeared to have sealed the Blades' fate.

Astonishingly, in the 89th minute, United were offered a reprieve— which they didn't take! Walsall substitute John Horne was adjudged to have handled the ball, Mr Flint again pointed to the penalty spot, and home supporters in the 16,000 crowd could hardly believe their eyes as Givens, making only his eleventh appearance since his £20,000 move from Birmingham in March, struck his kick so weakly that Walsall goalkeeper Ron Green had no difficulty saving the effort.

It has passed into local sporting folklore as the most debated penalty miss in United's modern history, and many still believe the course of history would have been different if Tony Kenworthy had not been absent from this game owing to injury. Six of Kenworthy's seven goals that term had come from penalties, and significantly, it was when he had been out of action earlier in the season that Ryan had wasted two opportunities. Yet, it will not be forgotten that events might not have taken the turn they did if John Matthews had kept his nerve when it mattered. Matthews, starting a game for only the second time since mid-October, had been nominated as penalty-taker that afternoon, but, as he admitted later, at the vital moment he could not face up to the responsibility. 'I didn't feel confident,' he said. The pressure, naturally, must have been enormous considering what was at stake; and Peters always said that he would have forgiven Matthews if he had failed with the kick, but his refusal to take it was unforgivable. At least Givens, a veteran of over 400 League games and with more than 100 goals to his name, had the courage to volunteer, but, while he couldn't remember when he had last failed from the spot, on this occasion he barely troubled the goalkeeper.

United had sunk to the lowest point in their Football League history and it was not without irony that the most ill-fated season they had known, coincided with the decision to finally demolish the old cricket pavilion and complete the last phase of the new South Stand development, with the provision of offices, dressing rooms and social and entertainment suites.

14

Jack Charlton: Owls 1977–1983

THE INSTALLATION of Jack Charlton as manager, within a few days of Len Ashurst's departure in the autumn of 1977, marked a long-awaited turning point in Wednesday's history. There was no instant transformation, but the genial Geordie giant's arrival inspired realistic hopes that the club's fortunes were finally set to improve; and those hopes did not go un-fulfilled. In nearly six years at Hillsborough, 'Big Jack' guided the Owls out of Division Three, and though he did not succeed in leading them all the way back to the top-grade, when he left, in the summer of 1983, Wednesday were within touching distance of a place among the game's elite—and he had helped restore financial stability.

'Big Jack' was already, at forty-two, one of football's most famous and respected figures. At the time of his move to Sheffield, he was a con-tender for the job as England's team-boss and accepted Wednesday's offer in the knowledge that the club would not stand in his way if the FA wanted him to manage the national side. In the event, in the following December, Ron Greenwood was appointed to the post.

Charlton had a natural flair for leadership, and one of his secrets was that responsibility never seemed to weigh heavily on his shoulders. After a long and impressive playing career with Leeds United between 1953 and

1973 (in which time he had won just about every honour in the game, made 770 appearances, scored 95 goals and collected 35 caps) he was an immediate hit as a manager. He led Middlesbrough to the Second Division title in his first season and was the first boss outside the top grade to be named Manager of the Year. He revelled in the role, yet it was entirely in character that, in April 1977, after four years, he chose to take a rest—going into a temporary retirement in which he pursued his passion for hunting and fishing, occasionally spoke at sporting dinners and worked as a television pundit: always the independent spirit who didn't have to depend on the game for a living.

But football was in Charlton's blood, for the Ashington product belonged to the famous Milburn clan. Four of his uncles (his mother's brothers) had all been leading professionals, and his cousin, Jackie Milburn, had a special place in Tyneside's sporting folklore. However, despite that pedigree, he did not have the easiest apprenticeship and needed patience and persistence to emerge as the outstanding centre-half who helped England win the World Cup in 1966, and figured in a great Leeds team under Don Revie. As a player he often lived in the shadow of his legendary younger brother, Bobby, of Man-chester United; yet he developed qualities that would ensure he made just as great an impact in the game. His time at Hillsborough was another step along the way to a unique place in football's managerial Hall of Fame, confirmed by his achievements in the late 1980s and early 1990s as the Republic of Ireland team-boss.

There was always about him a relaxed, contented and totally unselfconscious approach: he never lacked confidence in his own abilities, and boasted a toughness and honest realism which made people want to play for him—even though he had an embarrassing if endearing inability to remember their names on occasions! What mattered was that he epitomised the essential quality chairman McGee and his board sought in their new manager—he was 'a winner'.

Wednesday were not sure they could lure Charlton back into football but managed to persuade him to 'come and look at us' on Saturday October 8th 1977, the day the Owls beat Chesterfield 1-0 with a Tommy Tynan strike. Amusing as it may seem in retrospect, when the unmistakable giant and his wife Pat took their seats in the North Stand, they thought they might pass unnoticed; but, of course, within minutes, everybody in the 12,920 crowd knew 'Big Jack' was present—and hundreds of fans sitting in nearby seats spent the match urging him to accept the vacant manager's post.

Later, after he had walked round the ground at the end of the game, spent an hour talking to the directors, and agreed to join Wednesday, he told waiting reporters: 'If anyone convinced me to take the job, it was those fans. It certainly wasn't the team—there's an awful lot to be done

on that score, and I don't expect instant success.'

The Charlton era, which began modestly, was seldom uneventful and never dull. Wednesday played 298 games, won 118 and lost 87. Highlights included an FA Cup third-round marathon with eventual Wembley winners Arsenal in 1979, promotion in 1980, and an FA Cup semi-final in 1983. Along the way he fashioned a team which reflected his own durability. Acquisitions ahead of promotion included Brian Hornsby, Ray Blackhall, Mike Pickering, Terry Curran, Andy McCulloch and Ian Mellor; and later he recruited Yugoslavian Ante Mirocevic, the three Garys—Megson, Bannister and Shelton—and, amongst others, the popular veteran Mike Lyons. He also introduced such youngsters as Bob Bolder, Mark Smith, David Grant and Gordon Owen in his initial term; plus Kevin Taylor, Peter Shirtliff and Mel Sterland.

One of Charlton's secrets was choosing the right lieutenants. He inherited John Harris and had the wisdom to use the older man's experience by making him his assistant. The former Sheffield United boss was a steadying influence behind the scenes; a key figure in identifying likely signings and in urging the promotion of certain youngsters. A typical Harris suggestion was the one which prompted Mel Sterland's switch to the full-back role in which he made such a big impact.

Later, Charlton strengthened his coaching staff with the appointment of former Doncaster Rovers manager Maurice Setters—launching a partnership which survived long after both had departed Hillsborough. Setters was one of Football's great characters: a seasoned and indomitable campaigner, famed as an uncompromising player in his years as a half-back at West Brom, Manchester United and Coventry. He was not without humour: he once suggested to the chairman of Doncaster that he merited a gold watch for serving two years at a club where managers seldom lasted long. 'He didn't see the joke,' Setters chuckled. When Rovers sacked him after three years in November 1974, he brought a case of unfair dismissal against the club and was awarded £1,340. Alas, the money was swallowed up by legal costs, but for Setters it was the principle that mattered. He had been out of full-time football for four years when he joined Wednesday

It took Charlton time to get things going the way he wanted. However, after two victories and six defeats in his first ten matches, the outlook began to brighten around the turn of the year, with five wins in seven in a

spell coinciding with the promotion of goalkeeper Bolder and full-back Grant. Then, following six games without success, Wednesday ended the season with only two defeats in 12 to finish in 14th place. Meanwhile, in March, came Charlton's first important signing when £45,000 midfielder Hornsby, arrived from Shrewsbury. The ex-Arsenal apprentice was to clock up 124 games and 30 goals for the Owls.

The 1978-79 campaign, in which Wednesday again finished 14th in the Third Division, did not begin well, for while losing only two of their first 11 matches they managed a mere two victories. They also claimed only one League win in ten between November and early March (though, owing to a big freeze, they played only one League match in seven weeks after Boxing Day); subsequently they endured another run which produced a solitary success in 11 attempts, before ending the season with three wins in four games.

It was a season notable for the two major signings from Southampton (Mike Pickering, who cost £65,000 in October, and Terry Curran, £100,000 in March) who were destined to make a big impact; and a third-round FA Cup marathon which not only boosted finances but suggested Wednesday were not too far from having a side capable of promotion, sooner rather than later.

When Pickering, a centre-half who had started at Barnsley, made his Owls debut against Rotherham it gave him the distinction of having played in all four grades of the Football League at the age of twenty-two. He had helped Lawrie McMenemy's Southampton win promotion to the

Jack Charlton.

Jack Charlton congratulates Ian Porterfield, FA Cup marathon with Arsenal, 1979.

First Division the previous term, but then fell out of favour. Charlton spotted his potential as a captain.

Wednesday had required replays to beat Scunthorpe and Tranmere in the first two rounds of the FA Cup, but their duel with Arsenal went to five games—three replays being staged in the space of eight days at Filbert Street, chosen because Leicester boasted an 'anti-freeze' hot air balloon.

It serves to highlight the dreadful weather during this period to note that the first Arsenal game, on Saturday January 6th, was Wednesday's only home match between early December and the end of February, and it was one of just three FA Cup games completed throughout the country on that freezing afternoon.

Indeed it only went ahead after hundreds of volunteers had worked from dawn to clear snow off a pitch which was only just about playable. A 33,635 crowd saw the Owls emerge with a deserved draw after Jeff Johnson's 47th-minute header cancelled out Alan Sunderland's early strike for the Gunners. When the teams went to Highbury on the following Tuesday, Rodger Wylde shot Wednesday in front just before half-time, but Arsenal were spared a shock defeat with a last-minute equaliser from Liam Brady.

On the Monday of the following week, Wednesday, without the suspended Pickering, twice came from behind to earn a 2-2 draw in the second replay: their hero was Hornsby, who, having quickly levelled for the Owls in the first half, following a superb goal from Brady, went on to claim a second equaliser from the penalty spot on 76 minutes, after an Alan Sunderland header had restored Arsenal's lead seven minutes earlier. It was a gritty display which prompted Charlton to comment: 'We proved that on our day we can be a match for anybody'.

The third replay, and the second match played at Leicester, was staged within two days. It was witnessed by the smallest attendance in the five meetings (17,008), but it was a six-goal thriller which burst into life in a second half which featured a brilliant penalty save by Chris Turner from Liam Brady. Just before this, Dave Rushbury had headed the Owls in front, but barely 60 seconds after Turner's golden moment, Frank Stapleton equalised, and within ten minutes Arsenal grabbed the lead through Willie Young. Yet again Wednesday recovered. Ian Porterfield set up a chance from which John Lowey made the score 2-2 and sent the tie into another spell of extra-time. When Stapleton quickly put the Gunners 3-2 up, the odds were against the Owls coming back again, but remarkably, they did so, thanks to another Hornsby penalty in the 104th minute.

The saga finally ended seventeen days after it began, when Arsenal emerged 2-0 victors in the third Filbert Street clash, this time attracting a 30,275 crowd, which brought the aggregate attendance for the tie to more than 140,000. Wednesday again produced a performance full of pluck and persistence, but Arsenal had the boost of a fifth-minute goal from

Terry Curran.

Steve Gatting, and when Stapleton claimed a second, with a superb diving header just past the half-hour, the First Division side ensured they maintained the advantage, despite all the efforts of an Owls side afforded a standing ovation at the final whistle.

The consolation for Wednesday was that the income generated by the Cup games enabled them to finance Jack Charlton's first £100,000 signing for the club when, in March, he made winger Terry Curran his second buy from Southampton. The influence of Maurice Setters was evident in this deal, for he had been at Belle Vue when Curran started his League career at Doncaster in 1973. Curran helped Nottingham Forest win promotion in 1976 and had a spell at

Mick Pickering.

United—and the Owls were dismayed to collect only half of the £200,000 they wanted for him.

Ahead of the 1979-80 campaign, Charlton made three more important signings. Centre-forward Andy McCulloch, who had started with QPR in 1970 and boasted 91 goals in 258 League games, came from Brentford for £70,000; while midfielders Ian Mellor (£60,000) and Jeff King (£30,000) arrived from Chester and Walsall. The deals were financed by sales which included, £90,000 received from Sunderland for goalkeeper Chris Turner, and £60,000 from Swansea for Dave Rushbury.

If 1979-80 has passed into history as the season in which Wednesday finally turned the corner, they hardly looked promotion contenders at the outset. They won only two of their first seven games, and when they lost 3-0 at home to Blackburn in late August,

Derby, before making 39 appearances for Southampton after their return to the old First Division, including an appearance in the League Cup final shortly before moving to Hillsborough. He was a player who could be brilliant but he was also temperamental, and in truth, in a career then spanning nearly 200 games (37 goals), he had never fulfilled his potential. Setters felt he could get the best out of him, and in scoring 39 goals in 138 games, he became a big Wednesday favourite, emerging a key figure in the 1979-80 promotion success. He invariably excelled in a free role, and there was a phase in his time with the Owls when he was rated an England contender, but frustration often got the better of him. It was typical of his eccentric tendencies that, in 1982, he offered his services to Sheffield

Charlie Williamson.

Mark Smith.

Pickering suffered an injury which was to sideline him for ten weeks; while poor Bob Bolder had a nightmare afternoon and was promptly dropped. Charlton always preferred a big goalkeeper, which was why Turner's lack of inches cost him his place despite being a favourite with supporters and so often a hero. When Bolder blundered, the fans blamed the manager as much as the player, but it was to Bolder's credit that, after being displaced by Brian Cox for 15 games, he bounced back and in his remaining years at Hillsborough amply justified Charlton's faith.

As well as losing Pickering, the Owls were without McCulloch for 13 games in that modest first half of the season, and significantly perhaps, it was following their return that the outlook at Hillsborough took a dramatic upswing. Between December 21st and April 7th they enjoyed a run of 19 games in which they suffered only one defeat.

The second match in this sequence is the one which has passed into local sporting folklore as 'the Boxing Day massacre', the result remembered as the one which marked a turning point for both Wednesday and Sheffield United—the Owls' 4-0 defeat of the Blades before the biggest attendance in Third Division history. It was the 100th derby between the city clubs in League and Cup, and a 49,309 crowd packed into Hillsborough to witness a duel which mocked the form book. At the time United were top of the table and looking the far better bet for promotion, but as has so often happened on these occasions, there was an unexpected outcome and, remarkably, United's fortunes fell into a long-term decline. Mellor put Wednesday in front five minutes before half-time with a 25-yard shot, and, in a two-minute spell midway through the second period, Curran and King made it 3-0, with Smith (who ended the season with 11 League goals from penalties) completing the scoring with a spot-kick three minutes from the end. It was an especially memorable day for Owls back Charlie Williamson, aged seven-teen and making his second senior appearance; and, incidentally, Johnson, who was to emerge Wednesday's Player of the Year, had just returned to the side following suspension. The full line-up was:

Wednesday—Bolder, Blackhall, Williamson, Smith, Pickering, Hornsby, King, Johnson, McCulloch, Mellor, Curran.

United—Richardson, Speight (Cutbush 57 min), Tibbot, Kenworthy, MacPhail, Matthews, de Goey, Bourne, Butlin, Garner, Sabella.

In the light of events in a much later phase in the club's history, it is of interest to note that Wednesday's unbeaten 16-match run included a 5-1 home defeat of Bury in which the visitors had two men sent off—and one was Danny Wilson, destined to become a Hillsborough hero in the early 1990s. Incidentally, Ian Porterfield left Wednesday soon after the Boxing day derby and took over as manager of Rotherham; and when he returned with the Millers in February, his new team was crushed 5-0 on the day McCulloch claimed the Owls' first League hat-trick since 1973.

Wednesday finished the campaign with 58 points and went up with Grimsby (62) and Blackburn (59), just managing to pip Chesterfield (57) into the third promotion place. One of the six draws in their last 12 games was a 1-1 scoreline, in the return fixture with Sheffield United at Bramall Lane. This was the day when Curran brought his tally for the season to 24, with a memorable equaliser after John MacPhail had given United the lead.

Meanwhile, the most significant victory in the run-in was a 2-1 success at Blackburn in late April. It was a display which confirmed the team's character as they battled from behind and sealed the points with second-half strikes from Kevin Taylor and Ian Mellor—the latter's 82nd-minute diving header bringing his haul to eleven, just two behind McCulloch.

Wednesday did not exactly set the Second Division alight on their return in 1980-81, when they finished tenth, eight points adrift of the last promotion place, and they paid for

Mel Sterland.

inconsistency. They lost only three home games, but managed just three away victories. It summed up the sense of anti-climax when they ended the season with two wins and eight defeats in their final 12 matches. Ahead of the campaign, Jimmy Mullen had left to aid Rotherham's bid to

Wednesday 1980-81.
Back row: Ian Mellor, David Grant, Andy McCulloch, John Lowey, Jeff King, Brian Hornsby.
Centre: Tony Toms (coach), Maurice Setters (coach), Peter Shirtliff, Mark Smith, Mel Sterland,
Brian Cox, Bob Bolder, Brian Strutt, Jeff Johnson, John Honey (physio), Jack Charlton (manager).
Front row: Gordon Owen, Kevin Taylor, Charlie Williamson, Mick Pickering, Terry Curran, Phil
Campbell, Ray Blackhall, Denis Leman.

follow the Owls into the Second Division, while Wednesday's most interesting newcomer was Yugoslavian international Ante Mirocevic, who arrived from FC Budocnost for a record £200,000 fee. Unfortunately, in 70 appearances over the next three seasons, he could not be said to have made a big impact.

It was in Wednesday's game at Oldham, in September 1980, that the sending off of Curran, following an incident with ex-United man Simon Stainrod, provoked a pitch invasion which caused the game to be held up for more than half-an-hour. As a consequence, the FA inflicted a four-match travelling ban on Owls' supporters and Wednesday were made to compensate the home clubs, moreover, standing areas at

Bert McGee.

Hillsborough were closed for four games.

Happier news for the club came when the balance sheet for year ending May 31st 1981, revealed a significant move into the black with a surplus on the year of £219,553. Explaining the transformation in Wednesday's finances, chairman McGee said: 'We stopped spending and started earning. We kept a tight control on all overheads, instituted rigorous, sensible housekeeping, appointed sound management, and let them get on with it.'

The 1981-82 season was the one in which Wednesday missed promotion by a point, finishing in fourth place just behind Norwich. The irony was that this was the first year of three points for a win; under the old system, the Owls and not the Canaries would have gone up with Luton and Watford. However, despite three more victories and five fewer defeats than in the previous campaign, Wednesday were still dogged by a lack of consistency, illustrated in the way they started the season with four straight wins without conceding a goal, and then managed only three successes in the next ten. Then, when six wins in seven games in March and April revived promotion hopes, they managed a mere 2 points from 12 in the next 4 games.

Yet it was not a season without compensations, and one pleasing aspect was the arrival of three players who settled well and would emerge key figures in the promotion success of 1984. Striker Gary Bannister (Coventry) and midfielder Gary Megson (Everton) each cost £100,000 in the summer of 1981; while midfielder Gary Shelton, signed from Aston Villa for a modest £50,000, came in March 1982, initially on loan. Bannister, with only three goals and 22 League games to his credit at Highfield Road, ended up scoring 66 times in 143 matches in three terms at Hillsborough: his development was

such that he gained England Under-21 recognition, and 22 goals in his first season helped earn him the Player of the Year award. Megson clocked up 148 outings in the first and most successful of two spells with the club which his father, Don, had served so well; while Shelton, who was also to make the national Under-21s as an over-age player, became a big Owls' favourite in a six-year stay spanning some 240 matches. Moreover, in the summer of 1982 the Owls recruited another player who proved an outstanding acquisition, and a cornerstone of the team that finally climbed into the top grade within a year of Jack Charlton's departure. Mike Lyons was a centre-half who had already made some 460 appearances with Everton since 1970, but he had three more good years in him, and in 164 outings with the Owls, he proved to be a captain whose example and leadership greatly benefited younger colleagues.

Ahead of the 1982-83 campaign Wednesday also signed the Middlesbrough back Ian Bailey for £80,000, and, later in the season, another former Ayresome man, striker David Mills, and Aston Villa's left-sided defender, Pat Heard, were added to the squad. It was Bailey's misfortune that, having made 170 appearances with his home-town club, his Owls career was prematurely ended by injury after only 45 games; while neither Mills (Britain's first £500,000 footballer when he joined West Brom in 1979, but limited to 15 games for the Owls) nor Heard (33 outings) made much impact.

Although Wednesday began 1982-83 with nine wins and only two defeats in their first 13 matches, a solitary victory in the next 13 and

Wednesday 1982-83.
Back row: Mick Lyons, John Pearson, Andy McCulloch, Peter Shirtliff, Mick Pickering.
Middle row: Richard Beaumont, Mark Smith, Gavin Oliver, Dave Redfearn, Bob Bolder, Mel
Sterland, Ante Mirocevic, Trevor Matthewson.
Front row: Gary Shelton, Kevin Taylor, Charlie Williamson, Gary Megson, Gary Bannister,
Gordon Owen, Paul Shirtliff.

two victories in 19 games under-
mined their promotion ambitions.
Three wins in the final six League
fixtures did not prove enough to
enable them to seriously threaten
third-placed Leicester, who finished
seven points better off and went up
with QPR and Wolves, while the Owls
had to settle for sixth position in the
table.

For supporters, the only consolation was the excitement of the club's
first FA Cup semi-final since 1966—
and sadly, even that ended in anti-
climax; and it was all the more
disappointing because everyone knew
Jack Charlton had decided this would
be his last season at Hillsborough.

At the start of the Cup run, three
attempts were required to overcome
Third Division Southend, but victories
at Torquay and Cambridge, and a 5-0
defeat of Burnley in a memorable
Hillsborough replay, set up a semi-
final with First Division strugglers
Brighton at Highbury. When Wednesday avoided Arsenal and Ron
Atkinson's Manchester United in the
draw, their supporters felt they had
good reason to believe the Owls
could go all the way to Wembley.
However, on the day, Charlton's men
failed to rise to the occasion and
could hardly complain at being
defeated in a scrappy match which
they might well have won had they

shown a semblence of their true abilities.

There was a hint of impending doom ahead of the game, for, when the team started for the ground from their overnight headquarters, nobody noticed that David Mills and Pat Heard were not on the bus and had been left behind. Fortunately, the players had the foresight to hail a taxi and so reached Highbury in good time, but the incident created a sense of panic which may explain why, on the field, Wednesday did not get to grips with the game in the first half.

A week earlier, Bailey had suffered a broken leg at Bolton, and Heard was switched to left-back—a change which meant that Mirocevic, who had made only four appearances since the turn of the year, was recalled for what proved to be his final appearance for the Owls before returning to Yugoslavia.

Wednesday lined up as follows:

Bolder, Sterland, Heard, Smith, Lyons, Shelton, Megson, Mills, Bannister, McCulloch, Mirocevic.

The experience of Tony Grealish and Jimmy Case proved the difference between two modest sides, when, after 14 minutes, the Brighton veterans produced a goal which exposed Wednesday's poor marking. When Mills conceded a free-kick for a clumsy challenge, there ought to have been no danger from a set-piece 30 yards from goal. But Grealish rolled the ball to Case, and the former Liverpool man was left unchallenged

and with a clear sight of goal as he hammered an unstoppable shot, which screeched into the net off the underside of the crossbar.

It took Wednesday until 12 minutes into the second half to equalise through Mirocevic, and soon afterwards they went desperately close to grabbing the lead: McCulloch had a goal-bound header cleared off the line by Brighton skipper Steve Foster with a spectacular overhead kick; but, in the 78th minute, Case popped up again to contribute to what proved to be the matchwinner. His through pass sent Gordon Smith clear, and though Bolder advanced from his goal to block the Brighton forward's shot, the rebound fell just right for Mike Robinson to steer the ball into the net, thus ensuring there would be no romantic final twist to Jack Charlton's Hillsborough story.

The Geordie giant had always said five years was long enough for any manager to stay at one club, and when he made his mind up there was no sense in attempting to change his decision. Chairman McGee and his manager had done plenty of straight talking during their partnership, but this was one occasion when he knew no words of his could alter the situation. Charlton left on good terms and never lost his affection for the Owls—and nobody could ever say other than that 'Big Jack' had done a good job. Wednesday simply had to ensure that his successor was another man with the 'winning touch'.

Porterfield Blades, 1981–1986

AFTER Sheffield United's sensational slide into the Football League's bottom grade for the first time in their history in May 1981, the resignation of chairman John Hassall was not unexpected. His seven years at the helm had coincided with a fall from the First to the Fourth Division, and, though others clearly shared the blame, he had little choice but to acknowledge that the ultimate responsibility for the club's dramatic decline rested on his shoulders.

Hassall, a director for eighteen years, had been thrust into the top job in August 1974 when his friend Dick Wragg chose to step down and concentrate on Football Association commitments. He inherited what, in view of United's financial burden, was regarded as an acutely difficult task. Of course the situation was not impossible, but one demanding positive and imaginative leadership. Hassall gave it his all, but in the final analysis, the challenge proved beyond him for a variety of reasons, some of which, perhaps, were not of his own making. He did, however, tackle the job with an independence which exposed his inexperience, and many close observers felt that he did not compensate often enough for a lack of a deep football background by consulting colleagues with greater knowledge of the game and its ways. Of course, Wragg, as president, remained a key influence and a welcome ally to the new chairman,

but the opinions of such long-serving directors as Frank O'Gorman, Frank Melling and Ken Lee were seldom sought. Those who argued for the creation of a John Harris-Cec Coldwell managerial partnership, for instance, were ignored, and despite all their efforts, they were unable to prevent Harris being pushed out at a time when the Scot's wisdom and judgement might have been of immense value to a 'rookie' chairman.

Melling finally stepped down in 1978 after twenty-four years on the board, whilst Lee, a director for eighteen years, followed him into retirement in 1980. They left without rancour, though Lee's departure coincided with the double resignation of Professor O'Gorman and Bert Jackson, who took exception to Hassall's insistence that qualification for membership of the board should forthwith include personal guarantees to the bank. It was a new trend and an indication of the pressure the chairman was under to maintain faith with the bank; moreover, he wanted to make room for newcomers ready to promise financial commitment.

Few of those he brought in made the kind of contribution Hassall sought, but the boardroom changes of June 1980 proved significant in prompting the arrival on the scene of Reg Brealey, a man destined to play a major role in United's story over the next fifteen years. A Lincolnshirebased businessman with extensive interests at home and abroad, Brealey was then aged forty-two. He had been a director of Lincoln City for three years in the late 1970s, and, wise in money matters and full of enthusiasm and ideas for steering the Blades back to solvency, his credentials soon inspired Hassall to appoint him as financial director—and to agree to the newcomer's condition that he 'could have full control and run things in the way he thought best fit'. It was not without irony that, when Hassall quit barely a year later, he intimated that a disagreement with Brealey, who had given the go-ahead for the latest £500,000 phase of the club's re-development plans, had finally induced his decision to go.

At the time Brealey took over, United were set to reveal a record trading loss of £725,230 on the 1980-81 campaign, and were over £1 million in debt. The outlook was far from good. However, the new chairman had plans which he felt could not only ease current problems but bring long-term financial stability; and it was a source of great frustration to him when things failed to go as he had hoped. An early step was the launch of a new £1.25 million shares issue, but he ended up personally underwriting around 75 per cent of the shares. Other means of generating income were explored, and later, he produced an ambitious £6 million redevelopment scheme for the ground. The idea was to exploit the spare land and create a Bramall Centre featuring a shopping, sports and leisure complex and incor-porating an hotel. The income generated would benefit the football club. Naturally, he was 'bitterly

disappointed' when the Labour-controlled Sheffield City Council rejected the scheme. An appeal to the Environment Minister was rejected in December 1982: 'A golden opportunity to re-establish Sheffield United among the country's top clubs has been lost', he sighed.

All this lay in the future, and Brealey's priority in the summer of 1981 was taking the steps necessary to set United on course for a prompt promotion from the Fourth Division. When Martin Peters and Harry Haslam quit, Brealey recruited the former Wednesday and Sunderland forward Ian Porterfield as manager. Porterfield, then thirty-five, had celebrated his first full season in management by leading Rotherham United to the Third Division cham-pionship. His walk-out was not well received at Millmoor, and many were surprised by his move. However, the ambitious Scot was attracted not only by the potential at Bramall Lane but by the remarkable offer of a highly-lucrative 10-year deal, the promise he would be left to do the job without interference, and a guarantee that the chairman himself would ensure substantial sums were available to spend on players.

Porterfield was destined to remain with United for five years, in which time he led them to the Fourth Division title in his first term and to promotion from the Third Division two years later. The Blades won 94 and lost 64 of the 213 League matches played under him before his departure in late March 1986, but those bare statistics do not reflect the mounting sense of disillusion felt amongst supporters in the period of anti-climax which followed the early successes. Nor do they reflect the cost. In his first two years, United suffered trading losses of £852,975 and £690,949 (with a total deficit of over £590,000 on transfers), and after a profit of £107,923 in 1984, further losses of £129,188 and £289,751 followed.

Porterfield was still insisting, nearly ten years after leaving, that his achievements at Bramall Lane were never fully appreciated. He always contended he left United in better shape than when he arrived, and claimed he took the Blades up two divisions with a net outlay of less than half-a-million pounds and helped reduce the club's debt. He made several popular and successful signings, notably in his first three years (when United won almost exactly half of their League matches, compared with a third in the following two seasons), but he had his failures in the transfer market, too. High hopes gradually faded and, with levels of achievement sharply declining, he ultimately fell foul of supporters who dubbed his team 'Dad's Army' because of the later emphasis on recruiting older players who did not produce the results yet enjoyed long and lucrative contracts.

In 1981-82 however, Porterfield had little difficulty dispelling the gloom, raising spirits and creating the blend which enabled United to enjoy a fairly smooth run to the Fourth Division championship. They lost only four games and, in the first year of three points for a win, their haul of 96 comfortably captured the top prize. Their only embarrassment was an FA Cup first-round defeat at the hands of non-League Altrincham.

Bob Hatton, Stewart Houston, Steve Neville (he scored the first goal of the new season after only 35 seconds), Mike Trusson (named Player of the Year) and Tony Kenworthy were amongst the players Porterfield inherited who made important contributions. Newcomers Keith Waugh (a £90,000 goalkeeper from Peterborough), Jeff King (a free signing after being 'given his cards' by Wednesday), and especially forwards Keith Edwards (brought 'home' from Hull for £100,000) and Colin Morris (a £100,000 mid-season buy from Blackpool) played key roles. Incidentally, it was in this season that Julian Broddle, aged seventeen years and one month, became United's youngest-ever League player when he faced Halifax in January; but it was to be his only outing.

Buying back striker Keith Edwards in September 1981 was one of Porterfield's most astute decisions. In truth, United were dismayed by the tribunal-set £100,000 fee, but the twenty-four year-old not only went on to claim a post-war record with 35 goals in his first season but contributed another 33 when promotion to Division Two was gained in 1984. Moreover, he ended up boasting 134 goals in 222 League and Cup games in his second spell with the Blades, raising his overall record for the club to 163 in 297 matches. His career tally of 256 League goals in 549 outings with six clubs did not include any in Division One, and he was never the team's hardest worker, but he had speed and timing which made him a deadly finisher.

Edwards who promptly formed a profitable partnership with veteran Bob Hatton, scored seven in his first

Keith Edwards in aerial action, with Paul Garner (right) looking on, in a game against Walsall, 1984.

seven games—his return not only coinciding with the start of a 17-match unbeaten run which included 11 wins, but he finished on the losing side only twice in 41 League matches. Moreover, Morris, who was signed in January soon after the Blades' heaviest defeat of the season (5–2 at Colchester), began a Bramall Lane career which spanned 240 League games (68 goals) with a run of 23 matches in which he was a loser just once. Hatton and Kenworthy both finished with 15 goals (the latter's tally included nine from the penalty spot), and features of Trusson's

eleven strikes were late doubles which sealed vital successes at York and Northampton; whilst one of King's four was a last-minute winner at Crewe which all but sealed promotion in early May.

There was a sense of anti-climax about 1982–83, when attendances fell as the Blades endured a modest and disappointing return to the Third Division. They finished in mid-table, paying for poor away form which saw them win only three times and suffer 16 defeats on their travels. Their best sequence was five straight wins in March, but overall, they lacked the

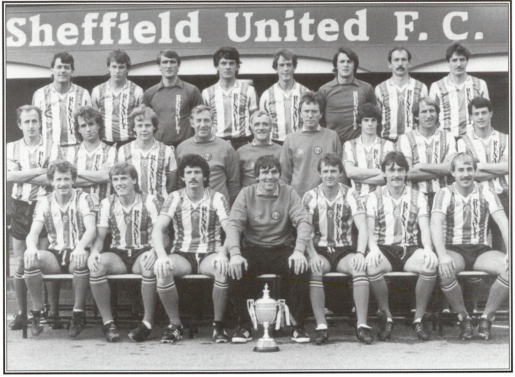

United 1982-83.
Back row: Kevin Arnott, Mike Trusson, Keith Waugh, John MacPhail, Stewart Houston, Steve
Conroy, Bob Hatton, Bob Atkins.
Middle Row: Mike Henderson, Steve Neville, Paul Garner, Cec Coldwell (chief coach), John
McSeveney (assistant manager), Jim Dixon (coach), Gary Brazil, Paul Richardson, Steve Charles.
Front row: Colin Morris, Keith Edwards, Terry Curran, Ian Porterfield (manager), Jeff King, Tony
Kenworthy, Ray McHale.

blend and spirit to maintain a decent run, and it was not without irony that some critics suggested the manager had too many players on his books!

Porterfield's excursions into the transfer market did not produce the expected dividends. Kevin Arnott, recruited from Sunderland without a fee under the new freedom of contract situation, was to make over 120 appearances and ultimately help United reach the Second Division, but initially he lacked consistency. Costly signings Alan Young (£160,000 from

Leicester) and Terry Curran (£100,000 from Wednesday) failed to fulfil expectations. Young was dogged with injuries, but Curran's failure was less easy to explain; indeed, it was all the more disappointing considering the remarkable circumstances in which he had arrived and been so determined to repeat his Wednesday success. Out of contract at Hillsborough, he audaciously knocked on Porterfield's door not once but three times and just begged to be signed. At first United officials questioned whether he was serious, but he insisted he was, and when an independent tribunal set the fee at half Wednesday's valuation, they felt they could only profit from the deal (though chairman and manager did not agree on the subject, with the deal causing friction with Wednesday). As it was, they were glad to get their money back when Curran moved on to Everton in September 1983 after only 33 League games. No doubt they were also consoled at suffering only minimal financial losses when Young, limited to 26 League outings, left for Brighton a month earlier.

Porterfield had better luck with his signings in 1983-84, when United enjoyed a sudden upturn in fortunes and clinched a place in Division Two in dramatic style by pipping Hull City into third place on goal-difference to go up with Oxford and Dave Bassett's Wimbledon. A modest outlay enabled him to recruit two new backs, former Spurs apprentice Tom Heffernan from Bournemouth, and ex-Sunderland favourite Joe Bolton from Middlesbrough, and both shone in the promotion success. However, the manager completed one of his most outstanding deals with a £100,000 investment in Paul Stancliffe. At twenty-five, the tall centre-back had already made 317 appearances at Rotherham, but the best was yet to come for a young man who would soon emerge an ideal captain and, in 337 outings over the next seven years, he became one of the club's all-time favourites as he shared in the long-awaited climb back to the top-grade, which he reached at the age of thirty-two after 560 League games.

There were other factors crucial to United's success. One was again the deadly finishing of Edwards, whose 38 League and Cup goals included two fours and two trebles; another was Morris' marksmanship, with half of his 20 League goals coming from the penalty spot; and the dramatic revival in the form of Arnott and ex-Chesterfield and Barnsley man, Ray McHale, gave the team the midfield sparkle lacking in the previous season. The £110,000 signing of attacking midfielder Glen Cockerill from Lincoln just before the March transfer deadline was another key piece in the jigsaw (it raised Brealey's personal investment to £1.25 million); but an unexpected hero was young goalkeeper Paul Tomlinson, who did so well after deputising for Waugh in November — he saved a penalty on his League debut — that he stayed in the side.

United began the season with five wins in an unbeaten seven-match run, but won only three of the next nine, and a spell in January and early February when they managed just one victory in seven games clouded their promotion prospects. However, a solitary defeat in a nine-game sequence up to the end of March kept them in with a shout. It was during the latter spell that Edwards scored three against Orient in a remarkable game in which United led 2–0, then trailed 3–2 before winning 6–3; and the striker also sealed a vital victory at Bournemouth with a goal often described as one of his best for the Blades.

With six matches remaining, United stood fourth in the table and promotion hopes soared when they won the first three of these (one was a victory achieved with a dramatic injury-time goal from substitute Bob

Chairman Reg Brealey (centre) lines up with the club's managerial and coaching staff: Denis Finnigan, Jeff Lees, John Stubbs, manager Ian Porterfield, John McSeveney and Jim McGuigan. (Brealey's chairmanship of United spanned the years from 1981 to 1995, apart from a spell when Paul Woolhouse briefly took control, but he finally confirmed the sale of his majority shareholding in late September 1995).

Atkins at Millmoor); but then dreams of glory faded following defeats at home to Wimbledon and at Bolton. Although the Blades ended their programme with a 2–0 home win against Newport, it looked like too little too late. Hull, with one game left, could pip them by winning 3–0 at Burnley on the following Tuesday. In the event, Hull scored after 80 seconds but finished with a 2–0 scoreline (both goals by Brian Marwood, later to play for both Wednesday and United), leaving them with exactly the same goal-difference (33) as United; but the Blades gained promotion having scored more goals (86) than Colin Appleton's Hull (71).

Unfortunately, once again promotion was followed by a contrasting season of gloom, with United winning only ten League games on their return to Division Two. They won just three of their first 19 games and collected a mere three points from their last nine fixtures; and in finishing 18th in the table, seven points clear of relegation, they were spared embarrassment as much by the shortcomings of rivals as through their own abilities. Edwards, troubled by injury and contractural problems, took his career haul past 200 goals but had a modest season; and though Mel Eves, a striker who had scored 53 goals for Wolves,

United 1983-84.
Back row: Brazil, Arnott, McHale, Henderson, Atkins, Kenworthy, Charles, Garner.
Middle row: Heffernan, Trusson, Stancliffe, Waugh, West, Bolton, Philliskirk.
Front: McSeveney, Morris, Porterfield, Edwards, Dixon.

arrived in December and contributed nine which included some superb strikes (notably a magnificent winner against Leeds), it did little to temper disappointment on the terraces.

Porterfield was having to show restraint in his spending. The recruitment in 1984-85 of veterans like goalkeeper John Burridge (aged thirty-two and boasting over 400 League games), former Liverpool captain Phil Thompson (aged thirty; 460 appearances) and the on-loan Dennis Mortimer (aged thirty-two; 615 games for Coventry and Aston Villa), suggested a short-term policy with the emphasis on experienced men at the end of their careers.

Porterfield hoped these players would enable him to fulfil Brealey's 1981 prediction of a place in Division One within five years. In the following season, the arrival of former Villa veteran Peter Withe (thirty-three), West Brom defender Ken McNaught (thirty) and Fulham midfielder Ray Lewington (twenty-nine), further raised the team's average age. Alas, gambling on the 'old brigade' paid no dividend and only increased the pressure on Porterfield.

The atmosphere in the early stages of the 1985-86 campaign was far from good. Porterfield's decision to leave Edwards (he did not start a game until late September) and Arnott on the

Keith Edwards on target in the 2-2 draw with Wigan in September 1983 on the day Tony Kenworthy equalised in injury time.

sidelines, was a source of dismay to fans whose patience snapped in early October when they greeted a home defeat by Millwall with jeers and verbal abuse. At that point United had won one game in 9, and though they followed it with 6 wins in the next 7 matches (they scored 5 goals in 24 minutes in a remarkable 5–1 victory at Oldham) and climbed into second place, four successive defeats in December (including a 5–0 defeat at Wimbledon, where McNaught and Withe were sent off) marked the beginning of the end for the manager with five years left on his contract.

His last major transfer deals, in October, were the sale of Cockerill to Southampton for £200,000 and the purchase of Steve Wigley, a winger, from Nottingham Forest for £90,000. Ironically, Wigley was limited to a handful of outings in Porterfield's remaining months because Morris was switched from a central striking role back to his more familiar wing position and he did so well that the newcomer could not get a regular place in the team. Wigley was to manage just 28 League appearances before moving to Birmingham in March 1987 and will be remembered largely for a tremendous solo effort in a 3–3 draw with Blackburn in November 1985.

The disillusionment of supporters was reflected in declining atten- dances, and gates which had averaged nearly 15,000 in 1981-82 had fallen by almost 30 per cent. Early in 1985-86 United boasted four 13,000-plus gates, but in January Bramall Lane had its lowest FA Cup attendance this century when only 7,004 watched the tie with Fulham (see footnote); in February the attendance for the visit of Brighton was 7,367, while the figures for the following home matches were 8,405 and 9,165.

When Second Division leaders Norwich visited Bramall Lane on March 22nd 1986, they arrived with the impressive record of one defeat in their previous 21 League matches and 13 wins in the last 15 outings. United boasted their best gate (11,894) since before Christmas, but there was little for home fans to cheer as the Blades crashed to a 5–2 defeat. It was the final straw. The furious anti-Porterfield demonstration which followed almost certainly sealed his fate, though chairman Brealey denied there had been any question of terminating the manager's contract until an hour into the board meeting on the following Tuesday.

Brealey emerged from that meeting to comment. 'It has become increasingly apparent over the past few weeks, to both parties, that the manager has lost the confidence of the supporters, and therefore, in the interest of all concerned, manager and club have parted company. Football is all about supporters and entertaining them. If you can't take them with you there is not much point in continuing. They do not run the club, but their views have to be taken into account. We cannot continue to have the sort of demonstrations we have had at the club recently.'

Porterfield did not accept that he had failed, and was permanently soured by his Bramall Lane axing. Late in 1986, he was appointed Alex Ferguson's successor at Aberdeen, a 'plum' post he quit in 1988 for family reasons. Later he managed Reading in between two spells with Chelsea (the second as team-boss from 1991 to 1993), and then spent some time abroad in the mid-1990s. He fancied the Wednesday job before it went to David Pleat in 1995.

Footnote: On the subject of attendances, United attracted only 4,075 for a League Cup-tie with Bury in September 1995, and in 1991 the gate for a Zenith Data match with Notts County was a mere 3,409.

Howard Wilkinson: Owls 1983–1988

WHEN WEDNESDAY recruited thirty-nine year-old Sheffielder Howard Wilkinson as Jack Charlton's successor in June 1983, he was not the 'big name' anticipated by the media and some supporters, but he proved to be an outstanding appointment—as much 'a winner' and the right man at the right time as his more famous predecessor. In five years at Hillsborough Wilkinson amply confirmed managerial talents which ultimately led him to the very top of his profession: dedication, discipline and determination were his keynotes, and he combined ability with a genuine passion for a club he had supported from boyhood and played with for over four years until 1966.

Wilkinson's time at the helm spanned 264 League and Cup games, of which 121 were won and 75 lost; he led Wednesday to promotion and five cup quarter-finals plus one semi-final. His first season brought the end of a fourteen-year wait for a return to the top-grade; his third term saw the Owls climb to their highest League position for twenty-five years and finish one step from Wembley in the FA Cup. If excellent early progress inspired high expectations which went unfulfilled in the following two seasons, it was largely due to financial inhibitions as the Owls failed to embrace the next stage of development. The irony was that when Wilkinson, frustrated by the board's lack of ambition and his inability to win the backing he felt essential to see the job through, accepted an offer to join Leeds, it set in motion events which subsequently induced a dramatic change of attitude in the Hillsborough boardroom—and others enjoyed resources he deserved but was denied.

The turnover in transfers in the Wilkinson years was around £9 million, and he recouped just about all he spent. He raised the club's transfer record to £475,000, which was modest compared with many of Wednesday's rivals; but he was restricted not only in buying the quality of players needed, but in attracting them with terms they could easily demand elsewhere. Moreover, many of his recruits who succeeded at Hillsborough (some had good reason to be grateful to see their careers revived with the Owls) readily exploited the new freedom of contract to move to where they could get more lucrative deals. The limitations of choice may explain the irony that some of his most expensive buys proved disappointing, and certainly confirms why, if Wilkinson's teams never lacked spirit, they were often short on the talent to reach for the very top. It was a mark of Wilkinson's loyalty that, though his hands were tied, he refrained from publicly exposing a boardroom policy he knew to be short-sighted and a self-imposed handicap.

Wednesday 1984.
Back Row: Lawrie Madden, Gavin Oliver, Iain Hesford, Martin Hodge, Mark Smith, Mick Lyons.
Middle row: Peter Eustace (assistant manager), Gary Shelton, Peter Shirtliff, John Pearson, Lee
Chapman, Imre Varadi, Nigel Worthington, Alan Smith (physio).
Front row: Brian Marwood, Mel Sterland, Charlie Williamson, Howard Wilkinson (manager),
Pat Heard, Chris Morris, Andy Blair.

Growing up in the Netherthorpe district, Wilkinson had been good enough to gain Yorkshire and England honours while attending Abbeydale Boys' Grammar School, and he later collected five Youth international caps; but he often insisted that, when he became a professional and a winger with Wednesday (22 League games after his 1964 debut) and Brighton (129) between 1962 and 1971, his abilities were modest. In truth, he was better than many and invariably took his football seriously,

but playing in the Third Division in his mid-twenties proved less than fulfilling and he seemed destined for a teaching career. Yet, prompted by Brighton colleague Steve Burtenshaw (later an Owls manager), he did find coaching rewarding. He was already progressing in that direction when, in 1971, fellow Sheffielder, ex-Blade Jim Smith, took him as a part-timer to Boston United, where he played while studying for a degree in physical education at Sheffield University. When Smith moved to Colchester in

November 1972, the departing player-manager nominated Wilkinson, then just twenty-nine, as his successor. 'Too young', said chairman Ernest Malkinson, but within a few months, he changed his mind, and Wilkinson, promoted from player-coach, marked his first season in charge by leading Boston to the Northern Premier League championship with a margin of nine points—the first of three triumphs in a six-year stay during which he rejected a chance to manage Lincoln City.

It was after a subsequent six months with Northern Premier League rivals Mossley, and a spell as Sheffield-based FA regional coach, that Wilkinson returned to League football in January 1980 as assistant to Notts County manager Jimmy Sirrel, who promised his recruit maximum freedom in training and team matters. In his first full season (1980-81), Wilkinson guided County into Division One for the first time since 1926—a success which prompted his formal confirmation as team-boss, plus the offer of two opportunities which he declined: the manager's job vacated by Ron Atkinson at West Brom, and the role of No. 2 to new England chief Bobby Robson. In the meantime, however, he did expand his horizons, knowledge and contacts as coach to England's Under-21s.

There were those in the game who were already aware of Wilkinson's promise and many believed he had a bright future. However, he was not Wednesday's first choice; indeed, it was only after Bert McGee had been refused permission to speak to Watford's Graham Taylor (who went to Aston Villa in 1987) that the Owls' chairman followed up a tip which turned his attention towards Meadow Lane. McGee got his man just in time. Had he delayed another twenty-four hours, County chairman, Jack Dunnett, would have had Wilkinson committed to a long-term contract.

Wilkinson always knew what he wanted and how he planned to achieve it, and he came 'home' armed with a formula for success shaped over twenty-one years in football. He surprised some people by bringing back Peter Eustace, who had been chief coach at Sunderland, for a third spell at Hillsborough as his assistant manager; and one of his wisest appointments was ex-Rotherham and Blackpool physio, Alan Smith. He wanted people around him who supported his philosophy, for his emphasis on fitness and tactics tailored to the strengths and abilities of the players at his disposal subsequently prompted images of his methods and style which he considered myths. The training sessions he introduced were undoubtedly tough (more than one newcomer described them as 'a shock to the system'), but he always insisted the cross-country runs in the local hills were intended to lend variety to fitness preparation, contending that players never did any more training there than at the ground. He was also invariably dismayed at being hailed 'a high priest of long-ball football': Wednesday's direct style provoked much criticism in the early days, but Wilkinson felt most of it unjust and believed it stemmed from envy of their success, echoing his friend Dave Bassett. Ironically, when the Owls consciously adopted a more 'cultured' approach, around 1986, it coincided with a decline in their

Martin Hodge . . . established record run of consecutive appearances.

Hodge was not only captain, but on stand-by for England's World Cup squad. The capture of striker Imre Varadi from Newcastle in a £150,000 deal was another inspired buy, with the ex-Sheffield United man contributing 19 League and Cup goals in his first term; while Lawrie Madden, signed from Millwall on a free transfer, proved one of the club's most dependable defenders in a Hillsborough career spanning 226 games. Wednesday's subsequent signings in 1983-84 were Barnsley striker Tony Cunningham (£85,000 in November),

fortunes—and exposed the shortcomings of a financial policy which prevented the recruitment of the quality players required to sustain a more sophisticated system.

Ahead of Wilkinson's first campaign in 1983-84, Wednesday made four signings which included three of his most successful deals, and moreover, by virtue of the £125,000 sale of Bob Bolder to Liverpool and the departure of McCulloch and David Mills, the net cost was barely £100,000. With Bolder gone, a new goalkeeper was a priority and, though Iain Hesford, a £25,000 buy from Blackpool, was the initial contender, circumstances conspired to thrust Martin Hodge, a £50,000 recruit from Everton (after a brief spell on loan), into a role he made his own over the next four years in a record-breaking run of 214 consecutive appearances. By 1986

Nigel Worthington . . . went on to become Wednesday's most-capped player.

who did not stay long; and Notts County's Nigel Worthington (£100,000 in February), a back destined to top 400 appearances and become the Owls' most-capped player with 50 games for Northern Ireland prior to joining Leeds in 1994.

Once the Wilkinson era kicked off, the new manager's meticulous planning and preparation, not least in the time spent on fitness and rehearsing set-pieces, were evident as the Owls started out with an unbeaten run of 18 League and Cup matches—their 15-match League sequence (11 wins and four draws) creating a club record. The last win in this run, a 4–2 home defeat of Newcastle watched by a 41,134 crowd in mid-November, saw Wednesday go six points clear at the top. Geordie hero Kevin Keegan, however, soured the mood with some harsh words about the Hillsborough team's style, and no doubt, he smiled a week later when the Owls suffered their first defeat, a 1–0 setback at Crystal Palace. Wednesday ended November with a Milk Cup triumph over First Division Stoke which prompted Stoke manager, Richie Barker, (seven years later he came to Sheffield as coach) to hail Wilkinson's team as good enough for the top-grade.

Wednesday suffered just six League defeats, and only once lost two games on the trot (at Grimsby and home to Middlesbrough over Christmas), and when Mel Sterland's penalty sealed a 1–0 success against Crystal Palace which clinched promotion in late April, a memorable season looked sure to end with the Second Division title. Alas, defeats at Middlesbrough and Shrewsbury and a home draw with Manchester City enabled Chelsea

Imre Varadi . . . scored some memorable goals in the first of two spells with the Owls.

to snatch that prize on goal-difference.

The feeling that the big-time was finally back at Hillsborough was compounded by progress which saw Wednesday reach the quarter-finals of both major cup competitions. They emerged with pride despite falling in away replays to champions Liverpool in the Milk Cup and Division One runners-up Southampton in the FA cup. In January a 49,357 crowd saw the Owls share a 2–2 draw with holders Liverpool (who salvaged a replay with a Phil Neal penalty) before losing 3–0 at Anfield; and in March, despite 'live' coverage by ITV, a 43,000-plus Sunday gate witnessed a 0–0 draw with Lawrie McMenemy's Southampton, whose 5–1 victory in

The Dell replay was a scoreline which did less than justice to Wilkinson's men. Incidentally, the home Southampton game saw Wednesday wear shirts bearing the names of sponsors (Crosby Kitchens) for the first time in their history.

That the contribution of the men Wilkinson inherited was significant is evident: Mike Lyons, an outstanding centre-half and skipper, and busy midfielder Gary Megson were ever-present; while Gary Shelton was voted Player of the Year, and Gary Bannister claimed 22 goals (eight in the cup matches). There were few more courageous players than Lyons, and symbolically perhaps, he started his men on the promotion trail with the first goal of the season—with a header from one of the set-pieces he said he didn't enjoy repeatedly practising in training!

The departure of Gary Bannister (to QPR, £200,000) and Gary Megson (Nottingham Forest, £175,000) in the summer of 1984 confirmed that while the spirit in the Owls' camp was high, the wage structure meant some players would always find the attraction of better personal terms elsewhere impossible to resist. Remarkably, Megson never played a League match for Brian Clough's Forest and returned to Sheffield via Newcastle two years later. Meanwhile, Wilkinson prepared for the challenge of Wednesday's first season in the top grade for fourteen years by investing £275,000 in recruiting three new men: Hull winger Brian Marwood, Sunderland's unsettled striker Lee Chapman, and Aston Villa's former Scottish Under-21 midfielder Andy Blair. A later arrival was teenager Siggi Jonsson, an Icelandic international

midfielder; and it is worthy of note that the season marked the start of apprenticeships for two local products of note, Kevin Pressman and Carl Bradshaw.

Marwood, who had scored 53 goals in 191 games over five seasons at Hull, was seen by Wilkinson as a player with the ability to find space on the flanks and provide precise crosses, and scoring 35 goals and making many others in 161 games, before his £600,000 move to Arsenal in March 1988, he proved for the most part a good investment at £125,000; though, in his last months at Hillsborough, he was caught up in a mood of disen-chantment which affected several key men. Marwood, a future PFA chairman, followed his move south with a brief appearance for England as late substitute (replacing future Owls hero Chris Waddle) in the same Saudi Arabia game in which Mel Sterland gained his only senior cap; and the winger later had a spell at Bramall Lane.

Chapman arrived with his career in the doldrums, for after starting off with 34 goals in 99 League games for Stoke, he managed four in 23 outings following a £500,000 move to Arsenal and three in 15 matches for Sunderland, where he knew his days were numbered when his old Stoke boss, Alan Durban, was replaced by ex-Owls manager, Len Ashurst, three months after the lanky striker had moved to the North East. Chapman proved good value for his £100,000 cost with 79 goals in 187 games with Wednesday, but he had cause to be grateful for the oppor-tunity to revive his fortunes in an atmosphere and circumstances which suited his strengths and enabled him

*Lee Chapman . . . his career was given a
new lease of life with the Owls.*

to remove some of the rough edges
from his game. Nobody ever doubted
his courage (he collected over 100
stitches in a succession of facial and
head wounds while with Wednesday)
and he certainly went through the
pain barrier in claiming 20 goals for
the first time in his career in 1984-85.
Moreover, after surviving the threat
inherent in Wilkinson's recruitment of
record signings Simon Stainrod (who
made only 15 appearances after his
£275,000 move from QPR in February
1985) and Garry Thompson (8 goals
in 44 games after arriving from West
Brom for £450,000 in August 1985),
Chapman deservedly claimed the
Player of the Year award in 1986-87.

Blair had a shorter stay than either
Marwood or Chapman, and his
Hillsborough career, limited to 75
games, ended abruptly in March 1986
when, after being substituted in an FA
Cup tie at Derby following a sloppy
pass which led to a home goal, he was
sold back to Aston Villa for £70,000
more than he cost. Blair did well in
his first term, and, though he scored
only seven goals for Wednesday, his
place in club records was assured
with a unique hat-trick of penalties in
the 4–2 Milk Cup defeat of David
Pleat's Luton in November 1984.

The new-boys helped Wednesday
enjoy a respectable return to the top
grade, where they finished eighth.
They might have done even better
but for four defeats in the last five
matches. An early-season unbeaten
run of eight games included a
memorable 2–0 victory at Liverpool,
and a subsequent 12-match sequence
without defeat (which lifted them
into the top four) featured a notable
2–1 success at Manchester United.
Varadi, who showed himself capable
of some stunning and exciting strikes
with ice-cool finishing, was on target
at both Anfield and Old Trafford, and
his tally of 21 for the season included hat-tricks in the 5–0 defeat of
Leicester and the 5–1 FA Cup triumph
over Oldham. Unfortunately, like
Bannister a year earlier, he chose to
leave at the end of the season and
joined West Brom for £285,000—a
tribunal fee which constituted a profit
but was painfully modest considering
it cost Wednesday nearly half as much
again to replace him with a man who
proved a flop.

The most dramatic match of the
1984-85 campaign was undoubtedly
the home Milk Cup quarter-final

replay with Chelsea in January. The first game, in London, had ended 1–1 after Hodge saved a Kerry Dixon penalty. Ironically, now it was an injury-time spot-kick which gave a final sensational twist to a match in which Wednesday had led 3–0 at half-time, then trailed 4–3 before Sterland, brought down by Scottish defender Doug Rougvie, hauled himself off the ground and hammered the ball past Niedzwicki to take the tie into extra time—it ended 4–4. Chelsea snatched a 2–1 victory in the second replay at Stamford Bridge with a Mickey Thomas strike in the closing seconds.

A Wembley final, however, again beckoned the Owls when they reached the last four in the FA Cup in 1985–86—a season in which Wilkinson's men also climbed into fifth place in Division One, their highest position since 1961. Alas, the prize of European competition was denied them, for in May of the previous year at the European Cup final between Liverpool and Juventus at the Heysel Stadium in Brussels, disaster had struck with the deaths of 38 spectators; the tragedy prompted a UEFA ban on English clubs.

It was not without irony that the major signings in 1985–86, striker Garry Thompson and winger Mark Chamberlain, were outshone by two free transfer players, Paul Hart and Carl Shutt. Like Stainrod, whose brief stay ended in September, Thompson somehow never fitted in. His role was too similar to Chapman's and he was not nearly as effective; while Chamberlain, who cost £300,000 from Stoke, made 21 appearances, 18 of which were as substitute. Only rarely did Chamberlain show anything remotely resembling the form that

had brought him eight England caps between 1982 and 1984, and he started in only 40 of the 88 games he played for the Owls before a £200,000 move to Portsmouth in 1988. Meanwhile, the arrival of defender Hart, a thirty-two year-old veteran of 490 League games with Stockport, Blackpool, Leeds and Nottingham Forest, enabled Wednesday to release Lyons to become player-manager at Grimsby. At the other end of the experience scale, Sheffield-born striker Shutt, recruited from non-League football at Spalding on the recommendation of youth coach Michael Hennigan and belatedly made a full-time professional at twenty-four, displayed surprisingly mature skills and had a remarkable impact, scoring 13 goals, including one with a magnificent header on his debut in October and a treble in the 5–1 defeat of Birmingham in March.

Wednesday won four of their first five games, and though crushed 5–1 by both Everton (at Hillsborough) and Spurs in the space of 18 days, they enjoyed another nine-match unbeaten run between the end of September and late November. They lacked the quality of serious title contenders but never fell below ninth, and five wins in an unbeaten six-match finale left them in fifth position.

Wilkinson knew their best chance of a trophy was in the cup competitions, and there were moments when the Wembley trail in the FA Cup promised fulfilment. Two attempts were required to dismiss top-grade strugglers West Brom in the third round. Then after Orient had been hammered 5–0, a Shutt double sealed a home replay success against Third Division Derby after a 1–1 draw in a

Baseball Ground game remembered for Blair's costly slip and Hodge's bravery. After collecting a high ball, the goalkeeper, newly installed as captain, crashed heavily head first on the icebound pitch. He played on despite suffering severe concussion; remarkably Derby boss Arthur Cox initially thought Hodge was 'making a meal' of his injury! The Hillsborough quarter-final with West Ham was a memorable duel between two teams bent on attack, with Worthington (using the right foot he normally

optimistic about the chances of overcoming the Everton hoodoo.

It so happened that a religious convention was being held at the team's headquarters, and the offer by some members of the clergy to bless the players before they left for the tie was accepted; alas, in the event, it failed to influence the result in the way Wilkinson hoped!

In fact, Wednesday might have led after only three minutes when Megson (he had returned via Newcastle a few months earlier for

Carl Shutt scoring in the 1986 FA Cup semi-final.

reserved for standing on!) and Shutt scoring in a 2–1 victory.

Howard Kendall's Everton, reigning League champions, Cup-Winners' Cup holders, and for so long Wednesday's 'bogey' team, provided the opposition in the Villa Park semi-final. With Marwood unfit and Chapman chosen, despite being still not fully recovered from illness, realists were not

£60,000) just failed to reach a ball knocked on by Hart; and when Alan Harper (the Owls thought he was offside) found the space and freedom to lob the ball over Hodge to give Everton the lead after 49 minutes, it was decidedly against the run of play. However, the Sheffield side bounced back and within four minutes a cross from defender Glyn Snodin (a

Chairman Bert McGee in conversation with Her Majesty Queen Elizabeth II in the directors' box when she visited Hillsborough to formally open the new covered Kop, December 12th 1986.

£115,000 summer buy from Doncaster) was headed on by Hart and Shutt nipped in to equalise with a splendid opportunists header.

As the game moved into extra time, Wednesday believed their superior stamina would prove decisive. Unfortunately, eight minutes into the added half-hour, they only partially cleared an Everton corner-kick, their marking was slack when the ball was hit back into the goalmouth, and Everton's Scottish striker Graeme Sharp settled the tie with a stunning volley which gave Hodge no chance.

There were those who predicted Wednesday's season would fall into anti-climax after their defeat, but in

fact, they showed as much tenacity and character in the remaining weeks of the League programme than at any stage of the campaign, and Wilkinson felt the Owls boasted the nucleus of a team on the brink of something good. Opportunity was knocking for a club that had not won a major honour since 1935, but did those with the power to authorise the next bold step recognise it?

In the summer of 1986 a start was made on putting a roof on and extending Hillsborough's Spion Kop at a cost of £1 million. Half the money was provided by the Football Grounds Improvement Trust, and this development would be formally 'opened' by

Sheffield Wednesday
Football Club plc

COMMEMORATIVE PROGRAMME

TO CELEBRATE THE
OPENING OF THE NEW
COVERED KOP

by HER MAJESTY THE QUEEN
on Friday, 12th December 1986

*Cover of official programme for Queen's
visit, December 1986.*

Her Majesty the Queen in the follow-ing December. Now, the manager told Bert McGee and his boardroom colleagues, was the time to provide the funds to also push the team into a new era by recruiting players to raise the overall quality and provide more tactical options.

In fact Wilkinson was left to launch his attempt to reshape the playing style in 1986–87 without any major change in personnel other than departures of Thompson, sold to Aston Villa for £450,000; Peter Shirtliff, who joined Charlton for £125,000; and, later, Hesford, for whom Sunderland paid £80,000. The only pre-season signing of note was David Hirst, a highly promising 18 year-old striker who cost an initial £200,000

David Hirst pictured with his father Eric and manager Howard Wilkinson (centre) after joining the Owls from Barnsley.

from Barnsley; though a contract was given to another striker with Oakwell links, Colin Walker, who had also served Doncaster and Cambridge. Hirst was to emerge an England player and top a century of goals in a career cruelly hampered by a succession of injuries in the 1990s. Walker, though he had the distinction of scoring a debut hat-trick in 16 minutes after coming on as second-half substitute in a record-breaking 7–0 defeat of Stockport at Maine Road in a Littlewoods (League) Cup tie in October 1986, could hardly be considered a long-term or First Division prospect. He was already twenty-eight and boasted barely 40 League games between spells in New Zealand and in non-League football. He played only twice in Wednesday's League side.

The 1986-87 campaign was one in which little went as planned off or on the field. Behind the scenes, for instance, Dick Chester, secretary since succeeding the long-serving Eric England, who retired after forty-seven years midway through 1983-84, announced he was returning to industry. The man appointed to replace him, Aston Villa's Steve Stride, gave back word soon after his appointment was announced. The upshot was that Graham Mackrell, then thirty-seven but thirteen years earlier the Football League's youngest club secretary when he started at Bournemouth, was recruited from Luton, where he had worked alongside team-boss David Pleat—the man destined to join the Owls as successor to Trevor Francis in 1995. Mackrell arrived in mid-December 1986.

Wednesday lost only one of their first nine games in 1986-87 and in early December climbed into the top six, but, going into the Christmas programme knowing good holiday results could lift them into second place, they saw their fortunes take a sudden and unexpected dip which marked a turning point in the Wilkinson era with the start of a phase which saw them win only six and lose 20 of 34 League matches spanning more than ten months.

On the 1986 Boxing Day visit to relegation-threatened Manchester City, the manager felt he had good reason to anticipate a quality performance. Instead he ended up angered by a lethargic display which brought a 1–0 defeat. He promptly dropped Hart (who did not play again), Megson and Shelton for the home game with Liverpool the next day—which the Owls also lost. In fact, those two defeats were amongst eleven suffered in the next 16 League matches. It was only three wins and two draws from the last six fixtures that enabled Wednesday to finish 13th in the table. One of those victories, incidentally, was a remarkable 7–1 crushing of QPR, whose manager was Wilkinson's old pal and Boston United boss, Jim Smith. (Shiregreen product Smith had been a Wednesdayite from boyhood, and if he had one regret in an eventful career in football it was that he never fulfilled his dream of managing the Owls!).

It said much for Wednesday's problems that Hodge was the team's only ever-present, and in fact, when he appeared in the FA Cup fourth-round replay against Chester in early February, he took a club record from pre-war hero Mark Hooper by making his 190th consecutive appearance. Yet even the normally dependable goalkeeper had his moments of anguish. In October, in the 2–2 home draw with Coventry, he conceded a freak goal when City goalkeeper Steve Ogrizovic's wind-assisted long clearance from the Leppings Lane end saw the ball bounce over him and into the net. Then in April, also in front of the Kop supporters, Hodge was again left blushing when, chasing an over-hit ball from Shelton in an effort to prevent Nottingham Forest gaining a corner kick on the right, he tried to dribble past visiting midfielder Johnny Metgod, lost possession, and watched in horror as the Dutchman crossed the ball which Nigel Clough turned into the unguarded net. Forest won 3–2. Somehow, 'Hodgy', who set such a fine example as skipper, was never quite the same again.

The promise of young Hirst, who scored a memorable winner against Manchester United in March with a devastating left-foot effort, was one of the few bright spots in a glum phase, though Chapman did well with 19 goals and Bradshaw's efforts earned him the Young Player of the Year award. Wednesday's woe was compounded when hopes of some compensation on the Wembley trail crumbled as they fell in the quarter-final, defeated at home by eventual FA Cup winners Coventry. (The Midlanders, incidentally, returned to Hillsborough to enjoy a memorable triumph over Leeds in the semi-final.)

The second half of Wednesday's campaign coincided with unexpected problems at the heart of the defence following the sale of Hart to Birmingham and a career-shattering injury suffered by Ian Knight. The availability of the long-serving Mark Smith and the outstanding promise of Knight (a 1985 free transfer recruit

from Barnsley who collected England Under-21 honours in 1986) induced Wilkinson to sell Hart in late December. Hart had been dropped over Christmas, but his sudden departure was still a surprise, and he must have been left pondering the strange and cruel mysteries of fate when, on his debut with his new club, he suffered a broken leg.

Ironically, within weeks Hart was consoling the youngster who had taken his place, for Knight, at twenty-one, saw his career wrecked by a double compound leg fracture suffered in the second minute of the February FA Cup replay with Chester. The odds looked in his favour as he went for a 60-40 ball with striker Gary 'Psycho' Bennett, whose challenge, as television replays confirmed, was reckless, high and late. Remarkably, referee Allison did not immediately react to the incident and it was a full minute before play was stopped for Knight to have attention. Owls' physio Alan Smith, who discovered that Knight's fibula had been forced through his calf muscle and was projecting out of his sock, described it as the worst injury he had ever seen on a football pitch. Smith subsequently helped Knight through a long battle to rescue his career, but while the Hartlepool product did eventually return to League football, he was a shadow of the player he had been and was limited to two further senior outings with the Owls and barely 20 with Grimsby and Carlisle. Bennett, meanwhile, was still thriving and playing First Division football in 1995-96 after moving to Tranmere following a spell at Wrexham.

Soon after the loss of Knight, Wilkinson recruited Larry May from

Nigel Pearson.

Barnsley for £200,000, but though the new centre-half had made a big impact at Oakwell, he proved a disappointment at Hillsborough, where the problems in central defence did not begin to ease until after the October 1987 arrival of Nigel Pearson, who cost £250,000 from Shrewsbury. Pearson was to make over 200 appearances and emerge an outstanding captain, but it was typical of Wednesday's ill-fate that his early progress was halted when he suffered a dislocated ankle after only 19 games.

That development only compounded Wilkinson's frustration for, long before signing Pearson, he had agreed terms with Southampton for England defender Mark Wright, and with Nottingham Forest for Chris Fairclough, but failed to match the financial packages the players demanded and were later offered, by Derby and Spurs respectively.

Newcomers at the start of 1987-88 (over £500,000 had been raised with

the sales of Smith, Shelton, Snodin and Chris Morris) included experienced Ipswich defender Steve McCall (£250,000), Spurs' once highly acclaimed winger Tony Galvin (£100,000), and a non-League centre-half, Greg Fee, who cost £20,000 from Boston United. In September Wednesday paid £250,000 for midfielder Mark Proctor, who had made 290 appearances with Middlesbrough, Nottingham Forest and Sunderland, and it cost £125,000 to bring former Sunderland and Watford striker Colin West from Glasgow Rangers. West was an unexpected choice as Chapman's partner, and he managed only eight goals in 45 League games over two seasons. When Pearson, the October recruit who proved the lone newcomer in this phase destined to make a lasting impact, was injured in March 1988, the Owls invested a record £475,000 in Ipswich central defender Ian Cranson, another disappointing buy, for he made only 35 appearances and stayed barely a year.

The gloom of the previous campaign continued deep into the autumn of 1987, with the situation exacerbated by a run of injuries, notably to McCall, who broke his leg in only his fifth game; and when Wednesday managed just one win and suffered eight defeats in their opening 12 matches to stand second from bottom of a reduced First Division in October, Wilkinson wisely withdrew from a commitment to take charge of the England 'B' team in Malta to concentrate on the more serious problem at home. (It is, perhaps, worthy of note that England boss Bobby Robson immediately recruited Graham Taylor, and Taylor

Wednesday 1987-88.
Back row: David Reeves, Siggi Jonsson, Larry May, Ian Knight, Kevin Pressman, Lee Chapman, Martin Hodge, Lawrie Madden, Ken Brannigan, Mark Smith, Andy Kiwomya.
Middle row: Clive Baker (chief scout), Peter Eustace (assistant manager), Mark Chamberlain, David Hirst, Gary Megson, Mel Sterland, Nigel Worthington, Carl Bradshaw, Steve McCall, Des Hazel, Mick Hennigan (Youth team manager), Alan Smith (physio).
Front row: Gary Owen, Carl Shutt, Glyn Snodin, Brian Marwood, Howard Wilkinson (manager), Gary Shelton, Wayne Jacobs, Tony Gregory, Colin Walker.

was thus set on a course which was to see him eventually installed as the next national team manager.)

Ten victories in their next 14 League fixtures lifted the Owls into ninth place, but five successive defeats (they conceded 14 goals and scored only two) in February and early March revived all the old pessimism on the terraces. Meanwhile, Wednesday had again reached the Littlewoods Cup quarter-finals only to lose at home to Arsenal, whose winner was a long speculative effort from Winterburn which somehow saw Hodge concede another 'soft' goal. The manner of the Owls' 5–1 home defeat against Everton (yes, again!) in the FA Cup third-round marathon a week later did nothing to raise the spirits of supporters. The latest lean spell cost Hodge his place in March and, after 249 games, his era was over, with young Kevin Pressman getting a late run which coincided with an eight-match unbeaten sequence that lifted the Owls into a final place in mid-table.

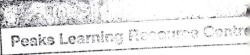

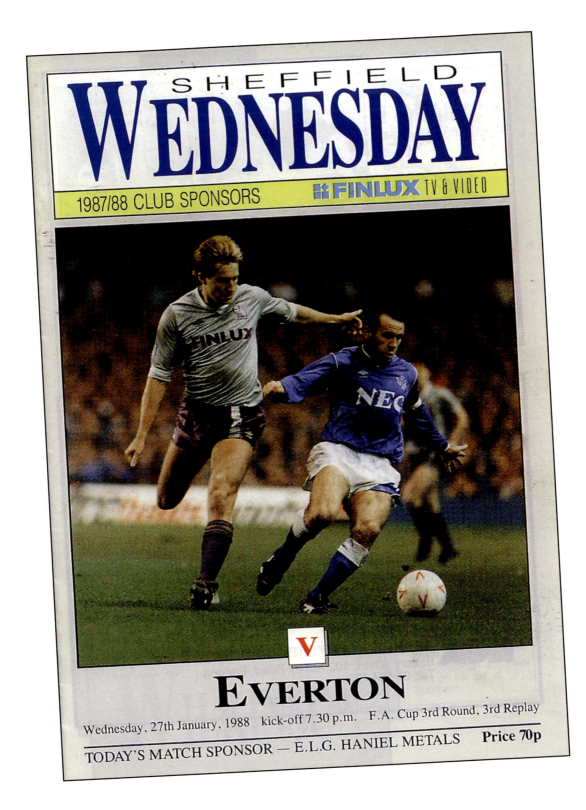

SHEFFIELD WEDNESDAY

1987/88 CLUB SPONSORS — FINLUX TV & VIDEO

EVERTON

Wednesday, 27th January, 1988   kick-off 7.30 p.m.   F.A. Cup 3rd Round, 3rd Replay

TODAY'S MATCH SPONSOR — E.L.G. HANIEL METALS   Price 70p

After the high expectations inspired by the success of his early years, Wilkinson was aware of the dismay felt by supporters at the reversal of the club's fortunes in the last two seasons but, though frustrated by the restraints under which he was operating, he said little, aware that the directors were the chief target of public criticism. Remarkably, whilst disagreeing with them and constantly seeking to encourage a change in policy, Wilkinson admitted he could understand their caution. Chairman McGee always said that, having rescued and revived a club which had been financially 'bleeding to death' in the mid-70s, he would not risk them ever again being at the mercy of the bank.

Of course, a dozen years had passed since those dark days, and many of the current staff (as well as supporters and shareholders) argued that a different time demanded a different philosophy. Some players felt they could wait no longer. Marwood, who went to Arsenal in March 1988, and Lee Chapman, who, astonishingly, was deceived into believing that greater riches and rewards awaited him at an 'unknown' French Second Division club called Niort in the following summer, were the latest players to express despair at Wednesday's lack of ambition. Their hearts were no longer at Hillsborough and ambition turned their thoughts elsewhere. Wilkinson had the chance to take the same route and seek more promising pastures when he received a lucrative offer from Greek club PAOK Salonika in July 1988, but as happened when he was sought by the Saudi Arabians in 1985 and Ipswich in 1987, he said 'no'. He was three years

into a five-year contract and expected to see it through.

As he prepared for the 1988-89 campaign and made Everton's Alan Harper (£275,000) his only major buy, Wilkinson was more concerned with the circumstances of the Chapman deal than his own interests, for the situation was developing into a remarkable and curious saga which left Wednesday feeling cheated. Initially, the Owls and Niort could not agree a fee, then, after a UEFA tribunal set the price at £275,000, it transpired the French club could not afford to pay. Meanwhile Chapman, discovering that neither the football nor the money were as conducive as he had anticipated, wanted to return to England. The upshot of all this was that Niort subsequently sold Chapman to Nottingham Forest for £400,000 in order to settle their debt, and Wednesday ended up with a fraction of what they might have got if the striker had gone straight from Hillsborough to the City Ground! Forest got their man on the cheap. The incident exposed a loophole in the system which UEFA promptly closed, but that was then of little consolation to Wednesday. Ironically, Chapman was destined to team up again with Wilkinson at Leeds, and help the Owls' Yorkshire rivals win the League Championship.

At least the other 1988 summer sales of Chamberlain (Portsmouth), Hodge (Leicester) and young Des Hazel (Rotherham), which raised around £450,000, were more conventional, and with the September departure of May, who went to Brighton for £100,000, Wilkinson was able to strengthen his goalkeeping cover by bringing Chris Turner back

to Hillsborough from Manchester United for £175,000. However, the return of another 'old boy', Imre Varadi, in a deal which took Carl Bradshaw to Manchester City, was much more significant. It was hoped he would solve a striking problem which had become so acute that defender Mel Sterland had been tried in attack, along with young David Reeves. Alas, it was soon evident that Varadi was no longer quite the player he had once been—though this was not fully confirmed until after Wilkinson had finally decided to depart.

When Leeds, struggling near the foot of the Second Division, sacked Billy Bremner in late September, it is doubtful whether anyone at Hillsborough thought Howard Wilkinson would be the next man in the Elland Road 'hot seat'. As the man himself said, on the face of it such a move seemed crazy, all the more so as a succession of managers (many old playing favourites at the club) had failed to survive in the shadow cast by memories of the golden Leeds era under Don Revie. However, Leslie Silver, the Leeds chairman, sought the opinions of some of the wisest figures in the game, and Wilkinson was the name that kept cropping up. Subsequently, Owls chairman Bert McGee was criticised by shareholders for giving Silver permission to speak to Wilkinson, for it set in motion developments which led to his formal departure on Monday October 10th 1988. The deal was as good as sealed before Wednesday's annual meeting on the previous Thursday, when ironically, shareholder Joe Ashton was given a standing ovation after praising

Wilkinson and saying: 'I hope the board will do everything in their power to keep him here.'

Wilkinson recognised that Leeds were a club capable of matching and ultimately surpassing anything Wednesday might hope to achieve in the climate which then existed at Hillsborough. He knew he had only one choice, and this was an opportunity he would be foolish to miss; yet as he noted in his excellent autobiography, the day he finally walked out he was heart-broken— and spent ten minutes in the Owls' boot-room sobbing into a towel and crying: 'If it wasn't for those bastards in the boardroom, I'd still be here'.

Though Wilkinson was not always the most popular of managers with the media or the fans, few ever questioned his abilities and the majority believed he was destined for the top of his profession. When he led Leeds to promotion in his first full season (by coincidence the year Wednesday were relegated) and then to the League championship two years later, the point was proved. It was typical of the man that, as he savoured that 1992 title triumph, he admitted his joy was tinged with a sense of sadness and regret that circumstances had prevented him from reaching the same goal with Wednesday.

At least he had the consolation that his departure led indirectly to the very change of policy he had been seeking, and though his immediate successor, Peter Eustace, survived barely four months, the subsequent arrival of Ron Atkinson would ensure Hillsborough boardroom attitudes would never be quite the same again!

Billy McEwan, 1986–1988

FOLLOWING Ian Porterfield's departure in late March 1986, Sheffield United unexpectedly promoted thirty-four year-old youth coach Billy McEwan to acting first-team boss. After he had guided the Blades through the remaining nine games of a 1985-86 campaign in which they finished seventh, 14 points adrift of a promotion place, the slim Scot was formally confirmed in his first managerial post, despite media predictions that the job would go to an experienced 'big name' brought in from outside. Alas, faced with severely limited funds and charged with the task of urgently reducing both the wage bill and the average age of the team, McEwan survived less than two years and emerged more a victim of circumstances than any lack of ability or effort. Like his predecessor, his exit came in the wake of a supporters' demonstration after a five-goal home defeat: his team did not reflect the spirit and character of its manager. He had been in charge for 79 League games.

McEwan, a product of Lanarkshire, was a dedicated, determined and disciplined football man, his skill and spirit had made him a popular midfield player in a career which spanned some 340 League and Cup games and six English League clubs following his 1973 move from Hibernian, where he had made his Scottish League debut while still an apprentice. After serving Blackpool, Brighton (he was signed by Brian Clough), Chesterfield, Mansfield (whom he helped win the Third Division title in 1977) and Peterborough, he concluded his playing days with some 100 appearances for Rotherham in a phase blighted by two serious spinal injuries which caused him to miss out on the Millmoor club's Third Division championship success under Porterfield in 1980-81.

However, McEwan was compensated for his long spell on the sidelines by influences which pushed him

Billy McEwan.

towards coaching and management. Porterfield used him as a scout reporting on forthcoming opponents, and later, he was encouraged to embark on courses in coaching and the treatment of injuries. In the meantime, he was made a player-coach at Millmoor, and by the time Porterfield recruited him to the backroom staff at Bramall Lane in the autumn of 1984, McEwan was equipped to fill the role of physio-therapist while coaching United's juniors. In 1985-86 he set the Blades' youngsters on course for the club's first Northern Intermediate League championship success in over twenty years, and his achievements at this level prompted his elevation to acting manager when Porterfield was axed. The day the chairman sent for McEwan to invite him to take over coincided with the Scot's wedding anniversary, and when he was called in to face Reg Brealey, he feared he was set to 'celebrate' a family occasion by joining the ranks of the unemployed!

It was, perhaps, an indication of both McEwan's individuality and natural modesty that he declined to use the manager's office whilst doing the job on a temporary basis. He recalled: 'I had a lot of respect for Ian Porterfield, and somehow didn't feel it right to work in an office that wasn't really mine. Deep down, I wanted the job and had faith in my ability to do it, but I was only the caretaker and while I retained that status didn't believe Ian's old office was the proper place for me to operate from'.

When he did finally take up residence after being confirmed as team boss, McEwan was under no illusions about the size of the task

before him. To lighten the Scot's load, Derek Dooley, elevated to managing director six months earlier, was put in charge of contracts and, with Porterfield's old assistant, John McSeveney, gone, Uruguayan Danny Bergara returned to the coaching staff. Plainly promotion had to be McEwan's goal, but his initial brief and priority was to reduce costs. The likes of Thompson, Lewington, and McNaught were released, Edwards was sold to Leeds for £250,000, and other departures included Kenworthy and Eves.

Meanwhile, incoming deals ahead of the new manager's first full season included defenders Andy Barnsley (Rotherham), Martin Pike (Peterborough) and Chris Wilder (Southampton), midfielder Mark Dempsey (Manchester United), striker Tony Daws (Notts County) and the costliest buy at around £30,000, twenty year-old winger Peter Beagrie (Middlesbrough). Later in the campaign midfielder Martin Kuhl, aged twenty-two and with around 100 League games to his name, was recruited in a deal which took Wigley to Birmingham; but attempts to sign two 'unknown' young strikers whom McEwan identified as stars of the future, Brighton's Dean Saunders and Leicester's Mark Bright, failed owing to the board's reluctance to add to the club's debts. The pair both fulfilled McEwan's expectations, but, as they were then battling to gain first team places, their names and potential were unfamiliar to United's directors.

The 1986-87 campaign was a moderate affair in which United spent most of the season in mid-table and ended up in ninth place, eight points adrift of the newly-instituted end-of-

season play-offs. The dismay of supporters was reflected in attendances which continued to fall. The League average was down to 9,990. The best gate was 19,166 for the visit of Second Division champions Derby in April, the worst 5,587 for a League Cup tie with Bristol City in October (United's lowest home attendance at a major cup tie since the 1890s). The 6,647 crowd at the Crystal Palace match in March constituted United's lowest home League gate of the post-war era. (Ironically, when a testimonial match was staged for former hero Tony Currie in October, the attendance was 17,500!).

The Blades won only three of their first 12 League games, and in one of these, at home to Reading, they lost a three-goal lead in the space of five minutes. They claimed three successive victories in November, but then collected maximum points only twice in the next 12 matches. One of those two successes came in a home match with Portsmouth remembered because four players—Beagrie and three visitors—were sent off, and the Blades just managed to beat eight men with a fortuitous own-goal conceded by Paul Mariner when Wigley's shot spun off the Pompey man's boot and the ball looped over the goalkeeper!

A run which brought 6 wins and only 2 defeats in 10 games followed. This pushed United into the top eight with five fixtures remaining, but a modest finale which brought just a single victory dashed any hopes of a shot at honours. Top League marksmen were Beagrie and Foley with nine goals apiece.

The storm clouds were again gathering over Bramall Lane, and the outlook turned even gloomier when United began the 1987-88 campaign with only one victory in their first nine matches and stood next to bottom of the table. They never really recovered from that dismal start. True, they briefly hinted at recovery with four straight victories (in which Philliskirk struck five times and young Clive Mendonca, one of the boys produced by McEwan in the juniors, claimed his first League goal), but six defeats (they failed to score in them all) in seven games followed and in fact, the McEwan era, which ended two days into the New Year, concluded with a run of 15 matches which brought ten defeats and a mere two victories. Just to compound United's woe, one of those defeats was at Birmingham, where the home side's goals were scored by Peter Withe—on loan from the Blades!

There were many reasons for United's failures, but overall, the plain truth was they weren't good enough, and the team's lack of quality and genuine experience was often cruelly exposed. McEwan, who admitted he was as frustrated as the fans, was especially dismayed by the circumstances which forced him to sell John Burridge to Southampton before the start of the season. Burridge was the one veteran he wanted to keep, but the player's financial demands were considered excessive, and the goalkeeping position was subsequently a source of concern. Andy Leaning was brought in from York on a free transfer, and later Roger Hansbury (Birmingham) and Hans Segers (Nottingham Forest) had spells at Bramall Lane on loan.

There was also disappointment that three youngsters tipped to excel—

Beagrie, Kuhl and new £135,000 recruit Richard Cadette—all fell below expectations. Beagrie, after a highly promising first term in which he had replaced the departed Edwards as the crowd's favourite, seemed to let the adulation go to his head and his form took a dramatic dip. He was one of those players who could delight with his genuine talent, but too often he flattered to deceive. He made 84 League appearances before joining Stoke in 1988, and significantly, all but two of his 11 goals came in his first term. United's consolation was that they sold him and made a profit of £180,000. Kuhl, installed as captain immediately upon his arrival in the previous March, seemed to find the responsibility too great a burden; though despite having limited success in only 38 League games for the Blades, he did mature into a very dependable player in later years, and when he was sold to Watford, in early 1988, United did well out of the deal.

Cadette was the biggest disappointment and never justified a fee partly financed by the sales of Burridge (£25,000), Tomlinson (£47,000) and Foley (£35,000). Having missed pre-season training he struggled to find fitness, and just when he started to hint at better things, he suffered an injury at Barnsley which sidelined him for 13 games. Then twenty-two, Cadette had scored 30 goals in helping Southend win promotion from Division Four in the previous season; and boasting 49 goals in 90 League outings, he was regarded as a striker of great potential. He spent only one year at Bramall Lane, scored just seven times, and was limited to 28 League outings. Ironically, when he returned from injury in December, he scored the only goal of the game against Swindon to give McEwan what proved to be his last victory as United's manager—though the occasion, which attracted only 7,248 spectators, is better remembered as the first League fixture played at Bramall Lane on a Sunday.

On Boxing Day 1987 United earned a home draw with high-riding Aston Villa: they might have won had Morris not missed the target with only the goalkeeper to beat. Looking back some years later, McEwan recalled that, after this game, Villa manager Graham Taylor praised the effort shown by the Blades. Little did he know that McEwan would be out of a job within a week. Defeats at Millwall and Blackburn followed the Villa game, and when United next played at Bramall Lane, against Oldham, it was the sheer lack of spirit and style which induced a 5–0 defeat and sparked the crowd demonstration which prompted McEwan's resignation.

McEwan had seen the writing on the wall for months, and recognised the end was near from the day in December when chairman Reg Brealey announced that he was putting his 62.3 per cent majority shareholding up for sale. Brealey had invested £2.5 million in the club, and while he had enjoyed his successes, somehow it had all turned sour and the smell of failure was again in the air, while debts had spiralled to around £3 million. He was ready to go, but, in the event, it would take him rather longer than anticipated to find a buyer, and remarkably perhaps, he was still at the helm as late as August 1995. As will be noted in more detail later, Brealey did eventually find a buyer, but circumstances were to

conspire to make his departure brief and he found himself back in control —and soon under fire. In the meantime, however, he was at least to have the satisfaction of finally seeing the Blades reach the top-grade.

How they achieved that goal after ending the 1987-88 campaign with a fall back into the Third Division belongs to an eventful chapter which began with the appointment of McEwan's successor and United's twelfth post-war manager—Dave Bassett.

United 1987-88.
Back row: Simon Copeland, Geoff Eckhardt, Peter Withe, Andy Leaning, Paul Heald, Paul Stancliffe, Andy Barnsley, Martin Pike.
Middle row: Chris France, Mark Dempsey, Brian Smith, Chris Wilder, Phil Henson (youth team coach), Ian Bailey (physio), Tony Philliskirk, Simon Grayson, Clive Mendonca, Chris Downes.
Front row: Danny Bergara (coach), Colin Morris, Mark Todd, Peter Beagrie, Martin Khul, Chris Marsden, David Frain, Richard Cadette, Billy McEwan (manager).

Dave Bassett and his back-up team: John Dungworth, Geoff Taylor (assistant manager), Derek French (physio), Keith Mincher.

18 Dave Bassett: A Blades Revival, 1988–1990

WHEN DAVE BASSETT breezed into Bramall Lane in late January 1988, few supporters could have imagined that, in less than three years, he would guide Sheffield United back to Division One for the first time since 1976. Indeed, the prospect of reaching the top-grade looked more remote than ever following their slide into the Third Division within months of the new manager's arrival. But Bassett was nothing if not a battler, and, though he offered to resign after relegation was confirmed in the play-offs in mid-May, the setback merely fired his determination to ensure the Blades bounced back—and to prove he was not a man to be kept down for long.

Bassett was known as the man who masterminded the remarkable rise of Wimbledon from the Fourth to the First Division on a shoestring budget in four sensational seasons between 1982 and 1986 — a feat achieved following a mix of promotion and relegation (the latter on goal-difference) in his first 18 months as a manager. He came north with a reputation as a great motivator, a man with as much flair for psychology as for tactics, and if Wimbledon's direct style had not pleased the purists, few could deny it was effective. Bassett argued that Watford and Sheffield Wednesday used similar styles and contended that the criticism of Wimbledon was rooted in irritation amongst pundits who felt the romance of his club's climb had lasted longer than they expected or wanted. However, on the field the Dons were more aggressive and uncompromising than most. Off the field, too, they delighted in refusing to conform to what others considered the traditional patterns of behaviour, invariably showing disrespect for reputations. They revelled in an anti-Establishment 'bad boys' image and in shocking some of their hosts at the top clubs (puncturing other people's dignity often gave them a psychological advantage), and it didn't take the media long to dub them 'the Crazy Gang'.

Looking back some years later, Bassett reflected: 'We had something special, and some of the players I had at Plough Lane were the kind who come along once in a lifetime. We had more ability than many credited us with, the spirit and camaraderie were tremendous. Yet it sometimes seemed that everybody hated us, but we took them all on and gained strength from not being liked. People enjoyed the novelty of our early success but expected the bubble to burst—and were upset when it didn't. There's nothing more guaranteed to bring players closer together than feeling the world is against them simply because of an envy of their success, and the more the so-called experts criticised us the more determined we became'.

Bassett's managerial abilities were reflected in statistics which showed Wimbledon won 136 and lost only 79 of 283 League games in climbing up four grades in his $6\frac{1}{2}$ years as team-boss. Yet, at the time of his move to Sheffield, his professional fortunes had taken a dip and his pride was dented: for while his Plough Lane achievements had prompted recruitment by Watford (then also in the First Division) as Graham Taylor's successor in May 1987, at Vicarage Road he immediately walked into a fiercely hostile environment and survived barely eight months before being sacked.

'Elton John, the chairman, wanted me as manager, but I got the impression nobody else did,' he recalled. 'By contrast, when I came to Sheffield I immediately felt comfortable and at home. Soon after I arrived, I told my wife, Christine, I thought we'd got a chance here. The atmosphere was all right, the people were all right, and there was something about this place, even after the trauma of relegation, that made me think I would stay a long time. I was right.' Perhaps his only frustration in the long term, apart from the lack of funds available to him even after he had taken United back to the top, was the way the pundits continued to associate him with Wimbledon and suggest the Blades were another version of the Dons.

Before his unexpected move to Bramall Lane, Bassett had always lived in and around London, close to the roots which had shaped his character and philosophy; and there were many who didn't believe he would settle in the north as well as he did. The man invariably described as 'a chirpy Cockney' by outsiders, was actually born in Stanmore, Middlesex, and it was in that region that he grew up and emerged as a youngster with a tenacious and terrier-like approach to life which was epitomised in the way he played his football. He was a 'natural' for the role of defensive wing-half, and while he has humorously suggested he was 'like Nobby Stiles but dirtier', he was good enough as a schoolboy to attract the attention of Chelsea and Watford. Tommy Docherty was the manager who dashed Bassett's hopes of a Stamford Bridge apprenticeship but by the time he was in his twenties, he had made his mark in non-League football with Hayes, St. Albans and Walton & Hersham. Indeed, he not only became Isthmian League Walton's skipper and led them to a FA Amateur Cup triumph when they beat Slough at Wembley in 1973, but collected ten amateur international caps between 1971 and 1974. It is of interest to note that it was at Hayes that he began his friendship with Geoff Taylor, later his lieutenant at Bramall Lane.

It was in 1974, at the late age of twenty-nine, that the opportunity finally knocked for him to become a professional, and when Allan Batsford, the Wimbledon manager, invited him to go full-time with the Southern League club, Bassett didn't hesitate to quit the security of his job as an insurance inspector. In his first season at Plough Lane he helped the Dons make FA Cup giant-killing history, with a third-round triumph over First Division Burnley at Turf Moor. At the next stage, they held mighty Leeds United to a goalless draw at Elland Road in a tie remembered for a brilliant save by Wimbledon goalkeeper Dick Guy from a Lorimer penalty—conceded by Bassett! In the replay at Selhurst Park in February 1975, the Dons finally succumbed to a Johnny Giles strike which was deflected past Guy off Bassett.

Bassett survived long enough as a Wimbledon player to figure in 35 Fourth Division games following their election to the Football League in 1977–78, but he was already graduating towards coaching, and it was following four years as coach that he succeeded Dario Gradi as manager in January 1981. It was a role which would bring more success and fame than he ever enjoyed as a player, simply because he ensured his team reflected his philosophy of total physical and mental commitment and made maximum use of individual and collective talents.

Before his move to Watford, Bassett had only once previously been tempted to leave Wimbledon. In May 1984, soon after Wimbledon (along with Sheffield United) won promotion from Division Three, he became manager of Crystal Palace, but resigned four days later, rejoined the Dons, and took them to sixth in Division One. He never lacked the courage to make what might seem an embarrassing turnabout if he felt it was the right thing to do. When he accepted Watford's offer in 1987 he soon recognised that this, too, was a mistake, but, on this occasion, it was others who decided he was the wrong man for the job—before he had been given a chance. The climate was hardly conducive to success, and Watford won just four of 23 League matches before Bassett's brief era ended.

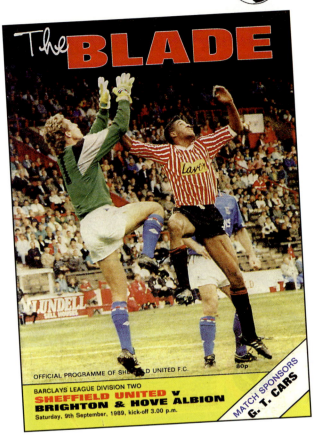

Bassett was out of work for only ten days, and his association with Sheffield United began halfway through that spell of unemployment when he took a call on his car-phone whilst driving with his wife and daughters to attend a production of the pantomime 'Aladdin' at Richmond. The caller was Reg Brealey, and the upshot of their conversation was a January 15th meeting with United's directors at the Chewton Glen Hotel, Bournemouth, on the eve of the Blades' League game in the town. Bassett stayed overnight and on the following afternoon paid to stand on the Dean Court terraces to watch United register a 2–1 victory. Five days later his appointment was formally confirmed, and so began the eventful Bassett era which by the end of the 1994-95 campaign had extended to nearly 400 League and Cup matches.

United had 15 League games left in their 1987-88 programme when he arrived; five were won and nine lost, and they finished third from the bottom. Defeats against fellow strugglers Shrewsbury (home), Birmingham and Reading were especially costly, and heavy setbacks at Leeds (0–5) and Middlesbrough (0–6) exposed the full measure of the task facing the new manager. They were spared automatic relegation, but the play-offs pitted them against Bristol City, who had finished fifth in Division Three. A 1–0 defeat in the first leg at Ashton Gate left room for optimism but, when former Owls' man Shutt's diving header made the Blades' deficit 2–0 sixteen minutes into the second leg on the following Wednesday, the odds were always against the Lane lads, for though Colin Morris, on his final appearance for the club, equalised in the second half it proved too little too late. Just to add a painful twist to Bassett's personal woe, a few days ahead of United's fall, his old club Wimbledon had captured their first major honour by defeating Liverpool in the FA Cup final.

Bassett always said he tried to do too much too soon in those early months, though at the time he no doubt felt he had little choice but to make dramatic changes in tactics and personnel. He was appalled by the poor quality and spirit of the team he inherited. 'When I came, the place was dead, the team was dead, and support was dwindling. I had to do

something—and quickly,' he recalled. He introduced almost a full team of newcomers, and if the fates were unkind at the outset, his consolation was that, of the first batch of signings, twenty-four year-old striker Tony Agana, who cost £40,000 in the deal which tool Kuhl to Watford, was to prove an outstanding investment. Also goalkeeper Graham Benstead (£35,000 from Norwich) figured prominently in the 1988-89 promotion success before being deposed by Simon Tracey; while defender Simon Webster, a £35,000 recruit from Huddersfield, was enjoying top form and might have achieved much more had he not suffered a broken leg in November 1988.

Webster's misfortune, incidentally, prompted one of Bassett's most popular free signings. Bob Booker, then aged thirty, looked set to bow out of full-time soccer after some 300 games with Brentford but, though he was not an instant hit with Lane fans and, in truth his talents were modest, he was destined to emerge a big favourite, making 126 appearances for the Blades and figuring in the climb to the top-grade.

The summer of 1988 brought further hectic transfer activity as Bassett, familiar with operating on limited resources and continuing the push to reduce the wage bill, plotted to produce a team equipped to revive the club's fortunes. Beagrie (Stoke, £215,000), Cadette (Brentford, £80,000), Philliskirk (Oldham), Withe and Chris Marsden (both Huddersfield) were amongst a string of departures. New recruits included wingers Alan Roberts (£15,000 from Darlington) and Ian Bryson (£40,000 from Kilmarnock), twenty-eight year-

Tony Agana on the ball against Blackburn, with Brian Deane ready to join the attack.

old ex-Wimbledon and Brentford striker Francis Joseph (free from Reading), and an 'unknown' young forward called Brian Deane (Doncaster), who cost an initial £30,000, with an extra £10,000 later, and was destined to become one of the Blades' biggest favourites. Notable signings during the season were a £12,500 goalkeeper, Simon Tracey, who had made only one League appearance with Wimbledon but played in that year's Charity Shield match; and £15,000 defender Steve Thompson (Leicester); whilst another successful 'free' deal late in the

campaign saw midfielder John Gannon come from Wimbledon and seize the chance to revive his career.

A major feature of the promotion run of 1988-89 was the impact of the remarkable Agana-Deane partnership, which produced 46 League goals plus 14 in the cup competitions in that memorable initial year, and between them, they claimed 95 in their first two seasons together. The irony is that they did not start the campaign as a deliberate pairing. However, in the opening fixture, at Reading, Francis Joseph had to retire after pulling a hamstring, Agana stepped

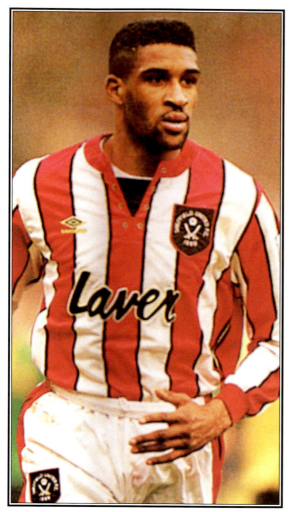

Brian Deane.

but, strange as it might seem, he did not shine on the May day in 1988 when Bassett watched him playing for relegation-bound Doncaster Rovers at Bristol City. Dave Cusack, the former Wednesday defender who had given Deane his first professional contract in 1985 during a brief spell as Belle Vue team-boss, was the man who alerted Bassett to the lanky young-ster's potential. Cusack insisted that Deane (he had then scored 13 goals in 70-plus outings for Rovers) was as good as John Fashanu if lacking the Wimbledon man's aggression. The lad was good in the air, could use both feet, and had surprising skills for someone so tall—if Bassett and his assistant Geoff Taylor worked on him they would unearth a jewel. In truth, the United manager was surprised at how quickly Deane fulfilled that prediction; and it was perhaps fortunate that the youngster, being out of contract at the time, had been wise enough to reject modest new terms offered by Rovers' boss Dave Mackay. Deane arrived for talks in that July week when Bramall Lane was staging two concerts by Bruce Springsteen (they attracted crowds of 40,000), and he always said the place had a look of the big-time which persuaded him this was where he wanted to play—even before he had discussed terms with Bassett.

The Blades spent a week of pre-season training on an army assault course, enjoyed a short tour of Sweden during which they won four games with an aggregate score of 40–2, and then started their Third Division campaign with nine victories and only two defeats in their first 12 matches. The run included a 6–1 defeat of Chester in which Deane and

off the substitute's bench to join twenty year-old Deane up front, and the duo 'clicked' immediately. The pace of Agana, whom Bassett had plucked from non-League football while at Watford, and the height and deft touches of the 6ft 3ins Deane proved a stunning combination.

Deane, a Leeds product, was destined to top a century of goals for the Blades and collect three England caps in his five years at Bramall Lane

Agana shared the goals—the club's first double hat-trick since Harry Johnson and David Mercer had done it in January 1926. Deane's treble came in the first half, and in fact he had retired with a slight injury before his partner equalled his feat—though Deane was quick enough out of the dressing room at the final whistle to claim the match ball as a souvenir!

Apart from the serious injuries to Webster and former Sheffield Boys defender Brian Smith (the latter's broken leg in April ended a promising career), it was a centenary season of happy memories, with a second-round League Cup triumph over First Division Newcastle and a run to the FA Cup fifth round (conceding a penalty and an own-goal, they were unlucky to fall to Norwich, who finished fourth in the top grade) pleasing bonuses. The Blades lost two games on the trot just twice, and on only three occasions did they go three matches without a victory.

Benstead, though displaced by Tracey late in the campaign, was a hero with four penalty saves; Peter Duffield, with 11 League goals (five from spot-kicks, including two in one game), enjoyed his best year; Pike, whose long run as first choice left-back was coming to an end, Roberts and Mark Todd all shone; while John Francis, a £5,000 buy from Emley, and local teenager Dane Whitehouse had their first taste of League football and showed promise. (It spoke volumes for Bassett's astute transfer dealings that, in January 1990, he sold Francis to Burnley for £90,000 after the player had scored six goals in 42 games, 28 of which were as substitute!). Agana claimed a hat-trick as United concluded their home programme with a

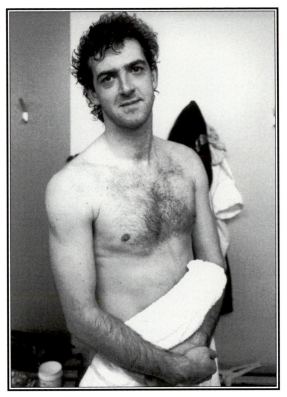

Paul Stancliffe.

5–1 defeat of Swansea, and he finished the club's top League marksman (24) with a strike in the subsequent 2–2 Molineux draw with champions Wolves. This enabled the Blades to miss the play-offs and pip Port Vale into second place on goal-difference.

Few people expected United to celebrate their climb back into Division Two with another promotion success. In fact the Blades probably surprised themselves by the way they began the 1989-90 campaign with a ten-match unbeaten run (their best start since 1971), suffering only two defeats in their first 23 League games, and leading the table from September to early December. They maintained their early pace despite occasional setbacks which threatened their ambitions and were only pipped to the championship on goal-difference by Yorkshire rivals, Leeds.

Moreover, Bassett's boys enjoyed the club's best FA Cup run for twenty-two years when they reached the quarter-finals where they were defeated by Manchester United, for whom Brian McClair scored the game's only goal in a Bramall Lane tie remembered for a linesman's failure to spot what millions of television viewers and most of the 34,344 spectators saw very clearly: that the ball had gone out of play immediately before the visitors were awarded the corner kick which led to the decisive strike. The Mancunians went on to win the coveted trophy in a Wembley replay; Bassett, meanwhile, reflected that the defeat was probably a blessing in disguise, for the Blades were left to concentrate on ending their long wait for a return to the top-grade—though they did have to endure the distraction of an unexpected twist in the saga of Reg Brealey's attempt to sell his majority shareholding.

Ahead of the campaign, Bassett strengthened his squad with four deals at a total cost of £225,000. He paid a club record £175,000 to Watford for central defender Mark Morris, who had figured in Wimbledon's rise from the Fourth to the First Division; and also bought full back Colin Hill (£80,000 from Colchester) and David Barnes (£50,000 from Aldershot), plus Huddersfield midfielder Julian Winter (£50,000). Morris was to make only 56 League appearances, but he missed only four games in his first term. Hill and Barnes each completed around

80 League games for the club, and former Arsenal man Hill, a versatile defender, was capped by Northern Ireland before the season was over. Winter, who faced a knee operation soon after his arrival, did not make the team.

Of the signings made during the season, undoubtedly the £50,000 capture of ex-Owl Carl Bradshaw, who initially arrived on loan from Manchester City in September, was the most successful long term. Bradshaw epitomised the never-say-die spirit which was a Bassett hallmark, and in his 150-plus games before he was sold to Norwich for a big profit in 1994, he matured into an adaptable and popular player, figuring at full back as well as on the right wing. Meanwhile, midfielder Paul Wood, who cost £90,000 from Brighton, veteran Billy Whitehurst, a £35,000 buy from Hull, and Wilf Rostron, a free signing from Wednesday who boasted over 400 League games with Arsenal, Sunderland and Watford, made an initial contribution which included some important goals, but between them managed only around 80 appearances.

Deane (with 24 goals), who missed only three of the season's 57 League and Cup matches, and Agana (12 goals), despite missing 16 games with injury problems, again topped the scoring charts. Others made important contributions, notable amongst these were goalkeeper Tracey (the only League ever-present), dependable and commanding skipper Stancliffe, and the busy Gannon. Bryson probably had his best season: one of his eleven goals was the spot-kick which pulled United level at 4–4 after they had lost a 3–0 lead in an incredible home game with Brighton which they finally won 5–4. He also scored an injury-time penalty winner at Barnsley—where Agana later sealed a similar success with a 91st-minute spot-kick which ended a three-match FA Cup fifth-round marathon. Duffield, though having the misfortune to be limited to seven outings and three goals, made a crucial contribution; in late October, coming on as substitute in the home game with Portsmouth, he converted two penalties as United came from behind to win 2–1, and six weeks later, at Swindon, he set the Blades on course for victory with an early strike—but broke a leg when scoring.

United remembered the games with Leeds with mixed feelings, for while the home match on Boxing Day was a 2–2 classic which 31,600 spectators savoured, the trip to Elland Road at Easter brought a comprehensive 4–0 defeat which left some critics questioning the team's promotion credentials and the Blades complaining about referee Allan Gunn's handling of a predominantly

Derek Dooley and Dave Bassett.

physical encounter. The Bramall Lane fixture, which came in a run which brought only one win in seven outings, did much to boost United's faith. Ex-Owl Mel Sterland hammered Leeds in front with a stunning 35-yard free-kick, but goals from Rostron and Agana gave the Blades a half-time lead before Shutt, the man whose strike had doomed United to relegation two years earlier, levelled the scores two minutes after the break.

The defeat at Leeds was the only one United suffered in their final seven matches, but it was also the third in five games and cost them a place in the top two for the first time since early season. This was an aggressive duel in which the Blades were overpowered and overawed in the intimidating atmosphere of Elland Road. The niggling tone was epitomised in the way Leeds, as in the Bramall Lane game in December, deployed striker Bobby Davison to 'sit' on Simon Tracey when he was in possession of the ball and seeking to kick it clear. Of course, there was nothing in the rules which said they couldn't do this. However, it unnerved the goalkeeper, put the whole defence on edge, and in the end, it induced Tracey to lose his composure and concede the 82nd minute penalty from which Gordon Strachan completed United's rout. Until the 74th minute the Blades had trailed only to an early Strachan strike. Then they suddenly succumbed and Lee Chapman, Gary Speed and, finally, Strachan hit three goals in eight minutes.

Fortunately, it was a setback which failed to knock Bassett's men off their stride, though, in promptly bouncing

back with a 2–1 home defeat of Port Vale (thanks to Deane's last-minute winner), they lost Stancliffe and Gannon with injuries which caused both players to miss the season's finale. Thus Booker was able to consolidate his popularity with supporters by taking over as captain on a final lap of the climb into the top-grade which also featured the return of Wilder and Todd.

United went into the last day of the season knowing they had to win to be sure of promotion, and in the event, made no mistake and showed remarkable composure and character in a memorable 5–2 triumph at Leicester, where they came from behind. Wood, Deane, Agana (2) and Rostron got the goals. Leeds, with a 1–0 win at Bournemouth, clinched the Second Division title, while Newcastle's 4–1 defeat at Middlesbrough meant the Blades finished second and five points clear of the Geordies—now managed by ex-Blade Jim Smith.

There was one unexpected and ironic twist to what had been an eventful and sometimes astonishing season for the Sheffield club, for on the same dramatic May day in 1990 that United finally made it back to the top, Wednesday were unexpectedly relegated on goal-difference after losing their last match. Earlier in the campaign, the Sheffield clubs had met in the Zenith Data Systems Cup, and though this was widely regarded as an unimportant tournament, a staggering 30,464 crowd (a record for the competition) had turned up at Hillsborough, where the Owls won a splendid game 3–2. It served to emphasise how badly local supporters wanted to see both

How Wednesday's official match programme celebrated the meeting of the Sheffield clubs in the Zenith Data Systems Cup in 1989 —the first cup derby in the city for almost 10 years.

the Blades and the Owls playing First Division derbies again. Now, alas, that prospect had been delayed for at least a further year.

To add to the drama of the season, in early March it suddenly looked as if Reg Brealey had finally found someone to buy his majority share-holding, which had been on the market since late 1987. However it was a curious and ultimately abortive episode, but one which set in motion a chain of events which were still influencing the club's fortunes in the mid-1990s. Even the chairman was taken aback when the news of his 'sale' was prematurely made public, and thirty-two year-old Sam Hashimi, a mysterious Iraqui-born business-man, revealed himself as front man of a Middle East-based group at a hastily-called press conference at Bramall Lane. Hashimi, it seems, had not only 'jumped the gun' but, in his haste, provoked the kind of reaction from the other directors that he could not have anticipated. Hashimi, purchasing a 51 per cent shareholding, was said to be moving in as vice-chairman and would be taking over as chairman when Brealey stepped down in June,

but his prospective colleagues were suspicious of the newcomer's motives and, led by Paul Woolhouse, a director since 1986, there was a furious boardroom battle to halt formal completion of a transaction which Woolhouse contended would have led to the end of football at Bramall Lane and seen the ground turned into a housing estate within a few years. It was an affair which dragged on but, before the Blades started their 1990-91 First Division campaign, Brealey had been persuaded to withdraw from the agreement. The way was thus left clear for negotiations to begin which would lead to a second, more prolonged and ultimately traumatic episode in the ownership saga, with Woolhouse cast in the role of the United saviour whose ambition, perhaps owing to circumstances he could not foresee and over which he had little control, outstripped his ability to finance the purchase of the control Brealey so badly wanted to relinquish at the right price.

It was against this background that the Blades spent four remarkable seasons in the top grade.

'Big Ron' Atkinson: Owls 1989–1991

Ron Atkinson.

ON THAT SECOND Monday in October 1988 when Howard Wilkinson drove up the M1 motorway to join Leeds United, you can be sure the last thing on Ron Atkinson's mind was the vacancy at Hillsborough— even though 'Big Ron', one of the most colourful and charismatic figures in the game, was hardly having the best of times in his second spell as manager of West Brom. He had been back at The Hawthorns barely twelve months, discovered that circumstances were much changed since his 1981 departure and, with Albion (the club he had once guided to within sight of the League Championships and into Europe) now languishing in the lower half of Division Two, knew he would have to look elsewhere to revive a career which had reached a pinnacle in six years at Manchester United. He wasn't, however, attracted by the Owls' job for a number of reasons, and the main one was revealed within another 48 hours when it emerged that he had negotiated a lucrative appointment as coach to Atletico Madrid in a deal said to be worth £500,000-plus over the next two years. He was not then aware that his great Spanish adventure would last a mere 96 days, end with the sack, and lead to an approach from Sheffield which proved an attractive oppor-tunity.

In the meantime, at Hillsborough, Peter Eustace, having rejected the chance to follow Wilkinson partly because he might not retain his No. 2 role after a switch to Elland Road, took temporary charge of Wednesday's team affairs, and within three weeks, was formally confirmed by chairman McGee as the new manager. Alas, just 110 days later, in mid-February, he was axed after guiding the Owls to only two wins in 17 League matches in which they scored eight goals, accumulated 13 points and slid to 18th in the table.

It was a disastrous spell. Eustace had such a passion for the club he had first joined as an apprentice in 1960, but he couldn't convert that into the immediate promise of success the job demanded. He did however make two decisions which proved beneficial to the club long after his departure. He gave Nigel Pearson the captaincy and recruited Frank Barlow to the backroom staff. When Pearson replaced crowd favourite Mel Sterland, the decision was not popular, but he emerged an outstanding skipper over the next five seasons. Meanwhile, Barlow arrived from Barnsley as assistant manager, and though he did not retain that role, the former Sheffield United half-back, and Chesterfield and Scunthorpe manager, stayed to enjoy notable success as coach to the reserves. Eustace had less luck with his signings: veteran defender Wilf Rostron, from Watford, made only nine senior appearances and later had a spell with Sheffield United; while £400,000 defender Darren Wood (Chelsea) was dogged by back trouble and limited to 14 outings. Also in this spell, Gary Megson was sold to Manchester City for £250,000, ending a family link with the Owls which had spanned 728 League and Cup games since his father Don's debut in 1959.

A Hillsborough board, criticised for allowing Wilkinson to go and finding themselves under fire for promoting Eustace, sought to compensate by lining up the biggest available 'name' in the game. Atkinson, now within a month of his fiftieth birthday, had been back in England barely four weeks when the chance arose for him to resume his managerial career in Sheffield. A few people remembered that, back in the mid-1970s, during his time with Cambridge United, 'Big

Ron' had been wanted by the Owls when they were struggling in the Third Division. On that occasion he had turned them down, and now, in truth, he took the job firmly believing his stay would be short and sweet. He welcomed the chance to get back to work, but only intended remaining long enough to try to steer them clear of relegation.

He surprised himself when he initially allowed three months to become fifteen with acceptance of a one-year contract. When circumstances then conspired to send Wednesday into the Second Division at the end of his first full term, he knew it was a matter of professional pride to hold on for another year. In the event, it was the extra season he hadn't bargained for which rebuilt his reputation as 'a winner': it brought Wednesday prompt promotion and their first major trophy for fifty-six years—and gave Atkinson the 'big time' call for which he had been waiting since leaving Old Trafford five years earlier.

The image of Atkinson as some kind of 'Flash Harry' who loved only jewellery and a champagne lifestyle was far removed from the reality. He was a down-to-earth guy, the essential football man with unbounding enthusiasm for the game. Ever the romantic at heart, he cared only for what he called 'proper football', and it was the reflection of this philosophy in his teams as much as his flamboyance and flair for publicity which made him a favourite with supporters. His secret, perhaps, was that he had a thorough grounding in the less glamorous regions of the game long before he reached the top, and the experience enabled him to appreciate

the rewards better than most.

Moreover, the man born on Merseyside but raised in the industrial Midlands was familiar with life outside football. As a teenager, he was enough of a realist to opt for the safeguard of an engineering apprenticeship when a six-month spell on Wolves' groundstaff didn't work out in 1954, and though Aston Villa soon discovered him playing for his firm's team, he elected to become only a part-time pro-fessional. Joe Mercer's arrival at Villa Park from Sheffield United in the 1958-59 campaign led to Atkinson's release, but in the event, it was a blessing because the twenty year-old was snapped up by Southern League Headington United—soon to become Oxford United—the club where it all began to happen for the big, solidly-built lad the fans soon dubbed 'The Tank'.

He soon turned full-time, was installed as skipper, and went on to make over 550 appearances spanning Oxford's rise from obscurity to the Second Division of the Football League. Then, in late 1971 at the age of thirty-two, he became player-manager of Southern League Kettering. Three years later he joined Cambridge, and led them to the Fourth Division title and to the brink of Division Two before accepting his first major appointment, in January 1978, as manager of West Brom. In Atkinson's three years at The Haw-thorns, Albion finished third and fourth in the First Division and reached the semi-finals of the FA Cup and the quarter-finals of the UEFA Cup.

It was in June 1981 that 'Big Ron' joined Manchester United. In his five years at Old Trafford he spent around

£7 million and led them to two FA Cup triumphs (1983 and 1985), a Charity Shield success (1983), a League Cup final (1983) and last eight in the UEFA Cup (1985). Though United never finished outside the First Division's top four, he was unable to give them the prize they most coveted—the League Cham-pionship. There was a famous occasion in 1983-84 when they led the chase with ten games remaining but finished with only two wins; and in 1985-86 they started the campaign with ten straight wins and were unbeaten in their first 15 matches before finally losing—to Wednesday at Hillsborough, where Lee Chapman scored the game's lone goal.

When Atkinson was axed by Manchester United in early November 1986, he boasted a remarkable record in League management with nearly 300 victories and barely 150 defeats in 600 League and Cup games with three clubs. However, if a modest spell on his return to West Brom (now in Division Two) somewhat blighted those statistics, he was still con-sidered a 'scoop' for the Owls when he started work on February 15th 1989.

Wednesday then had 15 matches left: they won five, lost six, and collected 19 points. In fact, they claimed only one victory in their final seven games, but it was just enough to seal safety; and while there was no overnight transformation, Atkinson's influence was immediately evident on and off the field. Not unexpectedly, he was soon active in the transfer market, with an initial turnover of around £2.5 million which, remarkably, left the Owls with a slight profit. The club's record was broken with a £750,000 deal which brought in 6ft 3ins midfielder Carlton Palmer and took Colin West (rated at £200,000) to West Brom; and while £250,000 striker Steve Whitton (Birmingham) and £220,000 winger Dave Bennett (Coventry) were signed, the sales of Mark Proctor (Middlesbrough, £300,000) and Mel Sterland (Rangers, £800,000) kept the books balanced.

Of the newcomers, Whitton (37 games, 8 goals) and Bennett (31 games, one goal) had an initial but not lasting impact, but 'Beanpole' Palmer was destined to remain for over five seasons during which he made 264 appearances and collected 18 England caps, being sold to Leeds

in 1994 for £2.7 million. The departing Sterland, big and strong and with 347 games and 49 goals to his name, had long been a Wednesday idol, but his sale provoked no criticism because most supporters knew him to be unsettled. Anyway, even as the Owls battled to stay in the top grade, 'Big Ron's mere presence and the promising change in the team's playing style suggested to most that an exciting new era was beginning. Already the Koppites were dubbing themselves 'Atkinson's Barmy Army'!

Alas, it was barely two months after Atkinson's arrival that a major tragedy occurred at Hillsborough which was so shocking and overwhelming in its

Carlton Palmer, Dave Bennett and Steve Whitton.

impact and implications, that it cast a huge shadow across English football and made such matters as seeking points and prizes seem trivial. The FA Cup semi-final between Liverpool and Nottingham Forest on Saturday April 15th lasted less than six minutes and will always be synonymous with the biggest disaster in British sporting history. At the time it claimed the lives of 95 Liverpool supporters and, in March 1993, the 96th victim, a youngster called Tony Bland, died after spending four years in a coma.

It happened in and around the standing areas at the Leppings Lane end of the ground and was sparked by a combination of circumstances, including the late arrival of thousands of supporters, the opening of a gate to relieve the fearsome crush which developed outside and, despite the availability of space in the side areas, the sudden flood of people pouring through a tunnel which led to the already congested central pens on the terracing behind the goal. This was a period in which hooliganism in the English game had induced the erection of high perimeter fences, and thus those spectators who had arrived early and claimed places at the front were the most vulnerable—unable to escape as the sheer weight of the increased volume of people behind crushed them. Some began scrambling over the fencing, whilst many at the back, unable to retreat, hauled themselves out of the heaving masses and into the upper seated areas.

The teams had appeared on the field and, amid the deafening noise of cheering and chanting which preceded and followed the start of the game, few people on the perimeter track and in other parts of the ground were aware of the anguish and suffering of the trapped spectators or of the full extent of the tragedy unfolding. Indeed, many believed the trouble was hooliganism prompting a pitch invasion, but, at five-and-a-half minutes past three o'clock, the game was stopped—and the enormity of the disaster became increasingly evident to all. The pitch, transformed into an horrific scene of human carnage, resembled a battlefield as the dead, the dying and the injured were carried, many on makeshift stretchers made out of advertising hoardings.

Here is not the place to debate the conclusions reached by Lord Justice Taylor in his inquiry into the disaster, other than to note that errors of judgement were evident in many aspects of a tragedy compounded in its depth because it occurred where it was not expected. It exposed shortcomings in communications, safety and other arrangements, and human reaction to horrific realities which are not always recognised for what they are until it is too late. It was a nightmare episode which remained an emotive subject for many years.

The lessons of the disaster were many, as were the long-term benefits to the game, with immediate improvements in safety standards at every major sporting venue in the country. The fences eventually came down and there was a prompt move towards making all-seater stadiums compulsory in top-class football in accordance with the recommendations of the Taylor Report. There was, perhaps inevitably, some over-reaction, but the over-riding emphasis was on ensuring nothing like it could happen again.

Dave Richards...quick elevation to chairman.

For some considerable time, the
Leppings Lane terracing remained
empty, a silent and somewhat haunt-
ing reminder, but in the summer of
1991 the area was upgraded and
seating installed. By mid-1993 with
the seating of the Kop, Hillsborough
had been converted into an all-seater
ground. As has to happen, life went
on, but the painful events of April
1989 would never be forgotten by the
generation who witnessed them, and
in Sheffield and Liverpool, permanent
memorials were created to ensure
those innocent victims of the disaster
would always be remembered. When
Liverpool paid their first visit to Hillsborough after the tragedy, in November 1989, the occasion was marked
by a dignified homage to the dead.

Ron Atkinson's first full season in
1989-90 did not go quite as expected,
for Wednesday made their worst-ever
start to a campaign, then enjoyed an
upturn which suggested they were
set for safety but, just when they
appeared to have escaped trouble,
five defeats in their last six games sent
them down. A 3–0 defeat in their final
fixture, against Nottingham Forest,

doomed them to relegation on goal-
difference after Luton squeezed clear
with an unexpected 3–2 victory at
Derby on the same afternoon.

One way or another, it was an
eventful term for Wednesday, for it
brought changes in the boardroom
and on the field which signalled a new
approach to the challenge of
improving the club's fortunes. Initially,
it was a phase played out under a
cloud, for although the Owls invested
£1.25 million on recruiting Ipswich
striker Dalian Atkinson, bringing back
defender Peter Shirtliff from Charlton,
and signing Shrewbury midfielders
Craig Shakespeare and Mark Taylor,
they began the season with a run
which produced one win and a mere
two goals in the opening 11 matches.
A record 8–0 League cup triumph at
Fourth Division Aldershot (Whitton
four goals, Atkinson three) did little to
temper the dismay of being firm
relegation favourites by late October.

This was the period during which
manager Atkinson's insistence, that
further investments in quality and a
loosening of the purse strings were
the only long-term solutions to
Wednesday's problems, inspired a
dramatic change of policy. The Owls
were destined to report a £1.7 million
loss in 1989-90, and perhaps it was no
coincidence that it was in this spell
that the first of several significant
board changes were announced.
The longest-serving director, Matt
Sheppard, stood down after eighteen
years, and was joined in retirement by
Stan Speight, a director since 1975;
with 'young blood' injected with the
appointments of Bob Grierson, a
forty-six year-old chartered accountant, and Dave Richards, managing
director of a local engineering group.

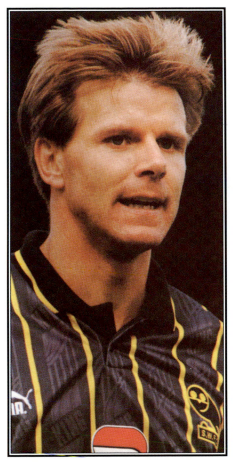

Roland Nilsson, arrived from Sweden and became a great favourite.

Richards, who was forty-seven in the month he joined the board, unexpectedly found himself elected chairman in the following March, when Bert McGee's long association with the club came to an end and his boardroom place was taken by Joe Ashton, Labour MP for Bassetlaw.

The first of the newcomers were thus installed when Atkinson completed the double deal which brought John Sheridan from Nottingham Forest for £500,000 and Phil King from Swindon for £400,000.

Neither man had played in the First Division, but both were immediately successful. Sheridan, twenty-five, Manchester-born but a Republic of Ireland midfielder then boasting five caps, had scored 51 goals in 262 games for Leeds, but remarkably, had been limited to just one senior outing after a £650,000 summer move to Brian Clough's Forest. He was what Atkinson called 'a proper player', a performer with perception and passing ability whose influence proved invaluable. On his Owls' debut he helped in a badly-needed 1–0 victory—at the City Ground! Moreover, his first goal, in only his fourth appearance, came with an unforgettable extra-time dribble and strike which gave Wednesday a 3–2 victory in a Zenith Data Systems tie with promotion-chasing Sheffield United which attracted a 30,464 crowd—a record for the competition. By mid-1995 he had scored 33 goals in 224 games and raised his haul of caps to 28. King, a left-back, was to make around 150 appearances and gain England 'B' honours.

The transformation which followed this double deal was quite remarkable, with Wednesday winning five and losing only three of their next twelve matches. They also enjoyed an 11-game unbeaten home run which extended to the end of March—by which time, thanks to four wins in five matches, the alarm bells had stopped ringing. In the meantime, Atkinson had added more quality to the squad with the £375,000 acquisition of Swedish international right-back Roland Nilsson (Gothenburg) in November, the loan of Forest winger Franz Carr in December, and the signing of former

Wednesday 1990-91.
Back Row: Peter Shirtliff, Chris Turner, Carlton Palmer, Kevin Pressman, Lawrie Madden.
Middle row: Roger Spry (training staff), Richie Barker (assistant manager), John Sheridan, Dave
Bennett, Phil King, Steve McCall, Nigel Worthington, David Hirst, Alan Smith (physio).
Front row: Roland Nilsson, Darren Wood, Paul Williams, Ron Atkinson (manager), Nigel
Pearson, Danny Wilson, Trevor Francis.

England striker Trevor Francis on a free transfer from QPR in late January.

Nilsson, who had chosen the Owls in preference to Manchester United, became one of the club's biggest favourites. He bore the stamp of class and epitomised the increased fluency in the side; indeed, his initial impact was such that he was applauded by the Hillsborough crowd every time he touched the ball! He arrived boasting 28 caps, a tally raised to 59 before his 1994 departure 'for domestic reasons'—and he made 186 appearances. Francis, at thirty-six, also brought unique talents, moving north after a brief and traumatic eleven months as QPR's player-manager.

When Wednesday moved into April with 40 points with five games left, nobody seriously believed they were any longer at risk, but they then collected just three points from a possible 15 and, moments after that last-day home defeat against Forest (who had won the League Cup the previous weekend), they knew they were doomed to relegation by Luton's surprise success at Derby. Luton had had three managers and four chairmen that season (one manager, Ray Harford, had been sacked because the chairman said he didn't smile often enough at supporters!), but at least they had survived thanks to a goal-difference superior by two goals. Meanwhile, new Owls chairman Richards who had been at the helm for nine games, witnessed a mere three wins and had seen his ambitious plans for the club rocked by a banana-skin slide into Division Two—a blow made all the more painful considering the investment reflected in the £1.7 million loss on the year. It didn't help either that Sheffield United had just climbed back into the top grade!

When Richards became chairman in March 1990, he made his priority persuading Atkinson to accept another one-year contract, and refused to listen when the manager offered to resign following the Forest defeat. He insisted 'Big Ron' should stay, and supporters echoed that view. Many managers in the same situation would have been the target of heavy criticism from the terraces, but the fans believed the fates had been cruel to the Owls and Atkinson—and they were convinced he was the only man capable of taking them straight back up. In any event, Atkinson's credibility was at stake; this was no time to walk away.

Ahead of their first Second Division campaign in seven seasons, Wednesday accepted a record £1.7 million offer from Real Sociedad for striker Dalian Atkinson, who had scored 15 goals in 45 games since his £450,000 move from Ipswich in 1989. The manager used some of this money to obtain two players destined to make invaluable contributions to

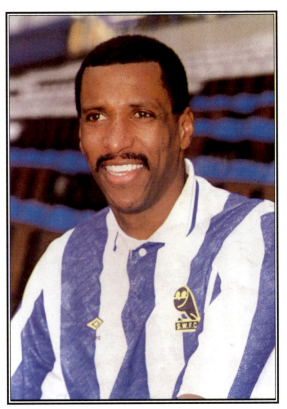

Viv Anderson.

the double success of 1990-91: Charlton's former England Under-21 striker Paul Williams (£600,000) and Luton's experienced Northern Ireland midfielder Danny Wilson (£200,000).

Williams, aged twenty-five, had scored 26 goals in 89 League games, and, though this slightly-built player moved north with some reservations, he enjoyed perhaps the happiest spell of his career in scoring 28 goals in 114 outing for the Owls—including 15 on the promotion run. He will always be remembered with affection as the unselfish little man who was probably the best partner David Hirst ever had. Hirst immediately benefited from the presence of his old England Under-21

John Harkes.

Wednesday. He was a player for whom a taste of glory came late, for he had been to Wembley three times with Luton and went twice more with the Owls. He left in 1993 to become player-coach at Barnsley. Later he was promoted to manager at Oakwell.

Subsequently, there were other signings of note: Viv Anderson, a veteran of some 650 games and remembered as the first coloured man to play for England, arrived on a free transfer from Manchester United in January (he was to make 95 appearances before becoming player-manager of Barnsley in 1993); and further imports from cash-strapped Charlton, the experienced Steve MacKenzie, who cost £100,000, and the teenage striker, Gordon Watson, was bought for an initial £250,000.

However, perhaps the most remarkable capture in 1990 was United States international midfielder John Harkes, who arrived on trial in the autumn and was ultimately signed from the U.S. Soccer Federation for £75,000. Harkes, born in New Jersey and the son of Scottish parents, also had trials with Celtic and Blackburn, but he settled on Hillsborough and made his debut as an emergency right-back, in a League Cup tie at Swindon in late October, after Nilsson suffered the knee injury which side-lined him for five months. Harkes' first goal in English football was a remarkable 30-yard rocket which set up a fourth-round replay victory at First Division Derby in the League Cup, and in April he had the distinction of being the first American to play in a Wembley Cup final.

Wednesday began the season with a 12-match unbeaten League run which included five successive away wins

colleague, and in notching 32 goals in 1990-91 he not only achieved the best individual haul by a Wednesday man since Roy Shiner in 1956, but gained the recognition which brought his first senior England cap in the summer of 1991. This, in fact, was the beginning of a phase in which the Barnsley product was ahead of Alan Shearer (then of Southampton) in the quest for a permanent international place. Sadly, in subsequent years, Hirst suffered a succession of injuries which set his career back.

Wilson, then aged thirty and boasting 536 games and 97 goals with six clubs since his 1977 debut with Bury, had already earned 18 of his 24 caps, but that he proved an astute buy is evident considering he clocked up 137 appearances and 14 goals for and, with their travelling form a feature of their progress towards promotion and their first major trophy success since 1935, they always had the look of a team destined to reclaim their top-grade place at the first attempt. They did, however, endure a spell when their home form gave cause for concern, for whilst they lost only once at Hillsborough, they conceded 23 points against visiting teams. In three games they let a two-goal lead slip and had to settle for a point, and there were other occasions when they ended up drawing matches they had dominated. A classic example came in the home match with West Ham in late September when, as Atkinson often recalled, they produced a stunning first-half display, managed just one goal, and the visitors somehow contrived to salvage a point after the interval. There were times, however, when Wednesday themselves were rescued by last-minute equalisers, and in thrilling home duels with Oldham and Ipswich they recovered from two-goal deficits.

Wednesday enjoyed another 12-match unbeaten run between mid-November and early February, but seven of these games were drawn, and they were grateful for two invaluable away victories of special merit against promotion rivals Notts County and West Ham in March. The victory at Meadow Lane came in one of those games which can make or break a team's promotion run, for it arrived at a moment when Wednesday, having just clinched a place at Wembley with a memorable two-legged semi-final triumph over Chelsea, were expected to be at their most vulnerable. County, managed by

Sheffield product Neil Warnock, were a fast, direct and physical side, and Atkinson admitted no team was more likely to bring the Owls down to earth. In the event, Pearson and his colleagues gave themselves the perfect psychological boost, and between then and the end of the season there were only two games in which their form was below par and threatened their promotion hopes.

League Cup success was never a priority, but naturally, it was more than welcome, and for skipper Pearson, it topped the most memorable season of his Hillsborough career. He was voted Player of the Year, took the Man of the Match award at Wembley, and earned a place in the club's Hall of Fame with outstanding leadership laced with 12 goals—five on the Cup run. The centre-back's strikes swung the balance in both legs of the second-round tie with Brentford, and he was the lone marksman in the triumphs at Swindon in a third-round replay and at First Division Coventry in the quarter-final.

In every season of triumph there are stories of players who have the misfortune to miss out on the final glory after playing key roles in the earlier stages, and in 1990-91 goalkeeper Kevin Pressman provided a classic example. In the previous term, when Wednesday were relegated, he had contributed to the team's mid-season revival with a 13-match run which was ended with damaged knee ligaments in the New Year's Day game with Manchester City. Now, after fighting back and figuring in the first 29 League and Cup fixtures, he tore a thigh muscle in the Boxing Day clash with Wolves, and was an onlooker as Chris Turner emerged a hero in the second half of the campaign. The irony, perhaps, was that this proved to be Turner's farewell run, though nobody could deny that he deserved his taste of glory more than most. As a local lad, he had joined the Owls from school, come to the fore in the bad old Third Division days, and then, after spells with Sunderland and Manchester United, returned to find the club again enduring a slide. He could appreciate what prompt promotion and capturing the first major trophy for fifty-six years meant to the fans. Turner emphasised his talents with an outstanding display in a memorable first-leg semi-final triumph at Chelsea, where the Owls survived an early onslaught and sealed a 2–0 victory with second half goals from Shirtliff and Hirst.

Wembley may have loomed large on the horizon, but Wednesday supporters, remembering Chelsea's famous fightback from a three-goal deficit in the same competition in 1985, resisted the temptation to start their celebrations before the second leg. As it happened, the outcome of the Hillsborough return was never in doubt after Pearson headed the Owls in front on 34 minutes and Wilson volleyed a tremendous second goal just before the interval. Chelsea claimed a consolation with Stuart's headed goal after 64 minutes, but just before the end, Williams collected a pass from McCall (another man to miss the final act) and nipped in between goalkeeper Beasant and a defender to make it 3–1 on the night and the aggregate score an emphatic 5–1.

In between the semi-final and the Wembley date with Manchester

Peter Shirtliff.

United on Sunday April 21st, defender Nigel Worthington underwent a cartilage operation from which he recovered surprisingly quickly, while Nilsson, out since October with damaged knee ligaments, managed to recover in time to return to the side two weeks ahead of the final. The Swede came back at Portsmouth on a day Palmer did not remember with pleasure: for the lanky and sometimes impetuous midfielder was sent off— and suspension coincided with the Rumbelows Cup final.

Wednesday players celebrate their Rumbelows Cup triumph of 1991 after the defeat of Manchester United at Wembley. It was the club's first major trophy success since 1935.

Wednesday went into the Wembley game, with Atkinson's old club, as outsiders expected to overwhelmed, but it was an occasion when the Owls' boss adopted tactics which nullified the threat of a Manchester side which played well below capacity, and a 77,612 crowd saw the game settled by a single goal from John Sheridan. It came in the 38th minute when Worthington swung a long free-kick into the goalmouth from the right, and United defender Gary Pallister, under challenge from Pearson, could only head the ball four yards outside the penalty area—where 'Sweet Sheri' struck a first-time effort which, though goalkeeper Sealey got a touch, sped into the net off the back post.

Before the game, the pundits had predicated that United's fast and tricky winger Lee Sharpe would expose Nilsson's lack of match-fitness, and that would be the key to the outcome, but in the event, with Harkes appointed to provide extra cover and the Swede using every ounce of guile and positional skill, the danger was defused. On the day Wednesday were rewarded more for hard work than their now customary flair, but the triumph (it was their 17th away win of the campaign) was just as satisfying. The closest United went to scoring was after 82 minutes

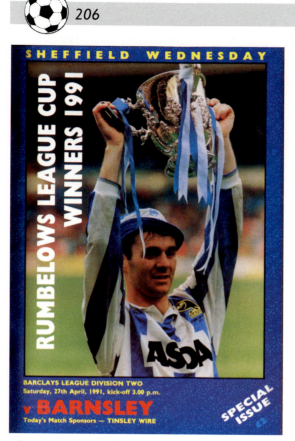

SHEFFIELD WEDNESDAY

RUMBELOWS LEAGUE CUP WINNERS 1991

ASDA

BARCLAYS LEAGUE DIVISION TWO
Saturday, 27th April, 1991, kick-off 3.00 p.m.

v BARNSLEY
Today's Match Sponsors — TINSLEY WIRE

SPECIAL ISSUE

Programme cover featuring Wembley scoring hero John Sheridan with the Rumbelows Cup.

when McClair's header forced a superb save from Turner. The teams were:

Wednesday: Turner; Nilsson, Pearson, Shirtliff, King; Harkes (Madden 88), Wilson, Sheridan, Worthington; Hirst, Williams. Unused sub: Francis.

Manchester United: Sealey; Blackmore, Bruce, Pallister, Irwin; Webb (Phelan 56), Robson, Ince, Sharpe; McClair, Hughes. Unused sub: Donaghy.

Referee: Ray Lewis (Great Bookham).

Atkinson's men celebrated in style at their London hotel that evening, but he insisted on postponing the civic reception planned for their homecoming on the following day. A

few weeks later he had reason to regret the delay, but at the time he said: 'We'll accept the plaudits when we've completed the job that really matters—getting back to the First Division'. That task took another seventeen days, a period during which the Owls won three and drew two of their five matches. Promotion was sealed with a 3–1 defeat of Bristol City in which Hirst (2) and Francis were the marksmen as Wednesday registered their 1,000th home victory in their Football League history. Three days later they concluded the season with a 3–2 defeat at Oldham, where the Lancashire side came back from 2–0 down to seal an injury-time win (with a penalty) which gave them the Second Division championship ahead of second-placed West Ham. To complete a memorable season, Wednesday's reserves won their first Pontins (Central) League title for thirty years under Frank Barlow, and the club's juniors, guided by coach Albert Phelan, reached the FA Youth Cup final for the first time.

Sheffield now boasted two top-grade clubs for the first time since 1968, but it soon emerged that Wednesday would return to Division One without Atkinson at the helm. During the season, 'Big Ron' had signed a two-year extension to his contract, but when the opportunity arose to take over at Aston Villa he found it impossible to resist—for personal as well as professional reasons. Villa sacked manager Dr. Josef Venglos in late May, and within two days, Atkinson was lined up to fill the vacancy—but he planned to defer any announcement until after Wednesday's delayed civic reception on the following Friday evening.

However, the news leaked out barely twenty-four hours before the Town Hall date, and the day of the event saw chairman Richards and director Cliff Woodward locked in talks with Atkinson as they tried to persuade him to stay, with members of the media and hundreds of fans waiting outside. Their meeting spanned several hours and ended in apparent success for Wednesday. Atkinson, confirming he had decided to stay, even went so far as to say: 'I'd have to be barmy to think of leaving this club'.

It was not however the end of the affair. Exactly one week later, 'Big Ron' invited chairman Richards out for dinner, and when they met he handed over an envelope containing his formal resignation. The next day he was installed as Villa's manager. Those close to him knew his departure was inevitable and most had insisted it would happen even after Atkinson had said he was staying. He was still living in his native Midlands, didn't want to leave the area, and had always stressed he never intended remaining at Hillsborough as long as he did. Moreover, he clearly believed the Villa post not only offered him fulfilment of a boyhood dream but an opportunity he didn't seriously think the Owls could match in terms of resources.

'I have to admit,' he said, 'that it really was a big wrench leaving, because I had been as happy in Sheffield as anywhere in my career; but it was a decision I had to take, and my consolation is that I feel I have done a good job at Hillsborough and leave the club in better shape than I found it. I hope that in years to come the supporters will look back

and say I set Wednesday on course for better things.'

At that moment, there were those who branded Atkinson 'a Judas', but, in fact, most acknowledged that he had indeed, inspired new attitudes within the club, not least in the boardroom, and he left behind a team full of ability and promise. In fact, Wednesday's overall League record in his time was not especially impressive, and it read:

	P	W	D	L
Div One	53	16	14	23
Div Two	46	22	16	8
	99	38	30	31

However, in leading Wednesday to their Rumbelows Cup triumph he had given the club the major trophy (with all its implications) which had eluded every other post-war manager, and the statistics did not reflect the dramatic improvement in the overall quality of the team he had created, or the potential of the side he had led out of the Second Division.

It is interesting to note that in little more than two years Atkinson spent approximately £5.1 million on 16 players compared with the £4.5 million Howard Wilkinson invested over five years on around 28 players. Both men balanced the books with their sales, but Wilkinson had come to a dead end when he left and it took the circumstances which followed and Atkinson's arrival to ensure new horizons were opened. Wednesday got good value from the majority of Atkinson's signings, and some (most notably Palmer) were sold at a profit when they moved on.

Atkinson was a high-profile manager who had raised Wednesday's image and ambitions at a crucial

moment in the history of English
League football and brought a touch
of colour and quality to Hillsborough.
Achievement, of course, is invariably
relative to what has gone before: in
that context most supporters were

grateful for the short but significant
era of 'Big Ron'. He had even recruited the man destined to succeed
him and face the challenge of taking
the Owls through the next stages of
progress—Trevor Francis.

20

Bassett's Blades at the Top: 1990–1994

SHEFFIELD UNITED were destined to spend four seasons in the top grade following their 1990 promotion, and, on and off the field, it proved one of the most remarkable phases in the club's history. The Blades fought a continuous battle to preserve a place amongst the game's elite, and life at Bramall Lane seldom lacked drama or interest as Bassett's team became experts in the art of bouncing back from the brink—until, just when they appeared to have survived yet again, they finally fell into the relegation trap in the staggering last seconds of the 1993-94 campaign with an injury-time defeat at Chelsea.

Moreover, the period coincided with an intriguing and unexpected episode in the club's ownership saga which induced a distracting and inhibiting climate of uncertainty that made Bassett's achievement in maintaining United's top status for so long all the more commendable. Metals dealer Paul Woolhouse took control in December 1990 after negotiating to buy Reg Brealey's 1,620 shares for £2.75 million. It raised his stake in the Blades to 75 per cent, and he ultimately installed himself as chief executive; but it all went horribly wrong. In October 1992 it was revealed he had defaulted on his payments, and by mid-1993 he had been forced out, with Reg Brealey, albeit reluctantly, back at the helm. Ironically, this development moved towards its High Court climax just as

United were enjoying their best FA Cup run for over thirty years and figured in the historic all-Sheffield semi-final with Wednesday at Wembley.

Bassett strengthened his squad for United's first term in Division One since 1976, with the recruitment of defenders Paul Beesley (Leyton) and John Pemberton (Crystal Palace), midfielder Jamie Hoyland (Bury), and goalkeeper Phil Kite (Bournemouth) at a total cost of around £925,000. The club record £350,000, paid for former Wigan man Beesley, proved perhaps the most rewarding investment considering he made more top-grade appearances than anyone else in the following four years and stayed with the Blades until 1995 when he joined Leeds. However, there were useful contributions from Pemberton, who, having started at Crewe and figured in Palace's 1990 FA Cup final team, remained until late 1993 when he was sold to Leeds for £250,000; and Hoyland (the son of former United favourite, Tom), who clocked up around 100 games before joining Burnley for £135,000 in November 1994. Kite, a £25,000 buy signed as cover following the £70,000 sale of Benstead, was limited to eleven games in a three-year stay, and seven of those came in the early weeks of the new season after Tracey suffered a fractured cheekbone 15 minutes into the campaign's first match—an occasion Pemberton had

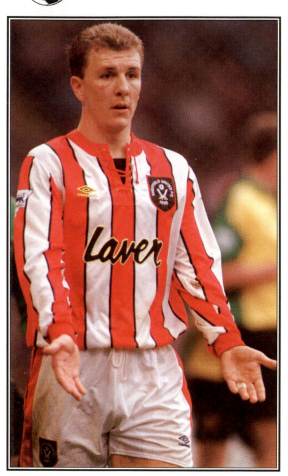

Jamie Hoyland.

cause to remember when he spent most of his debut in the role of emergency goalkeeper, as visitors Liverpool cashed in on United's misfortune to emerge 3–1 victors.

That setback was the one of twelve United suffered in a nightmare start which brought a paltry four points and not a single victory from their first 16 League matches. The long wait for maximum points did not end until three days before Christmas when, after leading 1–0 and then trailing 1–2, they beat Nottingham Forest 3–2

as headers from Bryson and Deane turned the tide. They then enjoyed the rare luxury of three wins in six games. Even better was to follow beginning in late January—for they registered seven straight wins, their best League sequence since 1903. Moreover, in losing only three of their last 16 matches, they were transformed from relegation certainties into a mid-table outfit who finished 12 points clear of the danger mark. Some of the Blades players may have started the season feeling inferior to the rest of the First Division, but they concluded it bubbling with the self-belief engendered by a regular taste of success.

Managing director Derek Dooley gave all the credit for the 'miracle' to Bassett. 'He is unique in football. When we had only four points on the morning of December 22nd, to the rest of the world we were not just dead—we were buried. But Dave had faith in our ability to survive, and the board had faith in him.'

Bassett put the sudden upturn down to rediscovery of their scoring touch, but in fact, they managed only 36 League goals all season and scored more than two in a game only twice (their biggest win a 7–2 defeat of Oldham in the Zenith Data Systems Cup). However, after notching a mere seven in their first 16 matches and once going 669 minutes playing time without finding the net, they made most of their subsequent strikes pay—as for instance when late goals by newcomers Glyn Hodges (on his home debut) and Brian Marwood clinched vital victories against Derby in late January and at Everton in April.

The first injection of new blood during the season came in September when, seeking to instil some iron and leadership into the team, Bassett paid £650,000 to recruit his old Wimbledon discovery Vinny Jones from Leeds, where the one-time building worker had fallen out of favour after helping Howard Wilkinson's side win the Second Division title. With creative skills also urgently required, the manager soon afterwards also bought Marwood, the former Wednesday winger soon destined to become PFA chairman, from Arsenal for £300,000; and, in January, Hodges, a Welsh international midfielder who, like Jones, had started out at Wimbledon, arrived on loan from Crystal Palace in a deal which involved a £410,000 fee when made permanent in April.

Neither Jones nor Marwood, who made only 56 League appearances between them, remained long, but both helped in United's recovery. Jones certainly lent his unique brand of physical and emotional commitment to the scene but, though Bassett argued that his captain was often the unjust victim of officials whose judgement was coloured by his public image, the player seemed intent upon enhancing his 'hard man' reputation. In a match at Manchester City in January, he was booked after only five seconds and later sent off for another reckless lunge at the same opponent in the second half. It was, perhaps, unfortunate that, before this game Bassett had collected a trophy because United had been judged by readers of a magazine 'the most sporting and best behaved' team in Division One!

The Blades never saw the best of Marwood, but Hodges, who was one of only a handful of the 50-plus

Glyn Hodges.

players used by United during their stay in the top grade to figure in a century of League games in that phase, did enough to show he was blessed with special talents. Unfortunately, he also had a flair for inconsistency, and at Bramall Lane he wasted the chance to become one of the biggest favourites since the Tony Currie era. He made his senior debut at the age of seventeen, nearly eleven years before moving to Sheffield, but in over 330 League games (fewer than a hundred with Newcastle, Watford and Palace, all of whom had invested heavily to get him), he had failed to fulfil his potential. He was not, however, lacking in a tendency to over-react when provoked: in only his seventh game for the Blades, at Sunderland in March, he was involved in a head-butting incident which subsequently cost him a £1,000 fine and a six-match ban which meant he missed the season's finale.

By the time the 1991-92 campaign kicked off, Bramall Lane boasted a magnificent new all-seater Kop, but, once again, the Blades started badly and managed only one victory in their first twelve matches. That the fates seemed to conspire against them all season is apparent in the injury problems which saw them call upon a record 35 players; and in the early weeks they often felt their luck was right out. Leading 2–0 with 14 minutes left in the opening game at Norwich, they ended up drawing; they lost 2–1 at Crystal Palace after being 1–0 up ten minutes from the end; and at Oldham in early September they had both Beesley and new free transfer signing Charlie Hartfield sent off by referee Terry Holbrook in the space of four minutes in the first half, and also had Whitehouse and Deane injured in a 2–1 defeat.

Bassett had sold Mark Morris to Bournemouth for £95,000 in the summer, and in late August he accepted (admitting he did so with mixed feelings) a £575,000 offer from Ian Porterfield's Chelsea for Vinny Jones. Meanwhile, the manager's only major pre-season buys were £110,000 striker Clive Mendonca, who came back from Rotherham, and £350,000 Tom Cowan, a promising left-back from Glasgow Rangers. He also paid £50,000 for Preston's Nathan Peel and offered trials to midfielder Hartfield

and striker Adrian Littlejohn, released by Arsenal and Walsall respectively. Mendonca, a former Bramall Lane apprentice whom Bassett had sold for £15,000 in 1988, had managed 27 goals in 84 League outings for Rotherham, but hopes that he had matured enough to adapt to the top-grade were soon dashed, and within a year he was sold to Grimsby for £80,000 after ten games and a single goal. Cowan, on the other hand, looked an astute buy at the outset but he was unable to maintain early progress and joined Huddersfield for £150,000 in 1994.

In the economic climate existing at Bramall Lane, Bassett had little room for manoeuvre or mistakes, and two deals in the first half of the 1991-92 campaign served to highlight the club's financial problems. In early November circumstances forced the reluctant sale of Tony Agana (who had claimed 51 goals in 149 games) to Notts County for £750,000, but the situation was already public knowledge after being highlighted in September when the club endured an embarrassing delay in completing the record £700,000 signing of defender Brian Gayle from Ipswich, because they could not deliver the required deposit after the deal had been announced.

Gayle was another Wimbledon old boy, but he was entirely different in character and style from the departed Jones, and Bassett identified him as exactly the central defender and in-spirational captain his team needed— and believed he would be popular with supporters (Bassett said that if the big skipper had not missed nearly 30 matches with a knee injury in 1993-94, the Blades would not have gone down). Gayle had not survived long at Plough Lane following Bassett's departure, and many considered him ill-used when new Wimbledon boss Bobby Gould left him out of the 1988 FA Cup final team after being a key figure in the run to Wembley. However, he went on to lead Mel Machin's Manchester City on their climb into the top grade in 1989, and before joining Ipswich in January 1990 he might have moved to the Blades—but Bassett could not raise a £330,000 fee which looked a snip compared with what he ended up having to pay.

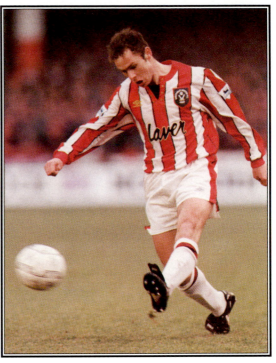

Dane Whitehouse.

Gayle's belated arrival did not coincide with an immediate upturn in United's fortunes. They were defeated in five of his first seven games and conceded 19 goals, and

when mid-November brought Sheffield's first Division One derby for twenty-three years there were few who did not fear that the Blades, with a mere two wins from 15 matches compared with seven by fourth-placed Wednesday, were set for a heavy dent to their pride. A 31,803 Sunday crowd at Bramall Lane, however, witnessed an occasion when Bassett's boys defied the form book and overwhelmed Trevor Francis's supposedly superior Owls largely because they knew these duels were more about passion than poise—and the team that triumphs is the one that wants success the most. The setback certainly taught Wednesday a few lessons!

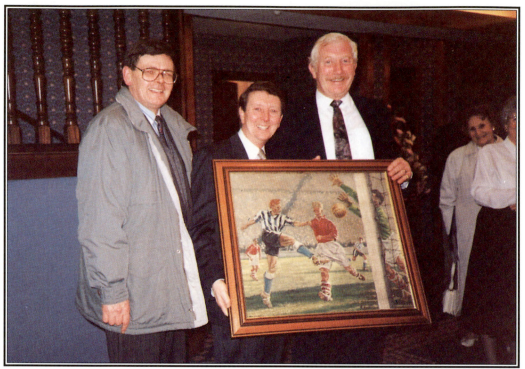

When Derek Dooley, United's managing director, finally went back to Hillsborough after 19 years, he was accorded a great reception, and, on a later return, Owls' chairman Dave Richards (centre) presented him with a painting of Dooley in action as a Wednesday player. Keith Farnsworth is on the left.

It was a great day for United's local lads, Carl Bradshaw, Jamie Hoyland and especially, Dane Whitehouse. The twenty-one year-old had seen his first derby at the age of nine on the occasion of the so-called 'Boxing Day massacre' in 1979, and long dreamed of avenging that defeat. Now it was he who gave United the lead just before half-time when a collision between Wednesday's Sheridan and Warhurst left Bryson in possession and the Scot's forward run ended with his shot being pushed aside by goal-keeper Chris Woods; Whitehouse pounced to score. After 72 minutes, Deane, back after missing eight games, made it 2–0 when he claimed his first League goal since early

September as his shot went through the legs of the unsighted Woods.

A week later, experienced defender Kevin Gage, yet another man with Wimbledon links, boasting 283 League appearances, made his debut on loan from Aston Villa, and celebrated by claiming the lone goal in the victory at Tottenham. He cost a £150,000 fee in February, by which time United's fortunes were improving. In January they enjoyed two remarkable away successes, winning 4–2 at Southampton and 5–2 at Nottingham Forest (Mike Lake, a modest buy from Macclesfield, only scored 4 goals in 35 outings for the club between 1989 and 1993, but three came in these two matches, with the one at The Dell an

astonishing first-time effort from 25 yards). When the return Sheffield derby came round in March they believed they could complete their first League double over the Owls for thirty years—even though Wednesday were by now harbouring hopes of proving the 'dark horses' in the Championship chase, and they certainly looked strong contenders for a UEFA Cup place for the first time in thirty years.

The Hillsborough duel, which attracted a 40,000 crowd, coincided with Derek Dooley's first visit to the ground for a Wednesday match since the club had sacked him in 1973, and though his heart was now very much with the Blades, Owls' fans gave him a tremendous reception when he appeared on the pitch before the game. On the only occasion that Dooley had played in a League derby, at this same venue back in January 1952, United had romped to a 3–1 victory. This was exactly the scoreline they achieved on that March evening in 1992. Once again it was Whitehouse who set them on course for success with a goal after four minutes, and Bobby Davison, making his debut while on loan from Leeds, scored after 28 and 67 minutes. (Davison subsequently made way for another debut, this time of United's latest 'free' signing, the Wimbledon veteran Alan Cork, and it is worthy of note that Paul Rogers, another bargain £50,000 buy from non-League football at Sutton, was making only his second League appearance).

Although the Blades lost 2–1 at Old Trafford on the following Saturday — Manchester's winner came eight minutes from the end — it was to prove one of only two defeats in 16

matches between mid-January and late April, for they promptly went into an eight-match unbeaten run which included six wins and shot them into the top seven. A feature of this sequence was a memorable double by Deane in the 2–0 defeat of Liverpool. His first goal bore the stamp of sheer class: when Bruce Grobbelaar dashed 40 yards from his goal, the striker won the challenge and delivered an instant, stunning long lob which saw the ball drop into the net over despairing defenders trying to atone for the eccentricity which was typical of their Zimbabwe-born goalkeeper.

That Liverpool game was also notable for the Blades' debut of Mel Rees, a goalkeeper who made only eight appearances yet earned a lasting niche in the club's records. Rees had had his first taste of League football aged seventeen nearly eight years earlier with Cardiff, his local team, but subsequently accumulated fewer than 80 senior appearances while serving five other clubs. He admitted his career 'had never taken off'. Bassett paid £60,000 to take him to Watford in 1987, but in 1992 the lad was languishing in West Brom's reserves just when the United boss, facing the loss of the injured Tracey, was searching for an emergency signing. The £25,000 deal was completed two days before Liverpool's visit. Rees had an outstanding game and, conceding only three goals in his first seven outings, made such a hit that he was called into the Welsh squad.

Alas, misfortune struck in United's final home game when Leeds ended the Blades' unbeaten run with a 3–2 victory which, coupled with Manchester United's defeat at

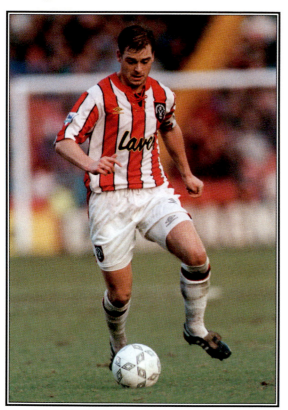

Carl Bradshaw.

Liverpool later the same day, took the League Championship to Elland Road. An injury to Rees, who played on when seriously handicapped with a heavily strapped leg, not only influenced the outcome of a vital match (settled by a crazy own-goal stemming from a misunderstanding between Gayle and his goalkeeper) but forced him to withdraw from his long-awaited international opportunity. Worse, however, was to follow, for during the summer, Rees fell ill and began a year-long fight against cancer of the bowel. Sadly, though at one stage he appeared to be winning the battle and was fit enough to make an appearance on the Wembley pitch

ahead of the all-Sheffield FA Cup semi-final in April 1993, he died late in the following month at the age of twenty-six.

Curiously in the light of what followed a year later, the FA Cup had provided Bassett with his biggest disappointment in the 1991-92 campaign for, when the Blades reached the fifth-round, he firmly believed they could go all the way to the final. 'We might not be equipped to seriously aspire to the Championship, but success in the knock-out competitions is not beyond us, and if we could do that it might generate the income which would enable us to stop having to always buy on the cheap,' he said. In the event, they crashed out at Chelsea when a stunning 25th minute strike from Graham Stuart beat stand-in goalkeeper Kite; but it was a day when the United manager was dismayed by his team's approach to a tie which he believed had been 'there for the taking'. The man nicknamed 'Harry' was seldom at a loss for words, and his players (and, indeed, the media) were never in doubt about his opinions!

A painful footnote to the Chelsea tie was a three-match suspension for Carl Bradshaw, who was caught by BBC Television cameras attempting to punch former team-mate Vinny Jones. The referee missed the incident, but earlier, barely five seconds after the kick-off, he had been quick to book Jones for a typically rash challenge!

Bradshaw was a passionate competitor and his emotional commitment sometimes provoked unexpected and, some would say, undeserved trouble. After the Sheffield derby in November, for

Alan Kelly.

at Tottenham, he was sent off, and suspension, then a succession of injury setbacks, saw him pushed out of the limelight for long spells.

Significantly, perhaps, United's most notable signing in the summer of 1992 was a new goalkeeper, and this time it was not someone destined to remain a stand-in. Alan Kelly, who came from Preston (for whom he had made 150 appearances) for an initial £150,000, seized his chance so well that, before the end of the season, he had gained his first Republic of Ireland cap. His debut came on the day of Tracey's dismissal (it was the first year of substitute goalkeepers, though Kelly actually replaced midfielder Hodges).

1992-93 marked the start of a new era in English football with the creation of the FA Premier League, a development with financial impli-cations that made it all the more imperative for the Blades to survive amongst the elite group who had broken away from the Football League and who were taking (and meaning to keep!) the lion's share of the game's income, which now included exclusive 'live' match coverage on BSB-Sky Television.

Bassett, whose attempts to maintain United's top-grade status were soon hampered by the distraction of the latest twist in the club's ownership wrangle, was never a man without a sense of humour, and conscious that United's first two terms after promotion had seen his side produce their best form in the second half of the season and their worst in the earlier months, he organised a Christmas party for players and staff—in August! Despite the summer weather, he said he

instance, he and Tracey found themselves at odds with the authorities for allegedly making gestures to Wednesday fans. Complaints were made to the police, the matter went to the FA and they fined the players but, not surprisingly, everyone at Bramall Lane felt a mountain was being made out of a molehill. Both men were very popular with supporters, and indeed, Tracey collected his second Player of the Year award that season; though, in fact, 1991-92 was the last term in which he could regard himself as automatic first choice. Early in the following season, hoped his men might be persuaded to believe it was already December and time for them to launch their customary mid-term revival.

Well, at least they kicked-off the campaign with a well-deserved 2–1 victory over Manchester United, but they lost five of their next six games and reached the turn of the year with a mere five wins (ten defeats) in 21 matches. Deane, who had signed a new two-year contract on the eve of the season and was soon celebrating his third England cap, had the distinction of scoring the first goal in Premier League history five minutes into the new era. After finding the net four times in the first three matches however, he endured a run during which he scored only once in 18 League outings. His luck finally changed in January when he bagged two hat-tricks in the space of five days; one sealed United's only win in a seven-match league sequence, while the other launched the Blades on the FA Cup run which took them all the way to the semi-final.

Wembley so dominated the Sheffield soccer story in 1993 that it makes more sense to devote a separate chapter to what was a remarkable episode. Here, therefore, it is sufficient to note that United's quest for Premier League survival coincided with FA Cup progress which included the Deane-inspired replay defeat of Burnley at Turf Moor, a narrow victory over Hartlepool, a more memorable one against Manchester United, and an unforgettable penalty shoot-out triumph over Blackburn in the quarter-final.

In between those days and nights of high drama and excitement, their League fortunes were often tempered by gloom, with occasional bright interludes. They began 1993 with one win and three defeats and dropped into bottom place in early February; then, though victories over fellow strugglers Oldham (2–0) and an out-of-sorts Tottenham (6–0) in successive home games hauled them out of the bottom five, home defeats against Norwich and Crystal Palace thrust them back into the danger zone. The turning point came in late March with a 3–1 success at Coventry (their last League fixture before the Wembley semi-final), for it was a desperately-needed morale booster and signalled the start of a sequence which saw them edge to safety with five wins and only one defeat in their last nine matches. During this run they failed for the third time that season to beat Wednesday, but the point gained at Hillsborough despite a red card for Hodges was invaluable; and they concluded the campaign in style with three successive wins—the 2–0 success at Nottingham Forest on May 1st dooming Brian Clough's side to relegation, and the 2–0 triumph at Everton three days later confirming survival. Not surprisingly, perhaps, the final match of the season, a 4–2 defeat of Chelsea, was played in a carnival atmosphere at Bramall Lane.

Bassett often felt the experience of reaching a semi-final and the knowledge that, at their best, United could match most of their rivals, raised the expectations of some supporters higher than was realistic. He knew that, with his present resources, the most he could aspire to was a place in the top half of the table—and even that was dependent upon what happened after the latest twist in the club's ownership saga. However, contrary to the image some

Paul Woolhouse.

At Christmas 1990, Woolhouse, forty-one year-old chairman of a group of companies dealing in metals, property and computers, had been hailed as a real-life Santa Claus and the club's saviour. He was the man who had persuaded Brealey to call off the planned £6.25 million Hashimi take-over which, he argued, would have 'led to United's demise and seen Bramall Lane turned into a building site'.

There was no disputing Woolhouse's passion for United. He had been a supporter since long before completing his education at King Ecgbert's School at Dore, and after joining the board in 1986 following the acquisition of 419 shares for the sum of £105,000, he readily made his own money available on a number of occasions to help ease the club's cash-flow problems when Brealey was abroad on business. Several key transfers might not have gone through when they did but for his intervention; and at the time he entered into his £2.75 million agreement with Brealey, he no doubt believed he could meet his obligations.

However, early in 1991 he was thrown off course by unexpected and potentially devastating business problems prompted by a sudden slump in the scrap market and, in seeking to save his business, he undertook financial commitments and reorganisation of his enterprises which started a chain of events that ultimately led to his downfall and a personal disaster which extended far beyond his links with Sheffield United. He was declared bankrupt in December 1993 and his subsequent disappearance added a mysterious

pundits were continuing to perpetrate about his team's style (he grew tired of saying 'We don't play anything like Wimbledon'), he did feel progress had been made and that there was cause for optimism—all the more so when, in the spring of 1993, he was promised he would not have to sell and would be given £1 million to spend. However, the 1992-93 season had been played out against a background of boardroom drama sparked by the October revelation that chairman and chief executive Woolhouse had failed to fulfil the terms of his deal for the purchase of Reg Brealey's shares. That set in motion a pattern of events which, by late June 1993, saw Brealey back in charge, and by mid-July the club had sold its most prized playing asset, Brian Deane, to Leeds for £2.7 million.

footnote to a strange episode. In 1995 it was still being suggested that he was emerging from hiding to turn up at Blades' matches in disguise!

In the late summer of 1992, Woolhouse persuaded Derek Dooley to retire as managing director and appointed himself chief executive. He stood down as chairman, in favour of vice-chairman Alan Laver, in October soon after Else 1982 Ltd (the Brealey family trust which sold the shares to him) announced they were taking legal action to reclaim them.

It was in February 1993 that the High Court ruled in favour of Else and ordered the shares to be returned to the Brealey family, but Woolhouse, despite being heavily criticised by the judge, took his case to the Court of Appeal, and it was May before the earlier judgement was confirmed. In the meantime, Woolhouse watched United progress to Wembley and, soon after the semi-final, made a public pronouncement in which he argued that if the club's bankers had allowed them to borrow the money to pay him what they owed him, he could have paid Else the outstanding £860,000. He also said that he could have met Else's demands if he had eased United's financial position by selling Deane.

When Woolhouse's appeal failed, the board felt it in the club's best interests to cancel his contract as chief executive and, while he was still technically a director, he was voted off the board within a few days at an extraordinary general meeting. Michael Wragg was removed at the same time, and as his father 'Dick' had died the previous November, the Wragg family's boardroom links with the Blades were ended after forty

years. Derek Dooley returned as temporary chairman, while Len Brealey, brother of Reg, was one of three new directors—and he remained on the board until August, by which time Reg was back in the chair.

Remarkably, amid all this activity behind the scenes, supporters expressed their confidence in the club with the investment of £1.5 million in advance season ticket sales, but Brealey was soon revealing that he had discovered a horrendous situation on his return, with a catalogue of unpaid bills and financial problems which he claimed would soon place United in dire straits unless something was done quickly. 'When I see what has happened to the club in the past two years I could tear my hair out,' he said.

Within days speculation increased that Deane would be sold, and the player submitted a formal transfer request while revealing that, when he signed a new two-year contract in August 1992, he had obtained an unwritten gentleman's agreement that he would be allowed to leave in 1993. Bassett disputed that, but when he left for a holiday in Italy, he insisted he had told the directors he did not want Deane to go and understood that the board had said they would not sell their biggest asset for less than £3.7 million. Thus at that point bids from Leeds and Sheffield Wednesday fell well below the asking price.

However, on July 14th, with Bassett still away, Deane, having rejected Wednesday, joined Leeds for £2.7 million. The offer from Elland Road split the board, with Reg and Len Brealey and newcomer John Plant the directors in favour, and Dooley, Laver and Bernard Proctor against, it was the chairman's casting vote which settled the issue. Boardroom opponents of the deal argued there was no pressure from the bank to sell, but Brealey claimed 'We would have been in serious difficulties within weeks without this sale'.

Bassett admitted he had been strongly opposed to the deal and thought United should at least have got more than they did from Leeds. Though angered by the news, he insisted it was never a resignation issue. 'I was disappointed at the way the Deane business was handled, but I never thought of jacking it in' he said.

The manager's consolation was that at least he was able to invest around £1 million in three major signings at the start of 1993-94: £350,000 defender David Tuttle (Spurs) and £400,000 midfielder Willie Falconer (Middlesbrough); plus 6ft 4ins Norwegian international striker Jostein Flo, who would eventually cost £500,000. More modest deals brought in Jonas Wirmola, a Swedish defender, and youngsters Mark Foran, from Millwall, and Robbie Scott from non-League Sutton. Bobby Davison was brought back on a free transfer from Leicester. Bassett, who raised £380,000 with the sales of Pemberton, Bryson, Peel and Barnes, subsequently recruited another Norwegian international, Roger Nilsen, a defender, in November, for £400,000, and in February he paid £300,000 for Cardiff striker Nathan Blake. For the record, towards the end of this season, Bassett claimed he had spent £6.4 million since his arrival at Bramall Lane and recouped £5.7 million, which left a deficit of around

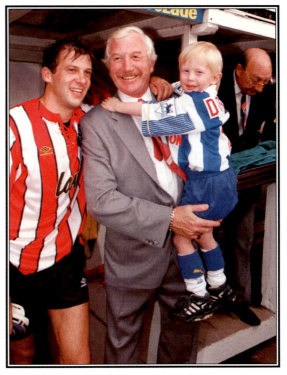

Derek Dooley, with his grandson Derek and United's Bob Booker, before the Dooley testimonial in August 1993.   Picture: Steve Ellis.

£700,000—'Not a bad price to pay for four years in the top grade', he said.

Flo, who enjoyed a memorable home debut against Wimbledon in September, made an immediate impact with five goals in his first eight games, but then endured a lean spell and finished the season with only nine in 33 outings. Late in the campaign, Blake, despite starting only seven games, was a success with five goals which at one stage looked as if they might help keep United in the Premier League. Tuttle, who suffered a serious injury late in the season, and Nilsen both did well, but Falconer proved a disappointment and soon moved on to Celtic.

United registered two victories in their first four games, but then failed to win any of their next twelve matches; indeed, they claimed maximum points only once in 19 fixtures and just twice in 30 between late August and late March. They drew 14 times in this period, and their final tally of 18 draws, which equalled a club record dating back to 1920-21, was one of the main reasons why they failed to escape the drop. Comparing United's record with those of rivals who escaped, it is intriguing to note that they lost seven games fewer than Southampton and six fewer than Everton.

Early in the season, Bassett had the satisfaction of seeing United beat his old club, Wimbledon, for the first time in seven attempts since his arrival at Bramall Lane; but almost from the onset, he felt the fates were conspiring against the Blades. At Everton young Whitehouse claimed the fastest goal of the season but the home men ended up 4–2 winners; Ipswich came to Sheffield and equalised in injury time; and at QPR United lost to a fiercely disputed penalty—an incident which prompted a typical volley of criticism for the referee from Bassett! Then when Spurs visited Bramall Lane and earned a 2–2 draw (the Blades twice came from behind thanks to a Littlejohn double), Bassett was justifiably angry after seeing Tottenham regain the lead while goalkeeper Alan Kelly lay on the ground after being knocked out by an opponent's elbow.

There were occasions when United's powers of recovery pleased the manager: notably when they came from 3–1 down at Southampton to earn a draw with a Flo double in the last ten minutes; and when, trailing 2–0 to Leeds (Deane returned to Bramall Lane to score his first goal in 15 matches), the Blades hit back and Gayle salvaged a point with an 89th-minute strike. However, a terrific fight back at Ipswich after conceding two goals in the first eight minutes ended in a 3–2 defeat, and, having twice led at Tottenham, United saw two points disappear when the home side equalised in the last minute.

The match at White Hart Lane in early March was the first of five successive draws, and when West Ham came to Sheffield at the end of that month and went 2–0 up after half-an-hour, nobody in the ground could have anticipated that United would stage a memorable recovery, scoring three goals in a game for the first time since the season's opening day, and registering a victory which inspired hopes of yet another great relegation escape. Optimism was at a peak on the following Saturday when the Blades went to Liverpool and claimed their first win at Anfield for twenty-six years, coming from behind to triumph with Flo's second-half double.

A home setback against Aston Villa followed, but newcomer Blake topped a splendid United display with the winner at Norwich. The Welshman again confirmed his outstanding finishing talents with a second-half double in another well-deserved 2–0 success against high-riding Newcastle, on the late April day when the old John Street stand was used for the last time prior to demolition. When, three days later, the Blades visited relegation rivals Oldham and emerged with a point despite the dismissal of goalkeeper Tracey, there was a

widespread feeling amongst supporters that, with one fixture remaining, Bassett's boys had done enough to retain their Premier League place.

Bassett, naturally, warned about the dangers of assuming the job was already done, but even he could never have envisaged the unexpected combination of factors which led to United's dramatic fall on the season's final afternoon. Southampton, Ipswich and Everton all looked more at risk, and the prospect of all three escaping at the Blades' expense seemed remote. Incredibly, that is exactly what happened. A 3–3 draw at West Ham saved Southampton, and Ipswich (who two weeks earlier had succumbed 5–0 at Hillsborough) defied the form book by scrambling clear with an unexpected goalless draw at Blackburn; but it was events at Goodison Park which produced the day's most remarkable episode. Everton, facing Wimbledon, were 2–0 down after 20 minutes but recovered to win 3–2. It was a dubious penalty earned by Swede Anders Limpar and awarded by referee Robbie Hart, which was converted by Graham Stuart that launched the revival, then Stuart grabbed an 81st-minute winner with a shot Hans Segers would normally have been expected to save.

However, none of those results would have mattered if United had got the result against FA Cup finalists Chelsea at Stamford Bridge—a solitary point was all they required. Flo put them in front after 29 minutes, and though Kjeldbjerg equalised after 57 minutes, Hodges quickly restored United's advantage. Even when Mark Stein pulled Chelsea level again, the outlook still appeared bright for the Blades; but, with the game drifting into injury-time, Stein mishit a near-post shot which beat Tracey and sealed a 3–2 victory that spelt disaster for United.

Bassett, reflecting on the events of the afternoon, said: 'That last goal will live with me forever. It's one of those unbelievable stories that happen in football. It's a cruel game. But if you play Russian roulette you sometimes get the bullet. People have said that the experience of fighting against relegation has made us experts at it, but when you do it year after year it doesn't get easier. Today we got caught. Now all we can do is take time off to recover from the blow, pick ourselves up, and try to bounce back'.

It was his third taste of relegation as a manager. Each of the two previous occasions had been followed by immediate promotion. He feared he might find it rather difficult to complete a hat-trick.

Trevor Francis.

21

Trevor Francis: Owls 1991–1994

TREVOR FRANCIS, then aged thirty-seven and already a favourite with supporters after eighteen months at Hillsborough during which he had made 60 appearances (24 as substitute), was a logical choice as Wednesday's player-manager following Ron Atkinson's mid-1991 departure; though, in fact, before he was given his second shot at management, the Owls did consider recruiting Ray Harford, the Wimbledon team-boss, but were refused permission to approach him.

Harford had a dour public image but was widely respected in the game, recognised as an outstanding coach; and many considered him harshly treated by Luton when, after leading them to three Wembley finals and their first major trophy, he was sacked in January 1990 by a chairman who said the manager hadn't smiled at the fans often enough! It is intriguing to speculate on what might have happened to Wednesday (and Francis) had Harford come to Sheffield, and worthy of note that, within a few months of the Owls' interest, he teamed up with Kenny Dalglish when the ex-Liverpool boss dramatically re-emerged from 'retirement' to launch the revolution which saw big-spending Blackburn climb from the lower reaches of the old Second Division and ultimately become Premiership champions in 1995. Ironically, Harford's name was again linked with Wednesday when

the Francis era ended after four seasons, but not surprisingly, he chose to remain at Ewood Park. Back in that summer of 1991, assistant manager Richie Barker (he had, incidentally, briefly worked under Harford at Luton) rejected the chance to take over from Atkinson. Barker had managed Shrewsbury, Stoke and Notts County, but since returning from spells abroad admitted he felt more comfortable in a No. 2 role. Moreover, he believed the front-line job needed another high-profile appointment; and on that count, had no qualms about the choice of Francis, who had the double advantage of being both a 'big name' and someone familiar with a Hillsborough backroom set-up which the board did not wish to change. Of course, Francis had had a traumatic and brief spell in charge at Queen's Park Rangers before his January 1990 arrival in Sheffield, but now the circumstances were different and there was no reason why he should not succeed and profit from the lessons of his Loftus Road setback.

Francis, a product of Plymouth, was widely recognised as one of the most gifted footballers of his generation: a striker boasting some 200 goals in 550 matches in English domestic football since bursting onto the scene as a sixteen year-old 'boy wonder' in 1971. An England star (capped 52 times between 1977 and 1986) he was assured of a lasting place in the game's history as Britain's first £1 million player when he moved from Birmingham to Nottingham Forest in February 1981, and had been a hero in American football with Detroit Express (coached by ex-Blades boss Ken Furphy), as well as spending five years in Italy with Sampdoria and Atalanta, before returning to the Football League with Queen's Park Rangers in March 1988, following a brief spell under Graeme Souness at Glasgow Rangers.

'Tricky Trev' had always enjoyed a special status from the start of his League career, and though success had made him wealthy, fame and fortune had not softened his commitment, he remained as enthusiastic and dedicated as ever. Most observers felt he had self-discipline and determination enough to play on at the top until he was forty. He certainly suggested so in the way he scored his first goals for QPR in September 1988—against Wednesday!

Jim Smith, the Sheffield man who had sold Francis to Forest, was also responsible for taking him to QPR and later, in December 1988, when Smith joined Newcastle, the former England man was promoted to player-manager. Francis appeared to have the ideal credentials for the job, yet survived for only eleven months and 48 League and Cup matches—of which 16 were won and 16 lost. In the final analysis his failure was not related to football, the team's results, or his knowledge of the game. Indeed, in many areas, including certain signings, he showed astute judgement; but unfortunately, for the first, though not the last time in this phase of his career, he was undone by criticism of his management style. Too many working relationships were blighted by a lack

of mutual understanding and tolerance.

A period which began promisingly, quickly turned sour largely because he discovered everyone did not have his single-mindedness nor share his philosophy, and his attempts to adopt disciplinary theories he had picked up in Italy were certainly not geared to gain the approval of English players familiar with a more relaxed and less regimented approach. Francis found it difficult to understand why highly-paid professionals thought nothing of arriving late for, or of missing training, because of minor domestic problems, and he sometimes felt their dedication was not in proportion to their incomes. There were players who had cause to be grateful for his help, but others found him inflexible and remote.

The first public hint that his methods were creating friction came in March 1989, with the revelation that midfielder Martin Allen had been fined £1,200 for absenting himself from the squad travelling to a match at Newcastle—because he chose to attend the birth of his child. The Football authorities subsequently halved Allen's penalty but, though they suggested a fine was justified, Francis emerged from the episode with damaging publicity; and this was subsequently compounded by further disharmony generated by criticism of his players in a tabloid newspaper—a lapse of judgement which prompted an angry response led by the club's PFA representative Nigel Spackman.

No doubt there were faults on both sides, and it didn't help that Francis got on the wrong side of some members of the London media. Some journalists found him the most

Trevor Francis the player.

beginning to feel his value lay in expressing his skills in a part, rather than the whole, of a match and knew it needed to be in a team more committed to flair than physique. So the opportunity to join 'Big Ron' in Sheffield fitted the bill perfectly and, despite relegation at the end of that first season, promotion and a Rumbleows Cup triumph (though he was an unused substitute at Wembley) in his second term, coincided with a spell in which he enjoyed his football and his talent brought new admirers on the Hillsborough terraces. He actually completed a full 90 minutes on only 14 occasions in this period, and all but one of his 29 outings after his elevation to player-manager came as a substitute: but he displayed enough moments of sheer class to leave the fans with memories they would always treasure. He never lost the ability to produce a pin-point cross, and while he managed only nine goals, most of them were gems.

Long before the dramatic managerial developments of mid-1991, there were those suggesting Francis should be groomed as Atkinson's eventual successor and given time to study the older man's leadership techniques; but when 'Big Ron' suddenly walked out he graduated into the 'hot seat' at a time and place he had not expected—and without the benefit of a period of preparation. Francis, very different in personality from his predecessor, knew some people would be waiting for him to fail, but was determined to prove he could succeed as a manager. He knew he would never get a better chance: Atkinson had left him with a strong squad, and just as important, had inspired a boardroom attitude which

helpful and genuine of people, but there were others who had a different view, and, once upset by what they interpreted as arrogance or deliberate lack of co-operation, they were only too happy to focus on the stories of dressing-room disenchantment. The situation could not last, and the inevitable upshot was his dismissal in late November 1989.

Francis, who did not then envisage an early return to management, sought to recover from the 'wounds' of QPR by concentrating solely on playing. In truth, he was already

David Hirst salutes his goal against the Blades in Derek Dooley's testimonial, August 1993.

would ensure the new boss enjoyed greater financial backing than any previous manager. No wonder some senior players rated him a lucky man.

The bare statistics of the Francis era show that Wednesday played 216 League and Cup games in his four seasons (won 89, lost 60, scoring 336 goals and conceding 264). In his initial term they finished third, their highest place in twenty-nine years and qualified for the UEFA Cup for the first time since 1964; in his second season they reached the finals of both League Cup and FA Cup; finishing outside the top seven just once (in 1994-95, a term discussed in Chapter 23.)

His first two years were memorable. Much more was achieved than anyone anticipated, and it coincided with a continuation of the exciting and entertaining style of play launched by Atkinson. Indeed, some of Wednesday's football in this period bettered anything that had gone before. Standards were set, however, which, for a variety of reasons, were not maintained in the longer term, and, ultimately, when progress began to falter optimism gave way to disenchantment. Some would suggest that a fleeting glimpse of Championship possibilities in 1991-92 and the 1992-93 taste of European competition plus four trips to Wembley in two months raised expectations to unrealistic levels. Others might point to injuries to certain key players which hampered the team and made seventh place in Francis's third term highly commendable in the circumstances.

Striker David Hirst was often considered the man whose frequent absence was the greatest handicap. He was at the peak of his form at the start of the Francis era, and indeed, had just gained England recognition (which meant paying Barnsley an extra £50,000). His value was probably never better emphasised than in that first term back in the top grade, when not once but on several occasions he returned after serious injury to score vital goals. It highlights the extent of problems exacerbated by four operations and prolonged Achilles trouble that Hirst started only 74 of Wednesday's 168 League games under Francis, and 55 of those outing were in the first two seasons of success—as were 29 of his 33 League goals.

There were other victims of untimely injuries. The influential John Sheridan missed more than half of Wednesday's League games between 1991 and 1994; Nigel Pearson had a run of bad luck, twice breaking a leg;

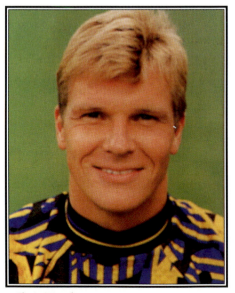

Chris Woods.

and later arrivals Chris Waddle and Andy Sinton had long spells on the sidelines.

Yet, in the final analysis, many felt Francis compounded his handicap by dismantling too quickly the squad he inherited; and, especially in the later stages of his tenure, he hurried the rebuilding he felt essential and recruited players who did not enjoy the impact or popularity of those they had replaced. He argued, some would say quite justifiably, that his four seasons as a whole did not add up to failure, and insisted that with time and a fully fit squad the dip in the team's fortunes would be reversed. For a combination of reasons how-ever, time was one commodity he did not have in great abundance as the patience of the fans and, ultimately, his employers began to run thin.

Investment of around £17 million (he recouped £10.5 million) had not paid the expected dividends, and once again, the spectre of QPR re-emerged in the form of allegations of dressing-room disharmony. Such tales lack the same sting when things are going well, but when they coincide with modest or poor results, they can prove a dangerous burden. The beginning of the end for Francis came when he started to lose the empathy of supporters—and a sudden deterioration developed in his relationship with chairman Richards.

All that lay in the distant future when Francis began his preparations for the 1991-92 campaign by persuad-ing Pearson, Palmer and Anderson to accept new contracts and by making his first major signings—Oldham's England Under-21 defender Paul Warhurst; and England goalkeeper Chris Woods, a veteran of over 570 games and 24 caps who arrived from Glasgow Rangers. Francis equalled the club's record fee by paying £750,000 for Warhurst, then surpassed it with the £1.2 million capture of Woods. During the season he raised his outlay to around £3 million in acquiring Nottingham Forest striker Nigel Jemson (£800,000), Leyton's exciting seventeen year-old midfield prospect Chris Bart-Williams (£350,000), and young Rotherham defender Julian Watts (£80,000). Bart-Williams, who was to have the distinction of making more League appearances (including substitutions) than any other player in the Francis years, was spotted by the player-manager in a League Cup game against the Owls, and other clubs were pipped to his signature because Leyton manager Peter Eustace wanted goalkeeper Chris Turner (Bart-Williams joined Nottingham Forest in the summer of 1995 with Leyton taking a cut of the £2.5 million fee).

One of those quirks of fate that football frequently throws up saw the Francis era kick off with a home date against Ron Atkinson's Aston Villa, and just to compound the irony, the visitors emerged 3–2 victors in front of a 36,749 crowd after Wednesday had led 2–0 with first-half goals from Hirst and Wilson. Ex-Owl Dalian Atkinson, back from Spain, scored the equaliser and laid on Villa's late winner.

However, that was one of only two defeats Wednesday suffered in their first seven games, and two of their four wins in this spell ensured a Boys' Own-style start for the new player-manager. When Everton came to Hillsborough, he stepped from the substitute's bench just long enough to set up Anderson's 87th-minute winner

(and immediately retired!); while on Forest's visit ten days later he topped another late appearance with an 88th-minute strike which sealed three points. In between these games, Palmer bagged a first-half hat-trick in a 4–1 defeat of QPR.

It was one of those seasons when, at some stage, every regular player confirmed his First Division credentials: Williams (a busy but not always lucky player), Worthington, Harkes, Nilsson and Anderson all contributed vital goals, and, though Jemson (signed after Hirst suffered his first serious injury in September) was rather a disappointment in the long term, he emerged the hero in victories at West Ham and Aston Villa, and notably with a two-goal burst in a home defeat of Manchester United.

There were however, several particularly painful setbacks. Sheffield United, again making a poor start in their second term back at the top, rocked the Owls by completing a double which defied the form book with a 2–0 success at Bramall Lane in November and a 3–1 triumph at Hillsborough in March. In between, Wednesday suffered a record home defeat when Howard Wilkinson's Leeds came in January and crushed them 6–1 (ex-Owl Lee Chapman scored a hat-trick); while a February trip to Highbury saw Arsenal turn a 1–1 scoreline at 70 minutes into a 7–1 drubbing.

Yet it summed up Wednesday's resilience that, after their November 'culture shock' at Sheffield United, they lost only four of 26 games and won 14. The later defeat at the hands of their city rivals was, in fact, one of only two inflicted upon Francis's team in their final 14 matches; the

Eric Cantona —taken while on trial with Wednesday.

sequence included a 2–2 draw at Luton which featured a memorable Sheridan strike (he flipped the ball up and hit a superb 25-yard volley), and a defeat of Notts County in which Francis again turned the tide as late substitute by providing the cross from which Hirst scored.

Wednesday's third place in the table behind Leeds and Manchester United far exceeded expectations and, until they dropped two points when conceding a late goal at Crystal Palace (the scorer was Mark Bright, soon to join the Owls) in the season's penultimate fixture, they retained slim hopes of pipping the front pair to the Championship. In the final analysis, however, a UEFA Cup place was a fine achievement—especially as West Ham and Notts County, two of the Owls' promotion companions, went straight back down, while

Oldham, the previous year's Second Division champions, only survived after a desperate struggle.

There was, perhaps, a touch of irony in that Leeds United's 1992 League title-winning team featured a player who had been on trial at Hillsborough in January—Eric Cantona. The controversial international, not for the first time, was in bother with French soccer authorities and, having responded to a long suspension by supposedly retiring, he then sought to rebuild his career in England. However, the weather here was so bad that Cantona's only public appearance in an Owls' shirt came in an indoor six-a-side match with Baltimore Blast at Sheffield Arena; and, when Francis suggested extending the trial until he could see Cantona play on grass, the impatient Frenchman walked out. It was assumed he was going home to France, but he ended up at Elland Road; Howard Wilkinson said he didn't need to watch Cantona on grass to know he would be an asset.

At that stage, Hirst was set for another earlier than expected comeback, which prompted Francis to mark time over Cantona; and there were, perhaps, other considerations. When the Frenchman followed his Leeds success by helping Manchester United win the Championship, Francis insisted he had no regrets. He questioned whether Cantona would have had the same impact at Hillsborough.

In the event, Francis turned his attention to France when seeking to strengthen his squad ahead of the 1992-93 campaign, but his target was a thirty-one year-old Geordie called Chris Waddle, who was brought home to England for a near £1 million fee

Chris Waddle, Footballer of the Year 1993, with chairman Dave Richards and manager Trevor Francis after collecting the trophy.

after three years in Marseille. Waddle boasted 62 caps, had made over 400 appearances and scored a century of goals with Newcastle and Tottenham before a £4.5 million move to France, and was acknowledged as one of the most gifted and perceptive players of his generation. At that stage he had fallen out of favour with England manager Graham Taylor but, appearing in 54 of Wednesday's 63 League and Cup games, he quickly won his way into the hearts of Hillsborough regulars in a memorable first term which saw the Owls make four trips to Wembley. He also captured the imagination of the nation's leading soccer writers, who could not

influence Taylor's opinion but named Waddle the 1993 FWA Footballer of the Year.

The first season of the new Premier League provided a remarkable mixture of drama, delight and disappointment for the Owls: it was a unique, eventful and exciting campaign, featuring a short-lived European adventure, an historic all-Sheffield FA Cup semi-final at Wembley, appearances in both domestic cup finals (the FA Cup final went to the last minute of extra time in a replay), and abundant tales of individual trials and triumph.

Yet, curiously, it was not a term which began well, though even in the disappointing initial phase, Francis insisted that results did not reflect his team's form or potential. A mere four wins in their first 19 League games left the Owls in the bottom six in early December, and some were even tipping them for relegation. However, an unbeaten ten-match run which included eight victories shot them into the top four by the end of February and, though they finally ended up in seventh place after concluding their League programme with only three wins in 13 fixtures (they played the last five in eleven days), they could at least use pre-occupation with the cup competitions as an excuse.

Wednesday's disappointing early-season results were partly due to injuries which interrupted Waddle's start and caused Pearson to miss several games, whilst the absence of Sheridan, whose first outing was delayed until late October following a knee operation, was a particularly crucial factor. Moreover, Hirst suffered the first of another series of setbacks in what he will always remember as a curiously mixed but largely frustrating campaign in which he figured in barely half of the club's matches. He was (albeit harshly) sent off on his European debut; scored one memorable goal in the November derby with Sheffield United, and another, his only FA Cup goal, in the Wembley final. In between, he was a £3.5 million target for Manchester United before boss Alex Ferguson switched his attention to Cantona—whose arrival at Old Trafford inspired a run which led to a long-awaited Championship triumph.

It is, perhaps, relevant here to note that Manchester United's matches with Wednesday that season had a significant influence on their title aspirations. In the first meeting, at Hillsborough on Boxing Day, the visitors looked anything but potential champions as the Owls romped to a three-goal lead after 65 minutes, but then United hit back to emerge with a 3–3 draw (Cantona got the equaliser) which marked a turning point in their fortunes. However, by the time the teams met at Old Trafford in early April, that familiar frown was back on Ferguson's face. United had won only one in five and their title hopes were fading. Now, Sheridan put Wednesday in front from the penalty spot, and United didn't equalise until minutes from the end. They would have been grateful for that, but linesman John Hilditch, who had taken over from injured referee Michael Peck during the game, elected to play eight minutes of 'extra time'—just long enough to enable Steve Bruce to head United's winner.

The initial loss of Hirst, who broke an ankle bone as the innocent victim of a clash with Arsenal's Steve Bould in late August, induced two developments which did much to shape the pattern of the season. One was the unexpected conversion of defender Warhurst into an emergency striker; the other the acquisition of Crystal Palace striker Mark Bright in a £1 million deal which took the £650,000-rated Paul Williams to Selhurst Park. Warhurst and Bright first formed an attacking spearhead at Nottingham Forest on a mid-September day when Wednesday recorded only their second win of the season.

The Warhurst saga was a remarkable episode with a surprising footnote. He had scored a mere two goals in some 130 League and Cup outings with Oldham and the Owls, yet now notched 18 (12 in the cup competitions); and it was after claiming 17 in 21 starts in two separate spells up front, that he was named in the England squad in March. Alas, he suffered a groin strain in training and had to withdraw. Subsequently, when injuries to central defenders Peter Shirtliff (broken arm) and Pearson forced Francis to ask Warhurst to again revert to his former role in the FA Cup final in May, the player was far from happy. Indeed, he admitted in a Sunday tabloid that he almost walked out on the eve of the Wembley game—a remarkable confession whatever the provocation. So many old Hillsborough heroes would have given anything for the chance to play on such an occasion. Warhurst's excuse was he 'was being treated like a piece of shit'.

According to Francis, between the final and the replay, Warhurst's agent sought talks about a new contract, was refused because the manager had other things on his mind, and started ringing other clubs to announce the player had fallen out with the Owls' boss and was available for transfer. That summer, Francis did arrange for Warhurst to talk to Blackburn, but called off the proposed move when plans to sign Brian Deane from Sheffield United collapsed. Warhurst, unfortunately, sulked despite signing a new four-year contract and, in early September, after an attempt had been made without success to create a Hirst-Warhurst strike partnership, the way was cleared for the former Oldham man to move to Ewood Park in a £2.7 million deal. He said he didn't care where Ray Harford played him!

Warhurst had gained Under-21 honours as a defender, but in this role often proved prone to error. His strength was his pace and, bursting from the back, he was an exciting player who caught the eye. Indeed, his forward dashes had contributed to Wednesday's success in his first term. With the benefit of hindsight, it is not difficult to see why his switch into attack seemed an obvious solution to Francis's front-line problems in the autumn of 1992. Yet, when the manager put the idea to him in training, Warhurst thought he was joking—and agreed to it with reluctance. He looked a natural striker from the outset. There was never any impression that he was a centre-half playing at centre-forward: he boasted an instinctive sense of anticipation, had the speed to get behind defenders, and the quality of his finishing was a revelation. When, in his second spell in attack, starting in late January, he scored nine goals in one run of seven League and Cup games, Francis suggested he was one of the top ten strikers in the country.

He did, however, suffer a major scare in only his second outing up front. It is often forgotten that Wednesday's 8–1 defeat of Spora Luxemburg, in their UEFA Cup match at Hillsborough, proved the last occasion on which Francis played a full game for the club, but it is always remembered as the night Warhurst might easily have died. He was knocked out in a collision with the visitors' goalkeeper as he headed his second goal in the 73rd minute, falling heavily head first, he moment-arily stopped breathing. The real hero of the night was physio Alan Smith, whose instant reaction averted a tragedy as he removed a blockage in the player's air passage. When Warhurst was taken unconscious to the hospital, few imagined he would recover in time to play in the second leg a fortnight later; but in fact, he scored with another brave header when the Owls went to Luxemburg and won 2–1 to become the first English team for nine years to reach double figures in a European competition.

Bright, who was already aged thirty and boasted 121 goals in some 340 League and Cup games with Port Vale, Leicester and Palace, was an experienced and widely admired striker who had enjoyed a successful partnership with Ian Wright at Selhurst Park. He was destined to score 56 in 136 outings in his first three seasons with the Owls, and the 20 he claimed in his first term included nine in the cup games.

He was not, however, eligible for the UEFA Cup, and Hirst was rushed back for the first leg of the second round tie in Kaiserslautern in October. Alas, after giving Wednesday an early lead, he was shown an undeserved red card, by French referee Quiniou, following a blatant piece of play-acting by Marco Haber three minutes before half-time. The Germans, who equalised from a disputed penalty, won 3–1, and though Wednesday, minus the suspended Hirst, managed a 2–2 draw (after twice leading) in the Hillsborough leg, they had to concede they had not only been beaten by a team better equipped in the wiles of European football, but one also boasting superiority in traditional soccer skills.

Wednesday were already progressing towards their second League Cup final in three years before their UEFA Cup exit, with Second Division Hartlepool defeated 5–2 on aggregate in the second round, and First Division promotion contenders Leicester surprisingly crushed 7–1 (Bright and Gordon Watson hit doubles on a night when Sheridan finally returned) at the next stage. Another impressive home success followed with a 4–0 victory over QPR, but then two games were required to dismiss Ipswich in the quarter-final. The first match, at Portman Road, not only saw the Owls denied victory by another dubious penalty decision, by referee Holbrook, seven minutes from the end, but Hirst suffered a thigh injury from which his recovery was so protracted that he started only one of the next 21 matches. In fact, both Hirst and Bright missed the Ipswich replay, but Warhurst sealed a narrow victory with a classic strike—a lob over the advancing goalkeeper after bursting through to meet Nilsson's superb through pass.

Wednesday's 4–2 victory at Blackburn in the first leg of the semi-final was the highlight of that Coca-Cola Cup run for, after trailing within ten minutes, they scored four in a breathtaking 16-minute burst of quality football. Harkes headed the equaliser, a Sheridan flick gave the Owls the lead, and then Warhurst struck twice in four minutes. Shortly before half-time, Palmer, attempting to intercept a high cross, looped the ball over the stranded Woods and into his own net, but the only unhappy note on a memorable evening was a broken leg which ended Pearson's season.

By the time of the second leg in mid-March, Wednesday's unbeaten League and Cup run had been halted after 16 games, and Shirtliff had been added to the injured list; but the Owls were still on course for a Wembley double. However, those who thought Coca-Cola success against Blackburn was a formality, adopted a more realistic view when Rovers pulled the aggregate back to 4–3 with a goal after 34 minutes. (It is often forgotten that, at this stage, the Lancashire club also had their sights on success in both major cup competitions—and their fate hinged on this game and an FA Cup quarter-final replay with Sheffield United at Bramall Lane two days later.) It was the appearance of Hirst as substitute ten minutes after the start of the second half which settled Wednesday's nerves and saw them through. Within 13 minutes, Hirst made it 1–1 on the night, and he then set up the chance from which Bright scored at the second attempt to give the Owls a 6–3 aggregate triumph.

As Wembley figured so prominently in the Sheffield soccer story in 1992-93, the Coca-Cola final and Wednesday's FA Cup run is discussed at length in the following chapter. However, it is relevant to note here that the Owls' progress to a unique FA Cup semi-final date with Sheffield United, saw them defeat Cambridge, Sunderland, Southend and, after a replay, Derby County. On the first of four Wembley visits, Wednesday defeated their city neighbours 2–1 in extra time, but they returned to the Stadium fifteen days later and lost 2–1 to Arsenal in the League Cup final; and in May, the Owls met the Gunners twice in the space of six days, and the North London club captured the FA

Cup with a dramatic winner in the last minute of extra time in the replay.

Yet, while Wednesday emerged from a marathon season with no trophies to reward their efforts, the club and supporters believed the brush with glory was an achievement which signalled that the Owls were on the brink of really big things with this the start of a phase in which the honours, already within touching distance, were bound to be grasped sooner rather than later.

In that context, the 1993-94 campaign was something of an anti-climax. Wednesday had another good run in the League Cup before falling in the semi-final to Manchester United, but they were knocked out of the FA Cup by Chelsea in a home fourth-round replay; and despite recovering from another poor start, to enjoy a spell in which they lost only one game in 15 and then finishing the season with a nine-match unbeaten run, they ended up seventh in the Premiership—too low for a UEFA Cup place. It was little consolation that their tally of 76 League goals was their best for thirty years—and this after they had failed to score in their first four matches.

It was a season of change, in that several familiar figures departed the scene. Ahead of the season, Viv Anderson and Danny Wilson left to form, albeit briefly, a new management team at Barnsley; others who went included Shirtliff (Wolves) and Harkes (Derby). Those sales brought in around £1.25 million, and that sum was trebled when Warhurst joined Blackburn in early September. None of these moves caused much surprise, and in fact, it was not a player's departure but that of a member of the backroom staff which created the biggest shock of the season. Physio Alan Smith's ten-year stay ended suddenly and unexpectedly in late January. He was one of the best men in the country at his job, but when Francis chose to dismiss him there was barely a murmur from supporters. However, the respect with which Smith was held in the game was soon evident when he was appointed to the England backroom team under new coach Terry Venables.

Francis again broke the club's transfer record in the summer with the £2.7 million acquisition of England and former Nottingham Forest defender Des Walker (346 appearances, 58 caps), who returned home after an unhappy spell in Italy with Sampdoria; and another centre-back, Andy Pearce, arrived from Coventry for a more modest £500,000. Soon after the start of the season another £2.7 million was invested in Andy Sinton, the England and QPR left-sided midfielder and a veteran of over 400 League games (10 caps) whom Francis had once taken to Loftus Road from Brentford for £350,000—and had long been trying to bring to Sheffield.

Unfortunately, it was a season in which Wednesday were again plagued by injury problems. Walker, who had an outstanding initial term, was the lone ever-present and Nilsson, Palmer and Bright (his 23 goals included 11 in one 12-game run) missed only a handful. Hirst however, endured another term of trauma with a mere seven League outings; Sheridan did not start a game between mid-October and mid-March; Waddle barely played after December;

Sinton's season also ended early; and in September, Pearson again broke a leg. Woods, too, was sidelined in October, but his return was delayed because Pressman deputised so well. Pressman, along with Bart-Williams, gained England 'B' recognition at a time when Woods, Walker, Sinton and Palmer looked to be at the end of their international careers. Palmer, by the way, started the season by getting himself sent off at Liverpool after only 12 minutes.

The Owls won only one of their first 13 matches and found themselves in the Premiership's bottom three at the end of October. They then lost only one of the next 12 games, and eight victories in this sequence shot them into the top six. The run featured a 5–0 home defeat of West Ham in mid-December when Waddle scored one goal and made three others in a vintage performance. Alas, within a couple of weeks, the former England man was in plaster and the victim of an Achilles injury which ruined his season.

Apart from the West Ham success, there were other highlights, and it was not a term without some moments to treasure, notably, impressive wins at Ipswich and Manchester City. Three individual strikes of note came in the League Cup run: Palmer's stunning late equaliser which earned a replay against Middlesbrough; a header from young Ryan Jones (a Sheffielder who qualified to play for Wales) which sealed victory at QPR; and a brilliant Bright volley which KO'd Wimbledon in the quarter-final.

Wednesday's cause was not helped by a habit of conceding late goals. In September they lost a three-goal lead

against Norwich, and there were seven matches during the season in which allowing the opposition to score in the final three minutes cost them a total of 18 points. There were only two occasions when they were soundly defeated: twice in a fortnight by Manchester United, losing 4–1 at home in the League Cup and 5–0 at Old Trafford in the Premiership.

There were many who felt that, all things considered, Wednesday had ended the season better placed than might have been expected when they were struggling in the relegation zone. The last lap of the campaign included emphatic defeats of relegation-threatened Everton and Ipswich, and the Owls did finally manage a League triumph over Sheffield United, who were destined to lose their top-grade status.

Yet there was also a sense in which it seemed things were not quite going as might have been hoped. A particular blow was the end-of-season departure of Roland Nilsson, who returned to Sweden for personal reasons. In November 1992 the £2 million-rated Nilsson had signed a lucrative three-and-a-half-year extension to his contract, but within less than a year, he asked for his release, revealing that his wife and children had suddenly become homesick and gone back to their native Helsingborg—and he wanted

to follow them. Wednesday, naturally, tried to persuade him to honour his contract but, when it became public knowledge that he planned to walk out in December, he and not the club had the sympathy of the fans. In the event, he was persuaded to remain until May on the understanding that the Owls would then release him without a fee to play with his home town club.

Nilsson, however, was not the only member of the 'old' brigade who did not remain to figure in Francis's plans for 1994-95. Worthington, whose long service had been rewarded with a testimonial in 1993, rejected new terms and, valued at £325,000 by an independent tribunal, joined Leeds—who also signed Palmer for £2.7 million. Pearson, too, was allowed to leave. Ex-Owl Viv Anderson, now at Middlesbrough as assistant to new boss Bryan Robson, had identified the deposed Wednesday skipper as the ideal man to lead the Teeside club's bid for a place in the Premiership. He proved a bargain at £500,000.

It was not without irony that while Pearson enjoyed outstanding success at Ayresome Park, and Palmer and Worthington helped bring UEFA Cup football to Elland Road, Francis was coming under increasing pressure in a campaign which turned sour and marked the end of his reign.

Sheffield Goes to Wembley: 1992–1993

THE 1992-93 SEASON marked a memorable milestone in the history of football in Sheffield, for United and Wednesday not only met at the semi-final stage in the FA Cup for the first time, but the most famous derby duel of them all was staged at Wembley Stadium, where a 75,364 crowd saw the Owls win 2–1 after extra time. Moreover, this was also the year when Wednesday paid four visits to Wembley but, despite having the rare experience of reaching the finals of both major domestic cup competitions, they ended up with no silverware to show for their efforts, being twice defeated by Arsenal— with the FA Cup final going to a replay which was decided in the last moments of extra-time.

It is intriguing to reflect on the circumstances which conspired to create that unique derby. It was United's eleventh semi-final, but they had not reached this stage since 1961; Wednesday were making their 16th appearance, and had been there twice in the 1980s; but the furthest both Sheffield teams had gone in the same year was in 1960 when they met in the quarter-final. Thus it would have been a special year in any event, but staging the match at the stadium synonymous with FA Cup finals since 1923 made it extra special.

Semi-finals at Wembley were a recent innovation, done to suit London clubs; and in 1993 the Football Association initially considered the venue appropriate for the clash between Arsenal and Tottenham but felt Elland Road more fitting for the all-Sheffield tie. They didn't know the dismay with which Sheffield supporters viewed the prospect of the biggest derby match in the history of the series going to Leeds. But then, few outsiders understood the intense rivalry between the Yorkshire cities, and they could hardly be expected to appreciate why Blades and Owls fans alike wanted the game staged anywhere but Elland Road. In any case, Sheffield folk felt the FA had failed to recognise what this event meant to the city. It was a match fit for nowhere but Wembley: the city's own cup final! Fortunately, strong protests from both clubs, and a campaign supported by civic leaders, members of Parliament and many others prompted a change of heart by the FA—though it was only after the occasion had proved an overwhelming success that the soccer authorities admitted they were glad they had given in to Sheffield's pleas.

The progress of the Sheffield clubs to the penultimate stage of football's greatest knock-out competition featured a mixture of grit, good fortune and flair—plus a few moments of high drama. The fates were kind to both in the third round. Wednesday came from behind to win 2–1 at First Division Cambridge, where John Harkes equalised with a 'soft' goal and Mark Bright sealed

Sheffield Wednesday squad at the time of the all-Sheffield semi-final, as featured in the Wembley programme.

Sheffield United squad at the time of the all-Sheffield semi-final, as featured in the Wembley programme.

victory with a superb header. Meanwhile, United, home to Second Division Burnley (managed by ex-Owl Jimmy Mullen), trailed 2–0 with only nine minutes left. Then Glyn Hodges reduced arrears, Littlejohn and visitors' goal-hero Heath were sent off following a touchline skirmish, and Paul Beesley salvaged the Blades' pride with a last-gasp equaliser. In the Turf Moor replay, that man Heath again gave Burnley the lead, but Brian Deane headed a first-half hat-trick to set up a 4–2 triumph.

In home fourth-round ties, one goal was enough for both Sheffield teams. United might have anticipated a bigger margin against Second Division Hartlepool, but they were content with veteran Alan Cork's solitary 47th-minute strike. On the following day, Wednesday looked like being held to a draw when First Division Sunderland, the defeated 1992 finalists, came to Hillsborough, but they were in luck in the 89th-minute when Tony Norman, in the visitors' goal, dropped a high cross to offer Bright a gift he could hardly refuse.

As expected, the Owls, fresh from their memorable midweek League Cup semi-final (first leg) victory at Blackburn, succeeded without much trouble when Southend visited Sheffield in the fifth round—Paul Warhurst, the defender-turned-striker, maintained his remarkable run with both goals in a 2–0 win. However, United produced the shock of the weekend when they came from behind to beat Manchester United in

Wednesday players celebrate the victory over Derby County which ensured an all-Sheffield FA Cup semi-final.

a Sunday game screened live by BBC Television. Ryan Giggs had given Manchester the lead after 31 minutes, but within three minutes, Jamie Hoyland had scrambled an equaliser. Hodges, whose clever free-kick had set up that chance, scored the decisive second goal four minutes before half-time with a delightful lob—a lesser player would have been tempted to hit a hard shot, but Hodges, so often guilty of failing to exploit his talents, showed a touch of class.

The sixth-round draw kept United and Wednesday apart, but testing ties at Blackburn and Derby did not seem to favour both succeeding. In the event, a double success came in replays—though only after much drama!

At Derby, Wednesday, despite leading twice through a John Sheridan penalty and another brilliant strike by

Warhurst, looked on their way out when County hit back to go 3–2 up. However, a flash of magic from Chris Waddle and a decisive touch by substitute Jemson set up an 85th-minute equaliser for Warhurst. In the Hillsborough replay, it was Warhurst's lone goal (his 17th of the season and a typical first-touch strike) after 23 minutes that clinched it.

The night before Wednesday's triumph over Derby, United had overcome Blackburn in a dramatic replay at Bramall Lane—completing a nightmare three days for Rovers, who, on the previous Sunday, had gone out of the Coca-Cola Cup in the second leg of their semi-final with the Owls at Hillsborough. United had emerged with a 0–0 draw in the first quarter-final game at Ewood Park on March 6th, and it is intriguing to ponder on what might have happened had the replay been staged in the week following this meeting—which is what would have happened in previous years. Alas, we had now reached that stage in sporting history when a 10-day gap was required by the police to make arrangements. Poor Rovers found their hopes of progress on both cup fronts hampered by having to play two crucial games between Sunday afternoon and Tuesday evening—and both in Sheffield.

In that Bramall Lane replay Blackburn led twice, and only seven minutes of 'normal' time remained when substitute Mitch Ward got United's first equaliser. Then three minutes from the end of extra-time, Ward again saved the Blades by making the score 2–2. The game went to a penalty shoot-out, and Ward set the lead by converting the first spot-kick. Alan Kelly saved a Jason Wilcox

penalty, and when John Pemberton became the fifth home man to convert, United were through on a 5–3 margin.

After Wednesday joined them in the semi-final, the battle to get the tie switched to Wembley began in earnest and, gratefully, it was a triumph for common-sense.

Saturday April 13th 1993 was undoubtedly the peak of Sheffield's season: United's first visit to Wembley since 1936, and Wednesday's first in the FA Cup since 1966—though the Owls had won there in the 1991 Rumbelows Cup final. Sheffield supporters turned the occasion into a carnival, creating a wonderful atmosphere, and while the rivalry was as keen as ever, it was a rare day when the circumstances of being together 160 miles from home, and at English football's most prestigious venue, ensured a good-natured gathering at which nobody really felt Sheffield could lose. Such a friendly occasion, indeed, that a week earlier the rival managers Dave Bassett and Trevor Francis had spent a short holiday together in Italy.

The Blades had problems which forced them to use Dane Whitehouse (he had missed much of the season with a serious leg injury) at left-back;

A duel between Mark Bright (Wednesday) and John Pemberton (United) in the Wembley FA Cup semi-final.

while Wednesday, having Pearson (broken leg) and Shirtliff (broken arm) out, were using Palmer at centre-back alongside acting skipper Viv Anderson. The Owls also chose to start with Bright and Warhurst up front. The men who figured in this famous game were:

United: Kelly; Gage, Gayle, Pemberton, Whitehouse; Carr, Gannon, Ward (Littlejohn 96 min), Hodges (Hoyland 91 min); Deane, Cork.

Wednesday: Woods; Nilsson, Palmer, Anderson, Worthington; Waddle, Wilson, Sheridan (Hyde 110 mins), Harkes; Warhurst (Hirst 60 min), Bright.

Referee: Kelvin Morton (Suffolk).

The game had an unforgettable opening, for within 62 seconds of the kick-off, after Pemberton had fouled Bright as they went for a high ball together, Chris Waddle shot Wednesday in front by hammering a 30-yard free-kick into the roof of goalkeeper Alan Kelly's net. Kelly and the Blades' players were not the only ones taken by surprise; so were Waddle's colleagues, and even John Sheridan didn't believe the Geordie when, as he placed the ball for the kick, he insisted he was going to have a 'pot' at goal from that distance.

The early breakthrough gave Wednesday confidence, and they went on to create abundant chances. Yet, as had happened in so many League games, they failed to profit from their superiority. Warhurst clipped United's bar and hit a post, and when, a minute before half-time, Franz Carr dispossessed Harkes down the right and found the unmarked Cork with a long pass, the former Wimbledon man's equaliser from just inside the penalty area prompted many to wonder whether the tide was

about to turn. Cork, incidentally, was sporting a beard he had started growing early on the cup run, and it had become a lucky omen.

In truth, United never showed the qualities which had so often been their strength in previous games with Wednesday. It was a marvellous occasion, but somehow it lacked the fire of a traditional derby. Perhaps the experience of Wembley proved too inhibiting, and the Blades must have wondered how different a story it might have been had the game been staged in more 'ordinary' surroundings (like Elland Road!). Wednesday continued to dominate and, though Hirst, coming on for Warhurst as 60th-minute substitute, showed his lack of fitness by missing a couple of chances he might normally have taken, United hung on thanks largely to the heroics of Kelly. The goalkeeper denied Hirst, Sheridan and Bright with a string of outstanding saves, as United forced the game into extra time and raised fears in the Owls' camp that the Blades were destined to snatch victory against the odds.

The breakthrough arrived 17 minutes into the extra half-hour, and came from a left-wing corner-kick—in fact it was to be from that very same spot that Arsenal would deliver the cross which denied Wednesday FA Cup final glory a month later. Harkes delivered his flag-kick perfectly to the front post and Bright, eluding marker Deane, headed his 17th goal of the season.

The former Crystal Palace striker later related that, before the game, Trevor Francis had told him: 'You'll be our match-winner today'. Ironically, player and manager did not always see eye-to-eye in later years.

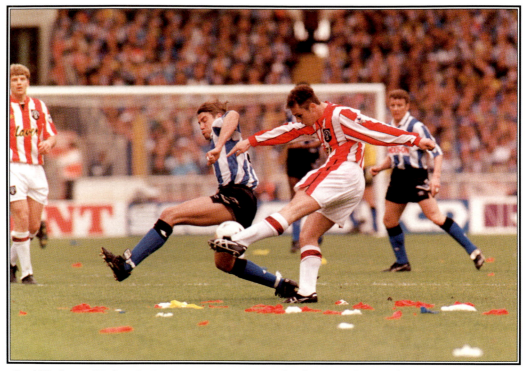

Paul Warhurst (Wednesday) tries to prevent Dane Whitehouse making a clearance on a Wembley pitch littered with burst balloons.

Wednesday learned within twenty-four hours of the match that they would face Arsenal in both cup finals, for George Graham's team beat Tottenham in the other Wembley semi-final—a poor game compared with the Sheffield match.

As was noted in the previous chapter, the Owls' run to the Coca Cola Cup final saw them defeat Hartlepool over two legs (aggregate 5–2), crush Leicester 7–1 and QPR 4–0, and then, after beating Ipswich 1–0 in a home replay, they ousted Blackburn Rovers in a semi-final in which the first leg at Ewood Park produced the performance of the competition.

So, a fortnight after their triumph over the Blades, Wednesday returned

F.A. CUP SEMI-FINAL
SATURDAY 3 APRIL 1993

SHEFFIELD

UNITED

v

SHEFFIELD

WEDNESDAY

KICK - OFF 1.00 P.M.

OFFICIAL MATCHDAY PROGRAMME £4.00

to Wembley on April 18th for their first final with Arsenal—a game, incidentally, watched by 1,300 fewer spectators than had been at the all-Sheffield game. The only change was at left-back, where Phil King replaced the suspended Worthington. Wednesday began splendidly, with Warhurst hitting a post after only four minutes, and Sheffield fans having a goal to cheer within less than ten minutes of the kick-off. Sheridan's free-kick sent King clear on the left, and Harkes pounced to score when the back's centre was not cleared. Unfortunately, Paul Merson not only levelled for Arsenal after 18 minutes, but began to prove a key influence on proceedings, and the omens were not good for the Owls when Anderson suffered a head injury and completed the game with his head swathed in a bandage. It was Merson who provided the centre which produced the winning goal after 67 minutes, for, when Carlton Palmer succeeded only in turning the ball into the path of Steve Morrow, the youngster (who had not scored a senior goal before and was preoccupied for most of the game tracking Sheridan) gratefully drilled the ball into the net from eight yards.

It was a day when Wednesday did not do themselves justice. 'We could have played much better', admitted Francis. 'We let Arsenal close us down, and in the second half we just didn't pass the ball properly. The result was all the more disappointing because we were beaten by a side that also didn't play particularly well.' The teams were:

Wednesday and Arsenal walking out for the 1993 FA Cup final.

David Hirst will not recall 1992-93 as one of his luckiest years, but he was delighted with his goal against Arsenal in the FA Cup final.

Wednesday: Woods; Nilsson, Palmer, Anderson, King (Hyde 83 min); Waddle, Wilson (Hirst 73 min), Sheridan, Harkes; Warhurst, Bright.

Arsenal: Seaman; O'Leary, Linighan, Adams, Winterburn; Davis, Parlour, Morrow, Merson; Wright, Campbell.

The referee was Allan Gunn (Sussex) and it is of interest to note that one of the linesmen was John Hilditch, the official who had taken over from the injured Michael Peck during the vital Premier League game with Manchester United eight days earlier—and played the 'extra time' which had enabled Bruce to give the Old Trafford club a vital victory that set them on course for the Championship.

When Wednesday met Arsenal in the FA Cup final on May 15th, the big challenge was to prove their North London opponents had not gained a psychological advantage from their earlier victory. Francis was confident. The Owls were boosted by the return of Worthington, while Hirst, starting his first tie since being injured at Ipswich in January, was brought back into the attack because the manager was keen to use Palmer in midfield. Warhurst, albeit with great reluctance, accepted a switch into central defence alongside Anderson; and King and Danny Wilson were the men to miss out.

On the eve of the big game, Waddle received his FWA Footballer of the Year trophy, but Arsenal ensured the

former England man did not have a chance to make an impact on a poor match which gave the 79,347 crowd little to enthuse about—but had the novelty of being the first final in which the teams wore shirts bearing their names and squad numbers.

Wednesday started well but fell behind after 21 minutes when Bright conceded a free-kick from which Davis flighted a ball into the goal mouth, Linighan headed it across the penalty area, and Ian Wright climbed above Warhurst to head beyond Woods. It was not until after half-time that the Owls regained the initiative,

but they got their reward within 17 minutes of the restart, when Hirst equalised with his first FA Cup goal of the season. The game dragged into extra-time but, though Wednesday's domination was reflected in a corner count of 20 to 7, they were unable to break the deadlock. The teams were:

Arsenal: Seaman; Dixon, Linighan, Adams, Winterburn; Davis, Parlour (Smith 65 min), Jensen, Merson; Campbell, Wright (O'Leary 90 min).

Wednesday: Woods; Nilsson, Anderson (Hyde 85 min), Warhurst, Worthington; Palmer, Waddle (Bart-Williams 112 min), Sheridan, Harkes; Hirst, Bright.

Referee: K. Barratt (Coventry).

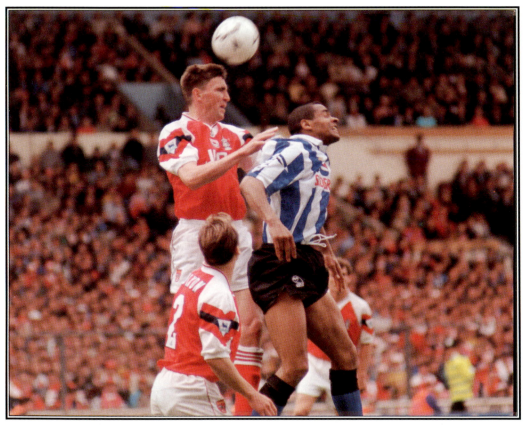

Arsenal's Linighan beats Wednesday's Bright in an aerial challenge in the FA Cup final. In the replay the big defender was to score the goal which gave the Gunners a dramatic victory in the last minute of extra time...and, ironically, Linighan had two brothers on the Hillsborough staff!

When the replay was staged the following Thursday, Wednesday were without the injured Anderson, and so Palmer took over the captaincy and reverted to central defence alongside Warhurst, with Wilson replacing him in midfield. The Owls had feared they might have to manage without Nilsson, who had no option but to turn out for Sweden, against Austria in Stockholm, on the previous evening, but the back flew to London straight after the international.

For the first time since 1923 the kick-off in a Wembley final was delayed, in this instance because a crash on the M1 motorway held up thousands of Sheffield supporters. When the latecomers arrived and the game began, Arsenal snatched the initiative after 35 minutes when Smith touched on a long ball and enabled Wright to dash between Palmer and Warhurst and clip the ball over Woods and into the net. The Owls equalised on 69 minutes, when a crossfield ball from Harkes found Waddle and he delivered a first-time shot which was deflected past the Gunners' goalkeeper off defender Dixon.

Bright subsequently hit a post and missed the target with a header, and the game, having again proved a dour affair and gone into extra-time, was looking set for a penalty shoot-out when Arsenal snatched victory with barely 50 seconds remaining. A fortuitous deflection took the ball out for a left-wing corner, and when Merson floated it in, defender Andy Linighan climbed to meet it with his head. Woods got his hands to the ball but was unable to prevent it spinning beyond him and across the line. In those agonising moments, Wednesday supporters in the 62,267 crowd watched in disbelief as the goal-keeper's fumble allowed their dream of glory to slip away. It was a night that ended in tears. Four trips to Wembley, and a 63-match season in which the Owls had lost only 16 times, scored 106 goals but had finished with nothing to celebrate except a brush with glory that whetted the appetite for a more substantial taste of success. Would it come soon? Expectations had never been so high.

Teams in the replay:

Wednesday: Woods; Nilsson (Bart-Williams 119 mins), Palmer, Warhurst, Worthington; Waddle, Wilson (Hyde 62 mins), Harkes, Sheridan; Hirst, Bright.

Arsenal: Seaman; Dixon, Linighan, Adams, Winterburn; Davis, Jensen, Campbell, Merson; Smith, Wright (O'Leary 83 mins).

Referee: K. Barratt (Coventry).

Blades and Owls, 1994–1995

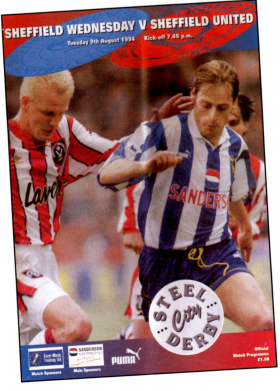

AT THE START of the 1994-95 campaign there were many observers who thought it would be no surprise if Dave Bassett did not see out the season at Bramall Lane, but few would have predicted that Trevor Francis was approaching the end of the line at Hillsborough. In the event, Bassett, though weary of struggling on a shoestring, rejected the chance to quit the Blades in December when nobody would have blamed him for moving on; while Francis saw a climate develop in which his position became the subject of increasing speculation and, long before the axe finally fell in May, he knew his days with the Owls were numbered.

It was one of those years when, unfortunately, the football was often overshadowed by off-the-field events, for it was a term dominated by an atmosphere of mounting discontent and protest on the terraces; with an independent Sheffield United supporters group leading demon-strations against chairman Reg Brealey, whilst some Wednesday fans made Francis the target of their frustrations when the season began and ended on a negative note.

United's hopes of regaining their Premiership status at the first attempt were dashed when a poor finale saw them finish in eighth place in the First Division. As a planned reduction in the size of the elite top-grade meant only one automatic promotion place (and big-spending Middlesbrough

Cover of programme for Steel City derby match, August 1994.

and Wolves were favourites to get that), the play-offs seemed to offer the most realistic route back up, and making the top five did not look beyond the Blades' capabilities.

True, they began the campaign badly, winning only two of their first seven games to find themselves in the bottom group in mid-September but, after enduring more gloom with three successive defeats in October, by the end of November they had launched

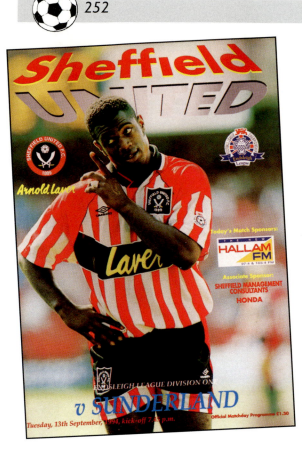

Sheffield United programme cover featuring Nathan Blake.

though such results at Bramall Lane against the likes of Middlesbrough and Wolves were not entirely disappointing, overall it was felt that the habit which cost them their Premiership status a year earlier had now torpedoed promotion dreams. Overall, they failed too often against struggling sides. Nathan Blake, who started only 28 matches, topped the scoring charts with 17 League goals, whilst newcomer Carl Veart, in his first season in English football, managed eleven.

Wednesday began the season even more badly than the Blades, for they won only one of the first 8 matches and 3 of the first 14. They were familiar with poor starts, but this time never really promised the kind of sustained recovery of previous seasons. Three straight victories in late December launched an unbeaten

a run of five victories in seven matches—which would have been six in eight had Wolves not forced a dramatic and sensational draw at Molineux with two goals in injury-time. One of the successes in this spell was a remarkable 6–3 triumph at David Pleat's Luton which highlighted United's potential.

By March, a mere two defeats in 21 games ensured they were well in contention for the play-offs, but sadly, they managed only two wins in their last 11 fixtures. In the final analysis, their undoing was again a tendency to draw too many games. In fact, nine of their 17 draws came in home matches and,

Sheffield United programme cover featuring Carl Veart.

Mark Bright.

Owls to a 7–1 record home defeat. Wednesday finished thirteenth in the table but the shadow of relegation loomed until almost the end of the season. Bright, with eleven goals, was the only marksman to reach double figures.

Sheffield United's relegation in 1994 had not diminished the high regard in which Blades' supporters held Dave Bassett, and aware of speculation that frustration over continuing limited resources might persuade him to leave, they were anxious to ensure he stayed. It was largely due to the messages of support from fans following the slide into Division One that Bassett accepted a one-year extension to his contract in 1994 and committed himself to the club until 1996. He did, however, decline a longer deal, commenting: 'It's important for me to see how ambitious the club is. I want to see they mean business. The board have got to be proving to me in the next two years that they really want to get back to the Premiership'.

With the John Street stand demolished and Bramall Lane a three-sided ground for the first time since the mid-1970s, Bassett hoped a new structure might be in place within a year or so as further concrete evidence of the club's aspirations. Bassett knew there were still only very limited resources available for team strengthening, but no doubt hoped something might happen to improve the situation; for the present, he was heartened by a promise made when he signed his new deal in 1994 that he could spend whatever he raised from sales. His only pre-season signings were two Australians, international striker Veart,

eight-match run, but they emerged with maximum points from only three of their last 15 games and suffered nine defeats; and their campaign seemed to disintegrate from the moment they went out of the FA Cup in a penalty shoot-out (losing 4–3 after leading 3–0!) in the fourth round replay against First Division Wolves at Molineux in early February. The gathering gloom was compounded when Nottingham Forest visited Hillsborough in April and sent the

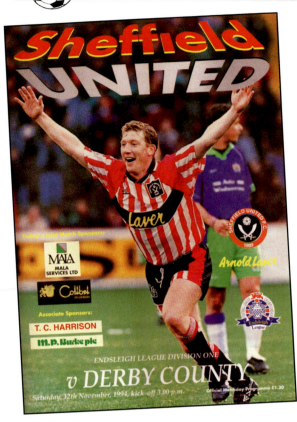

Sheffield United programme cover featuring Kevin Gage.

who cost £250,000 from Adelaide City, and defender Doug Hodgson, a £30,000 buy from Heidelberg (Western Australia), and in October, an independent tribunal put an initial £75,000 price tag on Billy Mercer, a young goalkeeper recruited from Rotherham United.

So, when the summer departures of Carl Bradshaw (Norwich, £500,000) and Tom Cowan (Huddersfield, £150,000) were followed by deals which took Franz Carr to Leicester for £100,000 and Jamie Hoyland to Burnley for £130,000, he believed a substantial sum was still available to invest. However, in November he revealed the board had told him 'that

due to financial limitations I cannot after all have the profit I've made on transfers'. (His only other major signing during the season, and one he had to battle to push through, was former Nottingham Forest forward Phil Starbuck, who cost £158,000 from Huddersfield in January after initially arriving on loan in October).

It was another broken promise and, naturally, Bassett was disappointed. Around this time he revealed that two years earlier he had rejected overtures from three Premiership clubs, and commented: 'Perhaps I should have jacked the job in then. I stayed because I felt a tremendous sense of loyalty to United. But with hindsight maybe I should have got out when the going was good and not let my heart rule my head. If I had known what was going to develop, I might have made a different decision'. It was typical of the man that he added: 'Yet, despite the financial restrictions I have had to work under, I have no regrets about staying, and nothing would please me more than to complete ten years here in 1998'.

The combination of circumstances, which some supporters did not believe inspired an optimistic outlook, had already induced the emergence of the Blades Independent Fans Association, a group who made their goal the removal of chairman Brealey. After the home defeat against Luton in late October, they staged a demonstration in the car park, and they again voiced opposition to the board before the game with Derby in mid-November. Most people recognised that Brealey had returned to the helm with great reluctance in 1993 when Paul Woolhouse defaulted on the payments of his purchase, and it was generally assumed he would sell up again if the opportunity arose. However, at half-time in the Derby game he formally announced on the electronic scoreboard: 'I have decided the time is right to make available the majority shareholding to a buyer who must be a man of substance'. He intimated that many of the so-called prospective purchasers he had dealt with before, and no doubt many he would hear from again, were 'publicity seekers' without the funds to negotiate a deal.

Brealey insisted he would not be forced into a hasty sale by militant supporters, and said: 'They may want a change, but I will not be rushed into a quick sell. If I can find someone to take over from me, I will, but I will not sell to someone without money who could come in, rip off the club, abandon our plans to build a new stand, sell the players and send us back to the old Fourth Division'.

When he indicated that he wanted £3.5 million for his shares, some were prompted to argue that, in view of what he had invested since his original arrival, he had every right to ask for what he considered an appropriate price. Others questioned whether he really expected to find a buyer at that figure. BIFA members, maintaining he was asking too much, went on with their demonstrations.

Brealey was quoted at one point as reflecting with dismay at the difference between the fans who had hailed him a hero, when he helped rescue the Blades at the start of the 1980s, and those who now cast him as the villain of the piece. He could perhaps argue that he had invested more in the club than any of his predecessors, and may well have

wondered whether any of his critics ever looked back into the more distant past and identified those who had set United on course for their initial slide twenty years earlier. Were those directors ever pilloried? Maybe it occurred to some supporters that it was others who had helped create the circumstances which allowed control of the club to pass into the hands of one individual.

Of course few people, and especially football supporters, care about cause and effect or what happened yesterday. They live for today, base their judgements on current performance, and though not in a financial position to buy control for themselves, they care passionately for their club and feel they can only influence events by voicing their displeasure at the apparent evidence of failure they see in the club's leadership. It is a means by which many a manager has been removed (and proved a lethal 'weapon' in prompting the departures of McEwan and Porterfield); but chairmen, especially those with a majority shareholding, are not so easily persuaded to depart. Reg Brealey had said he was prepared to go, but on his terms, and he not only felt he had good reason to feel his critics did not understand his dilemma, but believed that, were they in his shoes, they would act exactly as he had done.

Now BIFA's earlier 'red card' (a symbol of dismissal) demonstration was followed by one at the Southend game in late November when green (for 'go') cards were featured. Unfortunately, it made for a hostile afternoon which did not please manager Bassett, even though United won a poor game 2–0. When Veart scored United's second goal, home supporters celebrated by chanting 'sack the board'.

Said Bassett: 'The atmosphere at this club on match days is terrible. It is created by fans because of their frustration, but the players fear they are waiting for them to lose so they can beat up the stadium and smash it. If they've got a problem with the board, they should demonstrate before the game or after—not while the players are trying to perform. To be quiet and wait until we're 2–0 up to shout 'sack the board' is not helping the team'.

It was soon after this game that Brealey, perhaps not realising how it would be interpreted, intimated that he would not stand in Bassett's way if a top club came in for him. What the chairman actually said in reply to an interviewer was: 'The question is hypothetical because no club has contacted me, but basically I would always inform my manager first, and you cannot keep a discontented man. But I like to think we have a good relationship and Dave is not the sort of man to walk out on a job'.

It was not then widely known that Aston Villa, having sacked ex-Owls manager Ron Atkinson in early November, had Bassett on their wanted list—and 'Deadly' Doug Ellis, their chairman, actually spoke to him. However, Villa's top target was their former player, Brian Little, then manager of Leicester, and within a few days, he accepted the job—albeit in controversial circumstances which did little to enhance the image of the game. Bassett immediately emerged as the man being sought to fill the Filbert Street hot-seat, but though Brealey gave Leicester permission

to approach him, the United boss declined the opportunity to even talk about the vacancy. He showed loyalty when others in his situation might not have done, though in truth, it would have been a sideways and not upward move if he had gone to the Midlands.

Brealey remained under fire from some fans, and before the final game of the 1994-95 campaign, against Grimsby, he sought to appease his critics by announcing the go-ahead for the new £4 million John Street stand. The aim was to have it completed by January 1996. Unfortunately, problems arose which prevented United obtaining loan of the necessary finance, and when the Blades kicked off the 1995-96 campaign, work had still not started on the project. It was another setback, but Bassett remained remarkably philosophical. Indeed, he accepted another one-year extension to his contract and committed himself to stay until mid-1997. In the meantime, the ownership saga remained unsolved until late September 1995, when circumstances brought things to a head and Brealey sold his shares to Manchester-based Mike McDonald, a fifty-three year-old businessman with engineering and metals interests.

The irony of United's problem with the building of a new John Street stand was that, across the city at Hillsborough, Wednesday were proceeding with the latest £5 million investment in redevelopment due for completion ahead of the ground's use as a venue for the European Championships in the summer of 1996. What the Owls had managed to achieve on and off the field served only to rub salt in the wounded pride of every Blades' fan.

Dan Petrescu.

Aston Villa, and after striker Nigel Jemson was sold to Notts County for around £300,000 in September, centre-back Simon Coleman left for Bolton in October. Towards the end of the season, striker Gordon Watson was the subject of a £1.2 million transfer to Southampton.

Ahead of the campaign, Francis spent £4.6 million. Rumanian international defender Dan Petrescu, capped 41 times, arrived from Genoa for £1.3 million; left-back Ian Nolan, boasting 88 League appearances for Tranmere, cost £1.5 million; Port Vale midfielder Ian Taylor (83 League appearances, 28 goals) was rated at £1

However, 1994-95 had proved a far from successful term for Wednesday, and the decline in their fortunes had cost manager Trevor Francis his job. In this instance, the voice of the fans had influenced the board's decision to terminate his contract a year early in May 1995; Dave Richards was a chairman who prided himself on maintaining close links with sup-porters. As a humble kid from Walkley he had stood on the Hillsborough terraces himself and remained a fan at heart. He regularly sounded out Kop opinion.

As was noted in a previous chapter, Wednesday parted company with defenders Roland Nilsson, Nigel Pearson and Nigel Worthington and former England midfielder Carlton Palmer in the summer of 1994. Another defender, Phil King, joined

Ian Nolan.

million by an independent tribunal; and former Wigan defender Peter Atherton (296 League and Cup appearances) came from Coventry for £800,000. When, in September, the manager recruited Swedish international midfielder Klas Ingesson (51 caps) from PSV Eindhoven, it was initially believed he had cost £2 million, but in December Francis revealed the fee had been £50,000 down, with £750,000 to pay a year later.

It emerged that Ingesson, a pal of Roland Nilsson's, had arrived with a stomach injury which limited his appearances (he started only nine League games all season). Petrescu, too, managed fewer outings than might have been expected (20 plus 9 as substitute), but Nolan emerged an ever-present, and Atherton, who was voted Player of the Year by supporters, only missed one match.

Francis was over-endowed in midfield areas but short on players with a scoring touch. Taylor made only 14 League appearances (five as a substitute) and, with the tenacious Graham Hyde (one of the few senior players who had not cost a fee) and Sheridan excelling, he was unable to command a place in his preferred central midfield role. It was no surprise when Taylor departed in December, for with the manager desperate for an experienced striker but by now having exceeded his budget, it made sense to set up the deal which took him to Aston Villa for £1 million, with Wednesday getting Guy Whittingham for £600,000.

Hirst, again blighted by injury setbacks, was out of the side from late October until early April, and Wednesday, having scored five goals

Chris Waddle . . . proved a great favourite in his time with the Owls.

Andy Sinton.

in their first two matches (but losing both), managed only 14 in the next 17 Premiership games. Whittingham gave the team fresh impetus by scoring twice in each of his first two outings, as the Owls celebrated Christmas with victories at Everton (4–1) and at home to Coventry (5–1). Alas, they did not signal a lasting revival.

Frustration seemed to beckon at every turn, and even positive moments tended to be tempered by negative elements. Waddle's long-awaited return in December after a year-long battle with Achilles trouble coincided with a victory over Crystal Palace (it was the first time the Owls had managed two successive home wins all season), but this was the game at which 'Back him or sack him' leaflets were distributed to spectators when they arrived at the ground. The leaflets, which advertised a telephone poll allegedly intended to gauge support for the manager, were the brainchild of an anti-Francis faction, and while it was announced that profits from the exercise would go to charity, the organisers clearly extended no charitable feelings towards the subject of the vote.

It was not the first evidence that Francis was coming under increasing fire. In mid-September the *News of the World* had carried an 'exclusive' story under the headline 'We Want You Out Trev!' in which an unnamed player alleged he and his colleagues were critical of his man-management and tactics. The claims were subsequently refuted by several players, but the original story and follow-ups in every leading news-paper did untold damage. At the time, the official line was one of dismay that an insider would make such statements, yet lack the courage to identify himself. Even the by-line on the article was not the name of a 'real' person. It was suggested that the 'mole' would be weeded out, but he was never officially named, though it was generally recognised that he was still playing for the Owls long after Francis had gone.

There was never a time when Francis needed a good run of results more, but after the Owls had ended December with three straight wins they endured another modest spell—and hopes of a morale-boosting FA Cup run collapsed in remarkable circumstances. A home fourth-round date with First Division promotion contenders Wolves in late January seemed to offer the prospect of the kind of big occasion which could lift Wednesday and, with the right scoreline, mark a belated turning point in their season.

Alas, they emerged with a goalless draw in which the disappointment was exacerbated when Bart-Williams failed with an 88th-minute penalty. It was Wednesday's third spot-kick miss of the season, but not their last: for the Molineux replay would produce a dramatic hat-trick of failures. The replay saw the Owls come from behind to equalise through Bright, but the striker wasted a good chance to settle the issue in the last minute of extra-time. That old cliché which suggests it is in such moments that a manager's destiny can be shaped must have occurred to Francis for the first of several times at that point in the evening. But at least Bright had the courage to take the first penalty in the shoot-out; and when Whittingham and Kevin Pressman were also successful while Wolves failed with their first two attempts, a Wednesday triumph looked a formality. Alas, Andy Pearce then hit the crossbar, Bart-Williams saw his shot saved and, when the tie became a sudden-death affair, Waddle was unable to beat the goalkeeper. Wolves won 4–3.

The Sheffield supporters were stunned, and everyone in the

Kevin Pressman

Wednesday camp was devastated by the unexpected twist which had seen their fortunes plummet with painful suddenness. Nobody cut a sorrier sight as the players trooped off than Waddle, so often the darling of the fans. After a much-publicised failure in a penalty shoot-out in England's World Cup semi-final with Germany in 1990, he had vowed never to take another. Now he had, and the upshot was another unwelcome footnote to an otherwise memorable career.

Four days later the Owls visited title-chasing Blackburn, and suffered

Des Walker.

the first of three successive defeats in a match remembered for goalkeeper Pressman's second sending off in five weeks. In fact, Wednesday lost seven of the nine fixtures which followed their Cup defeat, and that sequence concluded with the heaviest home setback in the club's League history— a 7–1 crushing by Nottingham Forest, the club who had once paid the first £1 million transfer fee for Francis.

The manager's future was now the subject of open debate, and he knew he could not survive. He took the players away ahead of the next game, at home to Leicester, and those who were close to him knew the outward show of high spirits was the gesture of a condemned man. Wednesday returned to Hillsborough and, with several changes, beat Leicester 1–0; but a mere two points from their next four games left them facing their final match, at home to Ipswich, still mathematically involved in the relegation scramble. They won 4–1 and other results the same day meant they would have survived anyway but, perhaps significantly, Francis did not join in the traditional final day postmatch celebrations— and the fans who had so recently chanted 'We want Francis out' did not call his name.

Right to the end of his final Press conference, Francis refused to be drawn by questions about his future. The silence from within the boardroom was, perhaps, understandable, but while the directors preferred to neither deny nor confirm the rumours about the manager's fate until the season was over, the situation served only to increase speculation which spanned six or seven weeks. Unlike the directors (and the board was equally divided on the issue), Francis could not avoid the media, and it has to be said that, publicly, he emerged from a difficult final few weeks with dignity.

It was just six days after the formal end of the season, on the morning of the FA Cup final, that Wednesday confirmed his contract had been terminated. Exactly two years earlier it was Wednesday who had been at Wembley.

Before the start of the 1995-96 campaign, the Owls launched a new era by recruiting Luton manager David Pleat as Francis's successor. He brought in Danny Bergara as his assistant, and Richie Barker stood down from first-team duties within the new set-up.

It is relevant to note that 1995 saw the deaths of former chairman Bert McGee and ex-player and commercial manager Dennis Woodhead, while long-serving director Ernest Barron retired. They were a trio who had been involved in the revival launched in the mid-70s.

A footnote which traditionalists found somewhat painful, was the decision by both United and Wednesday to dispense with striped shirts in 1995-96. That, as they say, is progress, but perhaps what the players wear will not matter if the Sheffield clubs achieve the right results, give supporters plenty to cheer and, as the 21st century beckons, add lustre to the story of football in the city which was the birthplace of the organised game back in 1857!

Honours List

League Championship Successes

Sheffield United: 1897-98

Sheffield Wednesday: 1902-03, 1903-04, 1928-29, 1929-30

United were runners-up in the old Division One in 1897 and 1900; Wednesday finished second in 1960-61.

Division Two Successes

Sheffield United: Champions 1952-53

Promoted: 1892-93, 1938-39, 1960-61, 1970-71, 1989-90

Sheffield Wednesday: Champions 1899-1900, 1925-26, 1951-52, 1955-56, 1958-59

Promoted: 1949-50, 1983-84, 1990-91

Division Three Successes

Sheffield United: Promoted 1983-84, 1988-89

Sheffield Wednesday: Promoted 1979-80

Division Four Successes

Sheffield United: Champions 1981-82

Sheffield Clubs in FA Cup Finals

1890	Blackburn Rovers	6–1	Sheffield Wednesday
1896	Sheffield Wednesday	2–1	Wolverhampton W
1899	Sheffield United	4–1	Derby County
1901	Tottenham H	2–2	Sheffield United
	Tottenham H	3–1	Sheffield United
1902	Sheffield United	1–1	Southampton
	Sheffield United	2–1	Southampton
1907	Sheffield Wednesday	2–1	Everton
1915	Sheffield United	3–0	Chelsea
1925	Sheffield United	1–0	Cardiff City
1935	Sheffield Wednesday	4–2	West Bromwich Albion
1936	Arsenal	1–0	Sheffield United
1966	Everton	3–2	Sheffield Wednesday
1993	Arsenal	1–1	Sheffield Wednesday (after extra time)
	Arsenal	2–1	Sheffield Wednesday (after extra time)

Note: Wednesday have appeared in 16 FA Cup semi-finals, while Sheffield United have reached that stage on 11 occasions.

Sheffield Clubs in League Cup Finals

1991	Sheffield Wednesday	1–0	Manchester United
1993	Arsenal	2–1	Sheffield Wednesday

Note: Sheffield Wednesday won the FA Charity Shield in 1935.

Sheffield United 1970-71, Promoted from Division Two.

Appearances: Hodgkinson 24, Hope 17, Crawford 1, Badger 42, Hemsley 40, Powell 31, Colquhoun 40, Heaton 2 (1), Flynn 9, Salmons 25 (4), Barlow 13 (2), Addison 11 (1), Barnwell 9, Hockey 17, Woodward 42, Tudor 21 (2), Dearden 40 (1), Currie 42, Reece 27 (4), Ford 9 (2), Buckley 0 (1).

Goals (73 League): Woodward 15, Dearden 14, Tudor 9, Currie 9, Reece 8, Colquhoun 6, Hemsley 2, Barnwell 2, Flynn 1, Salmons 1, Addison 1, Powell 1, Hockey 1, Ford 1. own-goals 2.

Coach: Cec Coldwell

Sheffield Football Club: FA Vase Finalists 1976-77.

They lost to Billericay 2–1 in a replay at the City Ground, Nottingham, after the first meeting, at Wembley, had ended in a 1–1 draw after extra time. Sheffield's team in the final was: Wing, Gilbody, Lodge, Strutt (Hardisty in the first match, subbed by Strutt), Watts, Skelton, Kay, Travis, Pugh, Thornhill, Haines. Their run to the final featured victories against Tadcaster, Clitheroe, Arnold Kingswell, Friar Lane OB, Anson Villa, East Ham United, and Barton R.

Sheffield Wednesday 1979-80, Promoted from Division Three.

Appearances: Blackhall 35, Bolder 31, Cox 15, Curran 41, Fleming 7, Grant 43, Hornsby 33, Johnson 32 (3), King 32 (3), Leman 6 (4), Lowey 11 (2), McCulloch 30, Mellor 32 (5), Mullen 14 (1), Owen 4, Pickering 32, Porterfield 20 (2), Shirtliff 3, Smith 44, Sterland 0 (2), Strutt 2, Taylor 21, Williamson 3, Wylde 15.

Goals: Curran 22, McCulloch 12, Mellor 11, Smith 9, Wylde 8, Taylor 6, Grant 1, Hornsby 3, Johnson 1, King 3, Lowey 1, Mullen 2, Owen 1, Porterfield 1.

Note: Smith's goals were all penalties, and he also scored twice with spot-kicks in cup competitions.

Sheffield United 1981-82 Division Four Champions.

Appearances: Waugh 45, Ryan 19, Kenworthy 45, Matthews 24 (1), MacPhail 26, McAlle 18, Trusson 44, Tibbott 3, Neville 22 (8), Hatton 45, Charles 28 (2), Wiggan 3 (2), Garner 34, Moore 4, Richardson 19 (1), Edwards 41, Houston 27, Broddle 1, King 22, Morris 23, Casey 12, Conroy 1, Brazil 0 (1).

Goals: Edwards 35, Hatton 15, Kenworthy 15 (9 pens), Trusson 11, King 4, Morris 4, Neville 4, Matthews 3, Charles 1, MacPhail 1, Richardson 1.

Note: John McSeveney, the former Barnsley manager, was manager Ian Porterfield's assistant.

Sheffield Wednesday 1983-84. Promoted from Division Two.

Appearances: Bannister 36, Cunningham 26 (2), Heard 2 (3), Hodge 42, Lyons 42, Madden 38, Megson 42, S. Mills 1 (1), Morris 8 (5), Oliver 3 (2), J. Pearson 21 (6), Shelton 40, Shirtliff 36, M. Smith 29, Sterland 39, Taylor 1 (4), Varadi 35 (3), Williamson 9 (1), Worthington 14.

Goals: Varadi 17, Bannister 14, Sterland 8, Cunningham 5, Lyons 5, Shelton 5, Megson 4, Pearson 4, Smith 2, Heard 1, Madden 1, Morris 1, Shirtliff 1, Worthington 1, own-goals 3.

It is well known that, before Wednesday recruited Howard Wilkinson as manager in 1983 they tried to get Watford's Graham Taylor. Later, when Sheffield United were looking for a successor to Ian Porterfield, they also sought in vain to sign the man who subsequently managed Aston Villa and became England team boss in 1990.

Sheffield United 1983-84. Promoted from Division Three.
Appearances: Waugh 16, Atkins 13 (3), Garner 24, Arnott 46, Stancliffe 43, Henderson 21 (1), Morris 42, Trusson 11, Edwards 44, McHale 42, Brazil 8 (11), Heffernan 42, Bolton 45, Kenworthy 8, Charles 11, Philliskirk 20 (1), Tomlinson 30, West 24, Ross 4, Smith 2 (1), Cockerill 10.
Goals: Edwards 33, Morris 20 (10 penalties), Philliskirk 8, Arnott 6, Atkins 3, Trusson 3, Brazil 2, Heffernan 2, Bolton 1, Charles 1, Cockerill 1, Garner 1, Kenworthy 1, McHale 1, Stancliffe 1, own-goals 2.
Note: Paul Garner was the only survivor from the side relegated to Division Four in 1981, and in fact, he had played in the side that went down from the old First Division in 1976. Jim McGuigan, the former Chesterfield and Rotherham manager, joined United's coaching staff in November 1983, which was the same month as the long-serving Cec Coldwell's second testimonial game (the first had been in October 1966) at Bramall Lane.

Sheffield United 1988-89. Promoted from Division Three.
League appearances: Benstead 39, Powell 2 (2), Pike 45, Webster 12, Stancliffe 42, Smith 34 (1), Roberts 25 (4), Todd 39, Joseph 5 (8), Deane 43, Bryson 36 (1), Agana 44 (2), Wilder 29, Duffield 25 (13), Barnsley 1 (2), Williams 1 (1), Francis 3 (19), Dickinson 0 (1), Whitehouse 3 (2), C. Downes 2, Carr 9 (1), Booker 26, Ryan 2 (1), Thompson 20, Gannon 8 (8), Tracey 7, Moore 4 (1).
Goals: Agana 24, Deane 22, Duffield 11 (5 penalties), Bryson 8, Pike 5, Todd 4, Joseph 3, Stancliffe 3, Booker 2, Roberts 2, Webster 2, Carr 1, Francis 1, Gannon 1, Thompson 1, Wilder 1, own-goals 2.
Note: Deane scored eight cup goals, while Agana claimed six. Geoff Taylor arrived as assistant manager and Derek French as physio.

Sheffield United 1989-90. Promoted from Division Two.
League appearances: Tracey 46, Deane 45, Hill 42 (1), Morris 41 (1), Stancliffe 40, Bryson 39, Gannon 39, Booker 38 (5), Agana 26 (5), Rostron 24 (3), Barnes 24, Bradshaw 20 (13), Wood 15 (2), Francis 11 (12), Todd 10 (14), Webster 9 (12), Whitehurst 9 (5), Whitehouse 8 (6), Wilder 8, Roberts 6 (1), Lake 2 (5), Duffield 2 (4), Pike 2 (1), Ward 0 (2).
Goals: Deane 21, Agana 10, Bryson 9, Booker 8, Francis 5, Bradshaw 3, Duffield 3, Gannon 3, Morris 3, Rostron 3, Wood 3, Whitehurst 2, Stancliffe 1, Todd 1, Whitehouse 1, own-goals 2.
Note: Deane claimed three Cup goals and Agana two.

Sheffield Wednesday 1990-91. Promoted from Division Two and Rumbelows Cup winners.
League appearances: Anderson 21 (1), Francis 18 (20), Harkes 22 (1), Hirst 39 (2), King 43, MacKenzie 5 (7), McCall 13 (6), Madden 1 (4), Newsome 1, Nilsson 22, Palmer 45, Pearson 39, Pressman 23, Sheridan 45 (1), Shirtliff 39, Turner 23, Watson 1 (4), Whitton 0 (1), P. A. Williams 40 (6), Wilson 35 (1), Worthington 31 (2).
Goals: Hirst 24, Williams 15, Sheridan 10, Wilson 6, Pearson 6, Francis 4, Anderson 2, Harkes 2, MacKenzie 2, McCall 2, Shirtliff 2, Palmer 2, Worthington 1, own-goals 2.
Rumbelows Cup goals: Pearson 5, Hirst 3, Williams 2, Francis 1, Harkes 1, Sheridan 1, Shirtliff 1, Wilson 1.

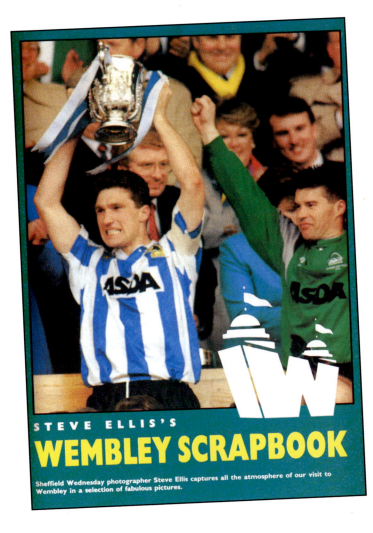

STEVE ELLIS'S
WEMBLEY SCRAPBOOK
Sheffield Wednesday photographer Steve Ellis captures all the atmosphere of our visit to Wembley in a selection of fabulous pictures.

Big Matches at Bramall Lane

Internationals:

March 10	1883	England	2–3	Scotland	7,000	
Feb 5	1887	England	7–0	Ireland	6,000	
March 29	1897	England	4–0	Wales	4,900	(Rec £912)
April 4	1903	England	1–2	Scotland	31,799	
Oct 20	1930	England	5–1	Ireland	39,064	(Rec £2,647)

FA Cup final replay

April 24	1912	Barnsley	1–0	West Brom (aet)	38,555	(Rec £2,615.9s)

FA Cup semi-finals

March 16	1889	Preston NE	1–0	West Brom	22,688
Feb 28	1891	Sunderland	3–3	Notts County	22,000
March 11	1891	Sunderland	0–2	Notts County	13,147
Feb 27	1892	Aston Villa	4–1	Sunderland	25,000
March 4	1893	Preston NE	2–2	Everton	26,000
March 16	1893	Preston NE	0–0	Everton	15,000
March 10	1894	Notts County	1–0	Blackburn	22,000
March 20	1897	Aston Villa	3–0	Liverpool	30,000
March 19	1898	Nottingham Forest	1–1	Southampton	30,000
March 9	1900	Bury	3–2	Nottingham Forest	11,200
March 27	1909	Manchester United	1–0	Newcastle	40,118
March 25	1911	Bradford City	3–0	Blackburn	36,479
March 29	1913	Sunderland	0–0	Burnley	33,655
March 27	1920	Aston Villa	3–1	Chelsea	37,771
March 19	1924	Aston Villa	3–0	Burnley	54,531
March 27	1926	Manchester City	3–0	Manchester United	36,450
March 26	1938	Preston NE	2–1	Aston Villa	55,129

Some other Bramall Lane representative games of interest:

Dec 27	1952	Sheffield FC	1–8	Pegasus
Oct 24	1957	Sheffield FC	2–2	Queen's Park
April 27	1977	England U21	1–0	Scotland U21
Apr 16	1980	England U21	1–2	Germany U21
Sep 21	1982	England U21	3–1	W. Germany
May 24	1984	England U21	2–0	Spain U21
Oct 13	1987	England U21	1–1	Turkey U21

Note: A Rugby League international was staged at Bramall Lane on September 25th 1911 when Yorkshire met the Australians; and Sheffield Eagles made their first appearance at the ground on April 10th 1988 when they played Doncaster.

On July 9th and 10th 1988 a Bruce Springsteen concert was staged at Bramall Lane.

Big Matches at Hillsborough

Internationals

April 10	1920	England	5–4	Scotland	25,536
Oct 3	1962	England	1–1	France	35,380

'B' Internationals

Jan 18	1950	England B	5–0	Switzerland B
Mar 23	1955	England B	1–1	Germany B
May 10	1994	England B	4–2	N. Ireland B

Under 23 Internationals

Feb 8	1956	England U23	3–1	Scotland U23
Sep 24	1958	England U23	4–1	Poland U23
Mar 16	1960	England U23	5–2	Holland U23

Under 21 Internationals

Feb 28	1984	England U21	6–1	France U21

Youth International

Nov	1957	England	2–0	Belgium

Inter-League

Oct	1951	Football League	2–1	Scottish League
Oct	1955	Football League	4–2	Scottish League

World Cup

July	1966	West Germany	5–0	Switzerland
		Spain	2–0	Switzerland
		Argentina	2–0	Switzerland
		West Germany	4–0	Uruguay
Sep	1973	Northern Ireland	0–0	Bulgaria

FA Cup Semi-Finals at Hillsborough (31):

1912	West Brom	1–0	Blackburn Rovers	20,050
1921	Tottenham	2–1	Preston NE	43,320
1922	Preston NE	2–1	Tottenham	49,282
1946	Derby County	1–1	Birmingham C	65,000
1948	Manchester United	3–1	Derby County	65,000
1949	Manchester United	1–1	Wolves	62,250
1951	Wolves	0–0	Newcastle	65,000
1952	Blackburn	0–0	Newcastle	65,000
1955	York City	1–1	Newcastle	65,000
1956	Birmingham	3–0	Sunderland	65,000
1957	Birmingham	0–2	Manchester United	65,000
1959	Nottingham Forest	1–0	Aston Villa	65,000
1962	Tottenham	3–2	Manchester United	65,000
1963	Liverpool	0–1	Leicester City	65,000
1964	West Ham	3–1	Manchester United	65,000
1965	Leeds United	0–0	Manchester United	60,000
1967	Tottenham	2–1	Nottingham Forest	55,000

1969	Leicester City	1–0	West Brom	53,207
1970	Manchester United	0–0	Leeds United	54,000
1971	Arsenal	2–2	Stoke City	55,000
1972	Birmingham	0–3	Leeds United	55,000
1974	Newcastle	2–0	Burnley	55,000
1975	Fulham	1–1	Birmingham	55,000
1976	Derby County	0–2	Manchester United	55,000
1977	Leeds United	1–2	Manchester United	55,000
1980	Arsenal	0–0	Liverpool	50,174
1981	Tottenham	2–2	Wolves	50,174
1987	Coventry	3–2	Leeds	51,372
1988	Liverpool	2–1	Nottingham Forest	51,627
1989	**Liverpool	0–0	Nottingham Forest	53,000
1992	Sunderland	1–0	Norwich	40,102

** Abandoned after six minutes

League Cup semi-final

| | Jan | 1972 | Stoke | 0–0 | West Ham | 42,424 |

League Cup final replay

| | March | 1977 | Everton | 1–1 | Aston Villa | 52,135 |

Hillsborough is scheduled to stage European Championship matches in 1996.

It will be of interest to note that in September 1989 the Wednesday ground staged its first Rugby League match when Sheffield Eagles met St Helens. Later in the same season the Eagles met Wigan at Hillsborough, having earlier faced Widnes at Bramall Lane.

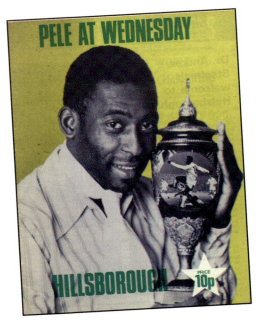

Programme of Wednesday match with Santos, February 1972, the second visit of the Brazilian champions.

Sheffield United: League matches with Wednesday since 1893.

Division 1

1.	16.10.1893	(h)	1–1	Hill
2.	13.11.1893	(a)	2–1	Drummond, Hammond
3.	27.10.1894	(a)	3–2	Hill, Hammond, Howell
4.	12.1.1895	(h)	1–0	Watson
5.	7.9.1895	(a)	0–1	
6.	26.12.1895	(h)	1–1	Watson
7.	26.12.1896	(h)	2–0	Priest, Howell
8.	2.3.1897	(a)	1–1	Needham
9.	16.10.1897	(a)	1–0	Bennett
10.	27.12.1897	(h)	1–1	Earp (own goal)
11.	3.10.1898	(a)	1–1	Priest
12.	26.12.1898	(h)	2–1	Beer, Morren
13.	15.12.1900	(h)	1–0	Field
14.	29.4.1901	(a)	0–1	
15.	2.11.1901	(a)	0–1	
16.	1.3.1902	(h)	3–0	Bennett (2), Priest (pen)
17.	1.9.1902	(h)	2–3	Priest, Lipsham
18.	11.10.1902	(a)	1–0	Priest
19.	12.12.1903	(a)	1–1	Lipsham
20.	9.4.1904	(a)	0–3	
21.	10.12.1904	(a)	3–1	Brown (2), Donnelly
22.	8.4.1905	(h)	4–2	Brown, Donnelly, Priest, Drake
23.	21.10.1905	(h)	0–2	
24.	18.4.1906	(a)	0–1	
25.	3.11.1906	(a)	2–2	Brown, Needham
26.	4.4.1907	(h)	2–1	Drake, Lipsham
27.	9.11.1907	(h)	1–3	Levick
28.	7.3.1908	(a)	0–2	
29.	25.12.1908	(a)	0–1	
30.	26.12.1908	(h)	2–1	Hardinge (pen), Peart
31.	6.11.1909	(h)	3–3	Brelsford, Simmons (2)
32.	19.3.1910	(a)	3–1	Hardinge (2), Evans
33.	22.10.1910	(a)	0–2	
34.	25.2.1911	(h)	0–1	
35.	4.11.1911	(h)	1–1	Kitchen
36.	9.3.1912	(a)	1–1	Wilkinson
37	26.10.1912	(a)	0–1	
38.	1.3.1913	(h)	0–2	
39.	25.10.1913	(h)	0–1	
40.	28.2.1914	(a)	1–2	Kitchen
41.	5.9.1914	(h)	0–1	
42.	2.1.1915	(a)	1–1	Davies

43.	27.9.1919	(a)	1–2	Tummon
44.	4.10.1919	(h)	3–0	Kitchen, Masterman, Tummon
45.	28.8.1926	(a)	3–2	Johnson (2), Hoyland
46.	15.1.1927	(h)	2–0	Tunstall, A. Mercer
47.	24.9.1927	(h)	1–1	Tunstall
48.	4.2.1928	(a)	3–3	Blair (2), Partridge
49.	22.9.1928	(a)	2–5	Gibson, Tunstall
50.	2.2.1929	(h)	1–1	Phillipson
51.	28.9.1929	(h)	2–2	Tunstall (2)
52.	1.2.1930	(a)	1–1	Dunne
53.	6.9.1930	(h)	1–1	S. Gibson
54.	3.1.1931	(a)	3–1	Dunne, Oxley, Tunstall
55.	21.11.1931	(a)	1–2	Dunne
56.	2.4.1932	(h)	1–1	Barclay
57.	24.9.1932	(a)	3–3	Oswald, Barclay, Dunne
58.	4.2.1933	(h)	2–3	Dunne (2)
59.	21.10.1933	(a)	1–0	Williams
60.	3.3.1934	(h)	5–1	Boyd (3), Pickering, Stacey

Division 2

61.	16.10.1937	(a)	1–0	Eggleston
62.	26.2.1938	(h)	2–1	Barton, Dodds
63.	29.10.1938	(h)	0–0	
64.	4.3.1939	(a)	0–1	
65.	17.9.1949	(a)	1–2	Hutchinson
66.	21.1.1950	(h)	2–0	Brook, Warhurst
67.	8.9.1951	(h)	7–3	Hawksworth (2), Brook (2), Ringstead (2), F. Smith
68.	5.1.1952	(a)	3–1	Ringstead (2), Hutchinson

Division 1

69.	12.9.1953	(h)	2–0	Hagan, Hawksworth
70.	23.1.1954	(a)	2–3	Brook (2)
71.	18.9.1954	(h)	1–0	Waldock
72.	5.2.1955	(a)	2–1	Cross, Ringstead

Division 2

| 73. | 4.10.1958 | (a) | 0–2 | |
| 74. | 21.2.1959 | (h) | 1–0 | Pace |

Division 1

75.	16.9.1961	(h)	1–0	Pace
76.	3.2.1962	(a)	2–1	Pace (2)
77.	6.10.1962	(h)	2–2	G. Shaw (pen), Pace
78.	15.5.1963	(a)	1–3	Pace
79.	14.9.1963	(h)	1–1	Simpson
80.	18.1.1964	(a)	0–3	

81.	5.9.1964	(a)	2–0	Birchenall (2)
82.	2.1.1965	(h)	2–3	Birchenall, Matthewson
83.	18.9.1965	(h)	1–0	Birchenall
84.	12.3.1966	(a)	2–2	Birchenall (2)
85.	24.9.1966	(a)	2–2	Woodward, Jones
86.	4.2.1967	(h)	1–0	Punton
87.	7.9.1967	(h)	0–1	
88.	6.1.1968	(a)	1–1	Hill

Division 2

| 89. | 3.10.1970 | (h) | 3–2 | Colquhoun, Dearden, Tudor |
| 90. | 12.4.1971 | (a) | 0–0 | |

Division 3

| 91. | 26.12.1979 | (a) | 0–4 | |
| 92. | 5.4.1980 | (h) | 1–1 | MacPhail |

Division 1

| 93. | 16.11.1991 | (h) | 2–0 | Deane, Whitehouse |
| 94. | 11.3.1992 | (a) | 3–1 | Davison (2), Whitehouse |

Premier League

95.	8.11.1992	(h)	1–1	Littlejohn
96.	21.4.1993	(a)	1–1	Deane
97.	23.10.1993	(a)	1–1	Hodges
98.	22.1.1994	(a)	1–3	Whitehouse (pen)

	P	W	D	L	F	A
	98	37	30	31	139	128

Sheffield United FA Cup Matches with Wednesday 1900-93

1.	10.2.1900	Round 2	(h)	0–0	(abandoned)
2.	17.2.1900		(h)	1–1	Almond
3.	19.2.1900		(a)	2–0	Nedham (pen), Beer
4.	31.1.1925	Round 2	(h)	3–2	Sampy (2), Green
5.	18.2.1928	Round 5	(a)	1–1	Partridge
6.	22.2.1928		(h)	4–1	Partridge, Johnson (3)
7.	9.1.1954	Round 3	(a)	1–1	Toner
8.	13.1.1954		(h)	1–3	Hawksworth
9.	12.3.1960	Round 6	(h)	0–2	
10.	3.4.1993	Semi-final		1–2	Cork *

* at Wembley after extra time

Sheffield United League Cup Matches with Wednesday

| 1. | 9.8.1980 | Round 1 | (1) | 0–2 | |
| 2. | 12.8.1980 | Round 1 | (2) | 1–1 | Hatton |

Sheffield Wednesday: League matches with United since 1893.

Division I

No.	Date		Score	Scorers
1.	16.10.1893	(h)	1–1	Spiksley
2.	13.11.1893	(h)	1–2	Miller
3.	27.10.1894	(h)	2–3	Spiksley, Davis
4.	12.1.1895	(a)	0–1	
5.	7.9.1895	(h)	1–0	Bell
6.	26.12.1895	(a)	1–1	Brady
7.	26.12.1896	(a)	0–2	
8.	2.3.1897	(h)	1–1	Brandon
9.	16.10.1897	(h)	0–1	
10.	27.12.1897	(a)	1–1	Spiksley
11.	3.10.1898	(h)	1–1	Hemmingfield
12.	26.12.1898	(a)	1–2	Hemmingfield
13.	15.12.1900	(a)	0–1	
14.	29.4.1901	(h)	1–0	Wilson
15.	2.11.1901	(h	1–0	Wilson
16.	1.3.1902	(a)	0–3	
17.	1.9.1902	(a)	3–2	Spiksley, Wilson, Davis
18.	11.10.1902	(h)	0–1	
19.	12.12.1903	(a)	1–1	Wilson
20.	9.4.1904	(h)	3–0	Chapman (2), Simpson
21.	10.12.1904	(h)	1–3	Wilson
22.	8.4.1905	(a)	2–4	Stewart (2)
23.	21.10.1905	(a)	2–0	Chapman, Stewart
24.	18.4.1906	(h)	1–0	Davis (pen)
25.	3.11.1906	(h)	2–2	Wilson (2)
26.	4.4.1907	(a)	1–2	Maxwell
27.	9.11.1907	(a)	3–1	Brittleton, Chapman, Stewart
28.	7.3.1908	(h)	2–0	Wilson, Maxwell
29.	25.12.1908	(h)	1–0	Simpson
30.	26.12.1908	(a)	1–2	Bradshaw
31.	6.11.1909	(a)	3–3	Kirkman (2), Chapman
32.	19.3.1910	(h)	1–3	Brittleton
33.	22.10.1910	(h)	2–0	Chapman
34.	25.2.1911	(a)	1–0	McLean
35.	4.11.1911	(a)	1–1	Wilson
36.	9.3.1912	(h)	1–1	Glennon
37	26.10.1912	(h)	1–0	Glennon
38.	1.3.1913	(a)	2–0	Robertson, McLean
39.	25.10.1913	(a)	1–0	Glennon
40.	18.2.1914	(h)	2–1	Glennon, McLean
41.	5.9.1914	(a)	1–0	Wilson
42.	2.1.1915	(h)	1–1	Wilson

43.	27.9.1919	(h)	2–1	Campbell, Gill
44.	4.10.1919	(a)	0–3	
45.	28.8.1926	(h)	2–3	Trotter (2)
46.	15.1.1927	(a)	0–2	
47.	24.9.1927	(a)	1–1	Trotter
48.	4.2.1928	(h)	3–3	Wilkinson (2), Harper
49.	22.9.1928	(h)	5–2	Hooper (2), Allen (2), Rimmer
50.	2.2.1929	(a)	1–1	Hooper
51.	28.9.1929	(a)	2–2	Seed, Allen
52.	1.2.1930	(h)	1–1	Burgess
53.	6.9.1930	(a)	1–1	Burgess
54.	3.1.1931	(h)	1–3	Ball
55.	21.11.1931	(h)	2–1	Ball, Stephenson
56.	2.4.1932	(a)	1–1	Ball
57.	24.9.1932	(h)	3–3	Ball, Rimmer, Hooper
58.	4.2.1933	(a)	3–2	Starling, Ball, Stephenson
59.	21.10.1933	(h)	0–1	
60.	3.3.1934	(a)	1–5	Burrows

Division 2

61.	16.10.1937	(h)	0–1	
62.	26.2.1938	(a)	1–2	Drury
63.	29.10.1938	(a)	0–0	
64.	4.3.1939	(h)	1–0	Fallon
65.	17.9.1949	(h)	2–1	Jordan, Quigley
66.	21.1.1950	(a)	0–2	
67.	8.9.1951	(a)	3–7	Woodhead (2), Thomas
68.	5.1.1952	(h)	1–3	Dooley

Division 1

69.	12.9.1953	(a)	0–2	
70.	23.1.1954	(h)	3–2	J. Shaw (2), Sewell
71.	18.9.1954	(a)	0–1	
72.	5.2.1955	(h)	1–2	Marriott

Division 2

| 73. | 4.10.1958 | (h) | 2–0 | Froggatt, Shiner |
| 74. | 21.2.1959 | (a) | 0–1 | |

Division 1

75.	16.9.1961	(a)	0–1	
76.	3.2.1962	(h)	1–2	Dobson
77.	6.10.1962	(a)	2–2	Layne (2)
78.	15.5.1963	(h)	3–1	Layne (2), McAnearney
79.	14.9.1963	(a)	1–1	Finney
80.	18.1.1964	(h)	3–0	Wilkinson (2), Layne
81.	5.9.1964	(h)	0–2	
82.	2.1.1965	(a)	3–2	Hickton, Fantham (2)

83.	18.9.1965	(a)	0–1	
84.	12.3.1966	(h)	2–2	Fantham, Eustace
85.	24.9.1966	(h)	2–2	Munks (own goal), McCalliog
86.	4.2.1967	(a)	0–1	
87.	2.9.1967	(a)	1–0	Ritchie
88.	6.1.1968	(h)	1–1	Fantham

Division 2
| 89. | 3.10.1970 | (a) | 2–3 | Craig, Sinclair |
| 90. | 12.4.1971 | (h) | 0–0 | |

Division 3
| 91. | 26.12.1979 | (h) | 4–0 | Mellor, Curran, King, Smith (pen) |
| 92. | 5.4.1980 | (a) | 1–1 | Curran |

Division 1
| 93. | 16.11.1991 | (a) | 0–2 | |
| 94. | 11.3.1992 | (h) | 1–3 | King |

Premier League
95.	8.11.1992	(a)	1–1	Hirst
96.	21.4.1993	(h)	1–1	Warhurst
97.	23.10.1993	(a)	1–1	Palmer
98.	22.1.1994	(h)	3–1	Bright, Pearce, Watson

P	W	D	L	F	A
98	31	30	37	128	139

Sheffield Wednesday FA Cup Matches with United 1900-93
1.	10.2.1900	Round 2	(a)	0–0	(abandoned after 50 min)
2.	17.2.1900		(a)	1–1	Brash
3.	19.2.1900		(h)	0–2	
4.	31.1.1925	Round 2	(a)	2–3	Trotter (2)
5.	18.2.1928	Round 5	(h)	1–1	Wilkinson
6.	22.2.1928		(a)	1–4	Hooper (pen)
7.	9.1.1954	Round 3	(h)	1–1	J. Shaw
8.	13.1.1954		(a)	3–1	Finney, Davies, Sewell
9.	12.3.1960	Round 6	(a)	2–0	Wilkinson (2)
10.	3.4.1993	Semi-final		2–1	Waddle, Bright*

* at Wembley, after extra time.

Sheffield Wednesday League Cup Matches with United
| 1. | 9.8.1980 | Round 1 | (h) | 2–0 | Taylor, Johnson |
| 2. | 12.8.1980 | Round 1 | (a) | 1–1 | Curran |

The following unique listing of certain junior honours in Sheffield and Hallamshire competitions, produced by Jason Dickinson, are of special interest to local enthusiasts who have not been able to find them in any reference book.

SHEFFIELD SENIOR CUP WINNERS

1877 The Wednesday	1926 Wath Athletic	1958 Bentley MW
1878 The Wednesday	Wednesday Res	1959 Bentley MW
1879 Thursday Wanderers	1927 Darfield	1960 Grimesthorpe Wel.
1880 Staveley	Sheffield United Res	1961 Frickley C.A.
1881 The Wednesday	1928 Frickley C.A.	1962 Hallam
1882 Heeley	Wednesday Res	1963 Frickley C.A.
1883 The Wednesday	1929 Ardsley	1964 Stocksbridge W
1884 Lockwood Brothers	Wednesday Res	1965 Hallam
1885 Lockwood Brothers	1930 S. Kirkby Coll	1966 Worksop
1886 Mexborough	Barnsley Res	1967 Frickley C.A.
1887 The Wednesday	1931 Mexborough	1968 Hallam
1888 The Wednesday	Wednesday Res	1969 Redfearns
1889 Rotherham Town	1932 Dinnington Athletic	1970 Worksop Town
1890 Rotherham Town	Wednesday Res	1971 Rawmarsh MW
1891 Doncaster Rovers	1933 Denaby United	1972 Kiveton Park U
1892 Sheffield United Res	Barnsley Res	1973 Worksop
1893 Sheffield United Res	1934 Mexborough Athletic	1974 Frecheville
1894 Mexborough	Barnsley Res	1975 Mexborough Town
1895 Wednesday Res	1935 Firbeck	1976 Emley
1896 Mexborough	1936 Denaby United	1977 Mexborough Town
1897 Sheffield United Res	1937 Upton Coll	1978 Maltby MW
1898 Sheffield United Res	Doncaster Rover Res	1979 Frickley
1899 Sheffield United Res	1938 Norton Woodseats	1980 Emley
1900 Wednesday Res	Doncaster Rovers Res	1981 Emley
1901 Sheffield United Res	1939 Rawmarsh Welfare	1982 Worksop Town
1902 Wednesday Res	Doncaster Rovers Res	1983 Mexborough Town
1903 Wednesday Res	1940 Beighton MW	1984 Emley
1904 Barnsley Res	Bolsover Coll	1985 Worksop Town
1905 Sheffield United Res	1941 S. Kirkby Coll	1986 Frickley
1906 Denaby United	Thurcroft	1987 Denaby
1907 Wednesday Res	1942 Manvers Main	1988 Frickley
1908 Sheffield United Res	RASC	1989 Emley
1909 Sheffield United Res	1943 RASC	1990 Frickley
1910 Denaby United	1944 RASC	1991 Emley
1911 Sheffield United Res	1945 Barnsley Res	1992 Emley
1912 Doncaster Rovers	Firbeck	1993 Stocksbridge PS
1913 Rotherham County	1946 Wombwell Town	1994 Sheffield
1914 Rotherham County	Thurnscoe Vic	1995 Worksop
1920 Rotherham Town	1947 Thurcroft Main	
1921 Wednesday Res	1948 Harworth CI	
1922 Wednesday Res	1949 Royston Soc	(Note: The Senior Cup was originally known as the Sheffield Challenge Cup — see page 32 of Volume One).
1923 Wombwell Town	1950 Upton Coll	
1924 Worksop Town	1951 Hallam	
1925 Rotherham Town	1952 Stocksbridge W	
	1953 Worksop Town	
	1954 Sheffield Wednesday A	
	1955 Worksop Town	
	1956 Beighton MW	
	1957 Frickley C.A.	

WHARNCLIFFE CHARITY CUP WINNERS

1879 Wednesday	1915 Wednesday Res	1952 Penistone Church
1880 Heeley	1916 Worksop Town	1953 Beighton MW
1882 Wednesday	1920 Retford Town	1954 ThorncliffeRec
1883 Wednesday	1921 Rotherham County Res	1955 Brown Bayleys & Greenhill
1884 Lockwood Brothers	1922 Wednesday Res	
1885 Heeley	1923 Doncaster R.	1956 Thurcroft Main
1886 Wednesday	1924 Sheffield United Res	1957 Wednesday A
1887 Staveley	1925 Wednesday Res	1958 Wednesday A
1888 Wednesday	1926 Sheffield United Res	1959 Wednesday A
1889 Staveley	1927 Doncaster Rovers Res	1960 Thorncliffe Rec
1890 Staveley	1928 Sheffield United Res	1961 Harworth Cl
1893 Wednesday and Sheffield United share	1929 Doncaster Rovers Res	1962 Retford Town
	1930 Sheffield United Res	1963 Harworth Cl
1894 Sheffield United	1931 Wednesday Res	1964 Swallownest MW
1895 Mexborough Town	1932 Sheffield United Res	1965 Maltby MW
1896 Barnsley St Peter's	1933 Wednesday Res	1966 Frecheville
1897 Sheffield United Res	1934 Doncaster Rovers Res	1967 Frecheville
1900 Wednesday Res	1935 Norton Woodseats	1968 Charlton United
1901 Monk Bretton	1937 Sheffield United A	1969 Swallownest MW
1902 Sheffield United Res	1938 Wednesday A	1970 Thurcroft Wel
1903 Wednesday Res	1939 Wednesday A	1971 Hallam
1904 Sheffield United Res	1941 Thurcroft Main	1972 Ecclesfield Red Rose
1905 Wednesday Res	1942 RASC	1973 Charlton United
1906 Wednesday Res	1943 RASC	1974 Heeley
1907 Sheffield United Res	1944 RASC	1975 Kiveton Park
1908 Wednesday Res	1945 ThorncliffeWelfare	1976 Harworth Cl
1909 Wednesday Res	1946 ThorncliffeWelfare	1977 Norton Woodseats
1910 Barnsley Res	1947 ThorncliffeWelfare	1978 Mosboro' Trinity
1911 Wednesday Res	1948 Hoyland Common	1979 Charlton Tavern
1912 Sheffield United Res	1949 Stocksbridge Works	1983 Frecheville CA
1913 Gainsborough Trinity	1950 Hoyland Common	1984 Kiveton Park
1914 Rotherham County	1951 Aughton Juniors	

SHEFFIELD JUNIOR CUP WINNERS

1910 Penistone Church	1925 Malin Bridge OB	1938 Stovin Ath
1911 Handsworth Rovers	1926 Park Labour	1939 City Surveyors
1912 Eckington R.R.	1927 Lopham Street UM	1940 Hoyland Low
1913 Valley Road B.C.	1928 Turton Platts	1941 Grimsthorpe
1914 Valley Road B.C.	1919 Lopham Street UM	1942 Attercliffe Radicals
1915 Nether Edge Am	1930 Tinsley Park Sports	1943 Attercliffe Radicals
1919 Kimberworth OB	1931 Tinsley Park Sports	1944 Thorncliffe Wel
1919 Oughtibridge Inst	1932 Tinsley Sports	1945 Heeley S
1920 Oughtibridge Inst	1933 Tinsley Park Sports	1946 Hoyland Comm H & S
1921 Grenoside	1934 Lopham Street UM	1947 Hoyland Comm Ath
1922 Grenoside	1935 Tinsley Park Sports	1948 Woodhouse Mill
1923 Nether Edge Am	1936 Fulwood Am	1949 Travellers Sp
1924 Attercliffe Vic	1937 Penistone Church	1950 Woodhouse Mill WMC

1951 Effingham Steel	1967 Brinsworth Albion	1984 Brodsworth MW
1952 Kendray Sports	1968 Lundwood WMC	1985 Walton MW
1953 Crookes WMC	1969 Barnsley GSOB	1986 Kingsley B
1954 Yotar Sports	1970 Bentley Vic	1987 Mexborough Northgate
1955 Ecclesfield Colley Rovers	1971 Monkton Coll	
	1972 Ecclesfield Red Rose	1988 Wharncliffe Arms
1956 Bellhouse Rd WMC	1973 Bentley Vic (*)	1989 Storthes Hall
1957 Dinnington MW	1974 Eldon YC	1990 Athersley Rec
1958 Yotar Sports	1975 Windsor BL	1991 Athersley Rec
1959 Ecclesfield Red Rose	1976 Eldon YC	1992 Athersley Rec
1960 Travellers Sports	1977 Ward Green WMC	1993 Darfield Road WMC
1961 Laughton Coll	1978 Upper Thong Social	1994 Darfield Road WMC
1962 Ecclesfield Red Rose	1979 Ward Green WMC	1995 Darfield Road WMC
1963 Brinsworth Albion	1980 Eldon YC	
1964 Ecclesfield Red Rose	1981 Cutting Edge	*(*) Trophy not awarded as winners played ineligible players.*
1965 Crookes WMC	1982 Redfearn NG	
1966 Northern Ideal Homes	1983 Upton Brookside	

SHEFFIELD AND HALLAMSHIRE COUNTY CUP

This competition was launched in 1920-21 and Sheffield United were the first winners, beating Wednesday in the final at Hillsborough in May 1921. When Wednesday first won the trophy, in 1927, they defeated Barnsley in the final. Wednesday won the competition three times on the trot between 1927 and 1929, United won it four times running between 1957 and 1960.

Sheffield United lifted the trophy in:
1921, 1924, 1926, 1930, 1931, 1933, 1952, 1954, 1957, 1958, 1959, 1960, 1964, 1965, 1967, 1969, 1974, 1978, 1980, 1982.

Wednesday's successes came in:
1927, 1928, 1929, 1932, 1934, 1945, 1946, 1950, 1951, 1953, 1973 1975.

The Sheffield clubs shared the trophy in 1939, and United shared it with Barnsley in 1971.

List compiled by Jason Dickinson

ERNEST KANGLEY, secretary of the Sheffield and Hallamshire County FA from 1949 to 1978 died in November 1980. When Kangley retired he was succeeded by Geoff Thompson. Kangley had worked at Firth Brown's and been secretary to Atlas & Norfolk before moving into full-time soccer administration. Thompson's initial links with the local FA started in 1968, when he left the Trustee Savings Bank to become Kangley's assistant. He was later secretary of the Durham FA, had a spell with Doncaster Rovers, and was secretary to the Birmingham FA before returning to Sheffield in 1977.

Sheffield FC team group in April 1989.
Back row: Stafford, Walshaw, McFadzean, Rogers, Milner, Worsfold, Barker.
Front row: Moorwood, James, Stenson, Jones, Lancaster, Maguire, Witham, Stewart.

Sheffield FC since 1961 (by Jason Dickinson)

The 1960s were a modest time for Sheffield FC in Yorkshire League football and they spent most of the time in mid table in Division 2 although promotion came in 1967 followed by relegation a year later. They dropped to the newly-formed Division 3 in 1972; then suddenly in 1976 a remarkable transformation occurred which brought double promotion (including the second division title in 1977), a trip to Wembley in the FA Vase final, and a Yorkshire League Cup success, 4-1 v Maltby at Bramall Lane, in 1978. The run to the FA Vase final in 1977 was a remarkable feat as they were still an amateur side and battled through seven rounds to reach Wembley. They lost in a replay, to Billericay at Nottingham.

When the Northern Counties East League was formed in 1982, Sheffield FC were placed in division one south, where they remained until 1985 when reorganisation saw them into the new division one. They finished second but promotion was denied owing to poor ground grading at their Abbeydale Park base. By the time the division one title was won in 1989 a move of ground to Hillsborough Park had occurred so they could take their place in the premier division. Lack of floodlights saw demotion to division one within a season. 1991 saw the club win the title, pipping rivals Hallam, and another move of ground, this time to the Don Valley Stadium, ensured premier division football would return to the club. The highlight of the 1990s came in May 1994 when Sheffield FC beat Worksop 6–5 on penalties at Hillsborough, after a 1–1 draw, to win the Senior Cup for the first time in their history. Sheffield FC's latest ground move, to Owlerton Stadium, occurred in the summer of 1994, but a turbulent season followed, with the loss of over half the side plus the manager, contributing greatly to a final position of 18th which was just enough to beat relegation.

Hallam FC since 1961 (by Jason Dickinson)

After winning the Yorkshire League's second division title in 1961, Hallam built on this a year later by winning the Senior Cup, for the first time in the club's history, when they defeated their great rivals Sheffield FC 1–0 in a replayed final at High Green (Hanwell got the goal). Hallam went on to lift the Senior Cup on two other occasions in the 1960s (they beat Thurcroft in 1965 and Norton Woodseats in 1968). Meanwhile in the Yorkshire League, Hallam staged first division football at Sandygate for twenty seasons, consistently finishing in the top half of the table, their best place being third in 1976, before the formation of the Northern Counties East League in 1982 when they were placed in division one south.

Hallam's best run in the FA Vase occurred in their penultimate season in the Yorkshire League, they reached the last 16 before falling to Guiseley in February 1981. Hallam's time in the NCEL has seen many changes of division. A League Cup semi-final in 1983 was an early highlight. In 1985, reorganisation saw a move to the new division two, from where they gained immediate promotion followed by a move up to the premier division a year later. Hallam achieved mid-table finishes in their three seasons of top flight football, but then experienced double heartbreak when they were demoted to division one because of their lack of floodlights and were denied promotion in 1991 for the same reason.

The Hallam ground was eventually equipped with lights in 1992 and the following season they clinched the runners-up spot — but incredibly, the expulsion of debt-ridden Bradley Rangers and the expunging of their record meant the Sandygate side's loss of points demoted them to third place and they missed promotion! However, they really did finish in second spot in 1994, there was no hitch this time. Yet their first season back in the top flight was a turbulent one with the loss of several players during the season and the manager at the end. Fortunately, relegation was avoided to ensure Premier football at the world's oldest club ground in 1995.

Vic Buckingham returned to Ajax (Amsterdam) after leaving Wednesday in 1964. He later managed Fulham and had spells in Greece and Spain. He died in January 1995 at the age of seventy-nine.

Monday 22nd October 1962.

Wednesday 2 Santos 4.
Teams
Wednesday: Springett, Johnson, Megson, T. McAnearney, Swan, Kay, Finney, Dobson, Layne (Young 35), Griffin, Holliday
Goals: Griffin (30), Layne (33)

Santos: Gilmar, Mauro, Dalmo, Olavo, Lima, Formiga (Carlos), Pageo, Mengalvio, Coutinho, Pele, Dorval
Goals: Coutinho (2, 28, 40), Pele (penalty, 45)
Referee: M. Kitabdjian (France)

Attendance: 49,058

Note: Wednesday also entertained Santos, and Pele, on 23rd February 1972 when a 36,996 Hillsborough crowd saw the Brazilians win 2–0 with goals from Nene (32 min) and Ferreira (78). The programme cover is shown on page 267.

Alan Brown spent five years at Sunderland after leaving Hillsborough in February 1968, and concluded his career in football with spells in Norway and at Plymouth Argyle.

The Springett brothers, goalkeepers Ron and Peter, were involved in a unique transfer swap in the summer of 1967 when Ron, Wednesday's most capped England international, returned to Queen's Park Rangers and Peter moved to Hillsborough, with the Owls making a £35,000 cash adjustment. Ron, a £10,000 buy in 1958, made 384 appearances for the Owls, Peter

207. Peter, incidentally, remained in Sheffield and, when his playing days ended, became a policeman—and ironically, in this role his duties brought close links with Sheffield United and Bramall Lane.

John Quinn, when he hung up his boots he opened a sports shop near the Wednesday ground and took over the running of a charity All-Stars team from Derek Dooley. Over the years this team has raised thousands of pounds for good causes.

It is of interest to note that on the same day in October 1975 that Wednesday sacked **Steve Burtenshaw**, former Sheffield United wing-half **Gerry Summers** was dismissed by Oxford United after seven years in charge. Later in the same month **Len Ashurst** was appointed to fill the Owls' vacancy, and his successor at Gillingham was Summers—

who subsequently chose his old Bramall Lane team-mate, Alan Hodgkinson, as his assistant. Hodgkinson later became a goal keeping coach and served the Scottish national team in this capacity, also working with a number of League clubs—including Wednesday.

Ken Furphy went to America shortly after being dismissed by Sheffield United in October 1975. He was appointed coach to the New York Cosmos in January 1976. He subsequently had a spell with Detroit Express, where one of his players was Trevor Francis—who, of course, later played for and managed Sheffield Wednesday. Furphy concluded his time in America with the Washington Diplomats. When he returned to England he spent some years working in local radio in the West Country. Eddie Colquhoun and Keith Eddy were amongst the United players who joined Furphy in America, and Alan Woodward not only went over there but eventually settled in the United States.

Peter and Paul Shirtliff when they appeared together in April 1981 they were the first brothers to figure in a Wednesday League side since **Tom** and **Jim McAnearney** in the late 1950s. Twins *Derek* and *Eric Wilkinson* had both played on one occasion in September 1958.

DEREK WILKINSON.

It is of interest to note, that when Wednesday visited The Dell in a Division One game in October 1988, South-ampton's team included the three Wallace brothers Danny, Rod and Ray. The Owls won 2–1. It was Peter Eustace's first match in charge after Howard Wilkinson's departure for Leeds—where he later signed Ray and Rod Wallace. Sheffield United's **Andy** and **Rob Scott** started a League match together for the first time against Watford (a) on August 12th 1995.

A milestone in Wednesday's move towards financial stability after the crisis in the 1970s (which led to the launch of a new shares issue and a change of emphasis in commercial activities under Dennis Woodhead) came in the annual report for 1980-81 when a £219,553 surplus was announced. Chairman Bert McGee explained the transformation thus: 'We stopped spending and started earning. We kept a tight control on all overheads, instituted rigorous, sensible house-keeping, appointed sound management, and let them get on with it'. Former Owls winger Woodhead, who was responsible for the club's commercial activities from 1971 to 1987 and was a key behind-the-scenes figure in the transformation, died in 1995. Bert McGee had died earlier in the same year. Ernest Barron, nominated for retirement in 1995 after nineteen years on the club's board, is remembered as the man who, in 1976, raised £1,000 by accepting a challenge to run from the Town Hall to Hillsborough in 30 minutes—at the age of fifty.

It is of interest to note that, when the Sheffield clubs achieved a promotion double in 1983-84, Dick Chester started the season as United's secretary but ended it as secretary at Hillsborough, where he succeeded the long-serving Eric England,

who had spent forty-seven years at Hillsborough. Chester's successor at Bramall Lane was Geoff Smith, who retired in December 1988 and was in turn succeeded by David Capper. When Chester left the Owls, his successor was Graham Mackrell. Incidentally, Norma Lane, secretary to every Wednesday manager since Jack Marshall, is one of the longest serving members of the Hillsborough staff.

Billy McEwan; after resigning as Sheffield United's manager on January 2nd 1988, he returned to the game within a few months as manager of Rotherham, whom he led to the Fourth Division championship in 1988-89. He left Millmoor in January 1991. Danny Bergara returned to Bramall Lane as coach during McEwan's reign, having previously been at the club from 1978 to 1981. Bergara, who later managed Stockport, was appointed to Wednesday's coaching staff in mid-1995 following the appointment of David Pleat.

Picture Note: *The photograph which appears on page 27 of Volume One has been identified as a Sheffield Wednesday team-group of 1874-75, and the players are:*
Standing: W.E. Clegg, J.C. Clegg, W. Wilkinson, E. Bowling, J. Morton, R. Gregory.
Seated: J. Housley, W.E. England, W.H. Stacey, W. Horton, G. Anthony, J. Hunter.

A Charity Match between old Sheffield United and old Sheffied Wednesday players at Owlerton Stadium in 1970. The two captains, Danny Williams and Cec Coldwell shake hands as referee George McCabe looks on.

Bibliography and Acknowledgements

Bibliography

Howard Wilkinson, with David Walker, *Managing to Succeed: My Life in Football Management,* (Mainstream 1992).
Lee Chapman, *More Than a Match: A Player's Story*, (Stanley Paul 1992).
Denis Clarebrough, *Sheffield United: The First 100 years*, (Sheffield United 1989).
Keith Farnsworth, *Wednesday!* (Sheffield City Libraries, 1982).
Keith Farnsworth, *Sheffield Wednesday: A Complete Record 1867-1987*, (Breedon Books, 1987).
John A. Steele, *The Countrymen: The Story of Hallam FC*, (1986).
Nicholas Fishwick, *From Clegg to Clegg House*, (Sheffield & Hallamshire CFA, 1986).
Keith Farnsworth, *The Blades and The Owls: A Pictorial History of the Sheffield Derby Matches,* (Breedon Books, 1995).

Newspapers:
Sheffield Star, Sheffield (Morning) Telegraph, Daily Telegraph, Yorkshire Post.

Other Reference books:
Various copies of the *Rothmans Annual, FA Year Book,* volumes in the excellent *Complete Record* series published by Breedon Books.

Acknowledgements

THE AUTHOR is grateful to the Sheffield Star for permission to reproduce Sheffield Newspapers pictures, which include some borrowed from the collections of several former players and local enthusiasts. I also thank, Keith Howard, Ralph Whitworth and Roger Oldfield for other pictures and illustrations. Steve Ellis, Wednesday's long-serving official photographer, has been especially generous in permitting use of pictures from his extensive collection.

The help of Sheffield United and Sheffield Wednesday has been appreciated, and information and background has been provided by many people, including Dave Bassett, Alan Birchenall, Tony Currie, Don Megson, Colin Prophett, Vin Kenny and Howard Johnson. I have, naturally, drawn upon notes of many interviews and conversations from across the years. In this context mention must be made of many former colleagues, including Benny Hill, Tony Pritchett, Peter Markie, Chris Wilson, Trevor Cook (an oft-unsung hero in the *Green 'Un* team!) and John Motson. It is appropriate, too, to thank my good friend Colin Gibson now sports editor of the *Sunday Telegraph*, for his help and encouragement, especially in his time as the *Daily Telegraph's* chief football writer. For, if

he had not been instrumental in developing the scope of my freelance career, I might not have maintained the journalistic links which led to the opportunity to write this history.

I have also much appreciated the enthusiastic statistical back-up of Jason Dickinson and help from John Brodie.

As always, I have especially appreciated the support of my wife, Linda, who has assisted in research, proof reading and ensuring a regular supply of cups of tea when writing has extended long into the night!

Last, but certainly not least, I once again extend my thanks to Pauline Climpson, Mark Glover and all the staff of The Hallamshire Press for the many hours they have devoted to the task of producing the two volumes of this history.

Programmes

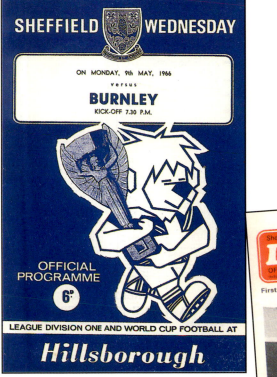

SHEFFIELD WEDNESDAY

ON MONDAY, 9th MAY, 1966
versus
BURNLEY
KICK-OFF 7.30 P.M.

OFFICIAL
PROGRAMME
6ᴅ

LEAGUE DIVISION ONE AND WORLD CUP FOOTBALL AT

Hillsborough

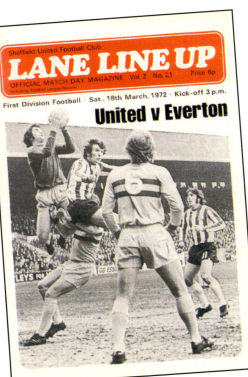

Sheffield United Football Club

LANE LINE UP

OFFICIAL MATCH DAY MAGAZINE   Vol. 2   No. 21   Price 6p
Including Football League Review

First Division Football · Sat., 18th March, 1972 · Kick-off 3 p.m.

United v Everton

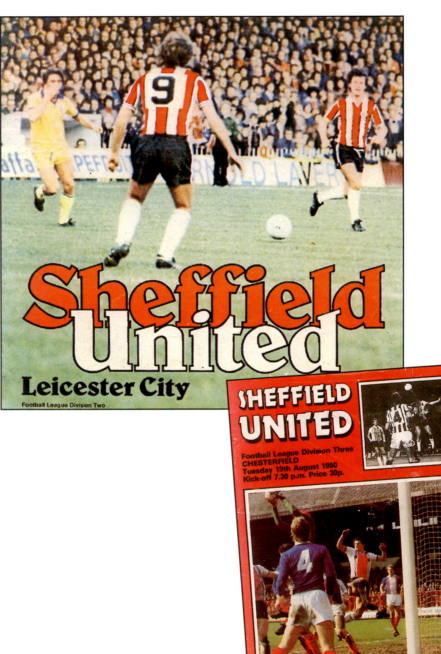

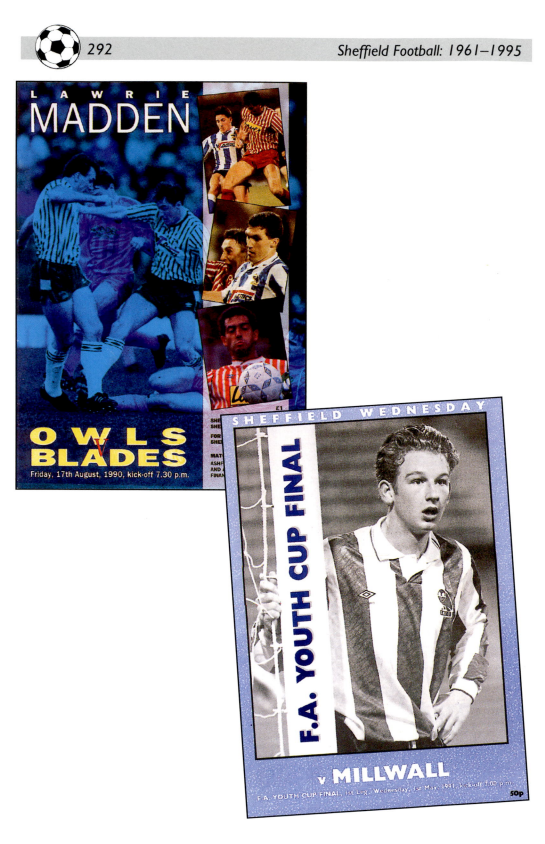

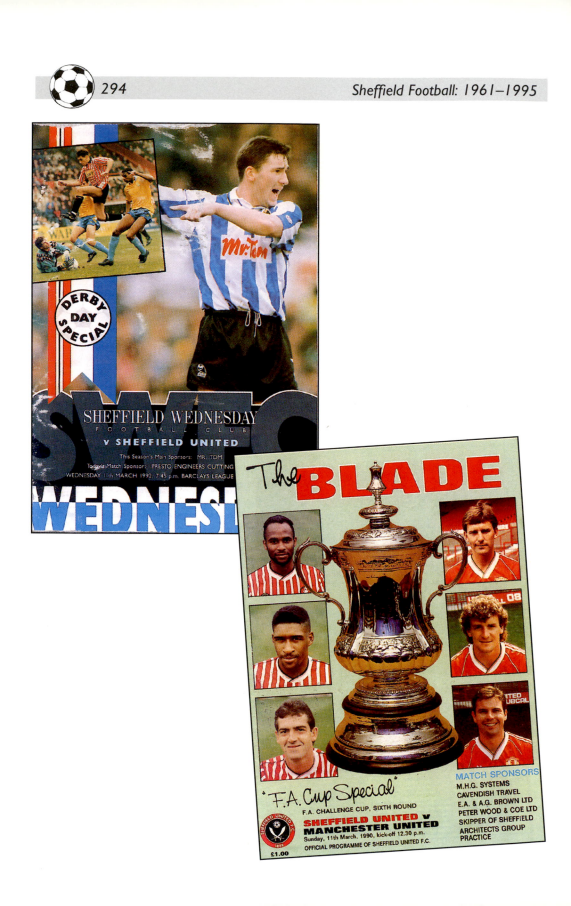

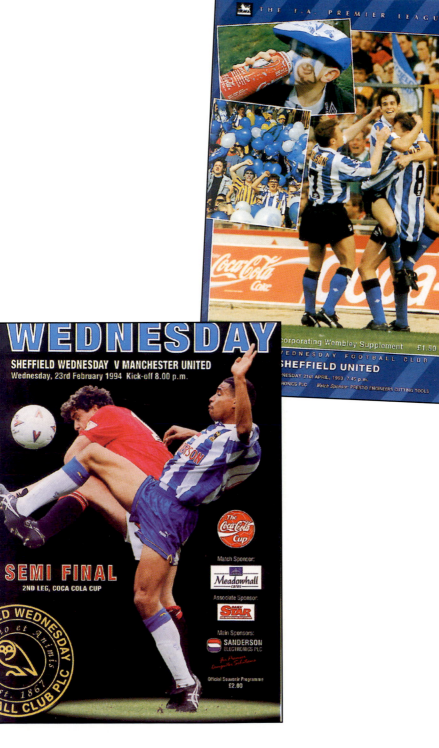

v CRYSTAL PALACE
Saturday 28th December 1991, kick-off 3.00 p.m.
BARCLAYS LEAGUE
DIVISION ONE
OFFICIAL PROGRAMME
THE FAMILY CLUB
£1.20

Sheffield
UNITED
Blade
THE FA PREMIER LEAGUE
Sheffield United v Nottingham Forest
SATURDAY 24th OCTOBER 1992, KICK-OFF 3.00 p.m.
Today's Match Sponsor: M. P. BURKE p.l.c.
OFFICIAL PROGRAMME
£1.20

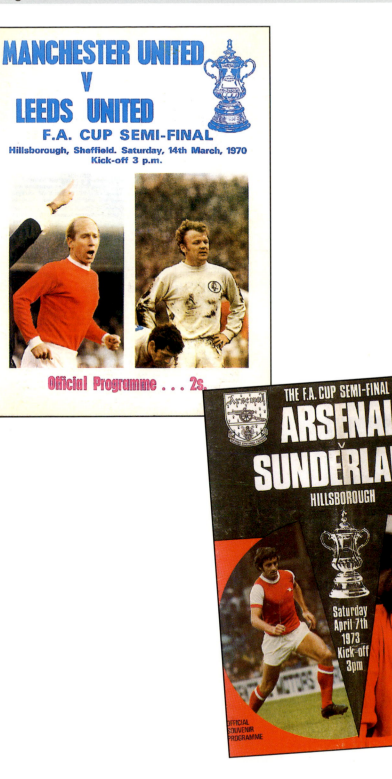

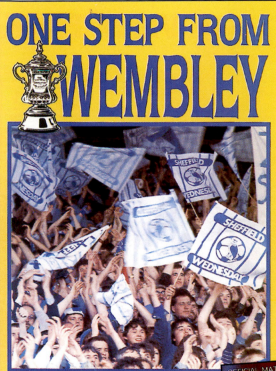

A souvenir of our 1986 Semi Final app

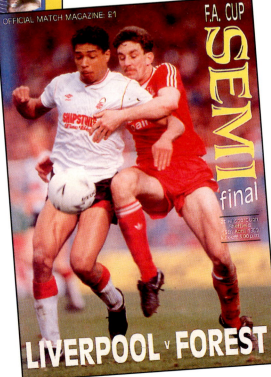

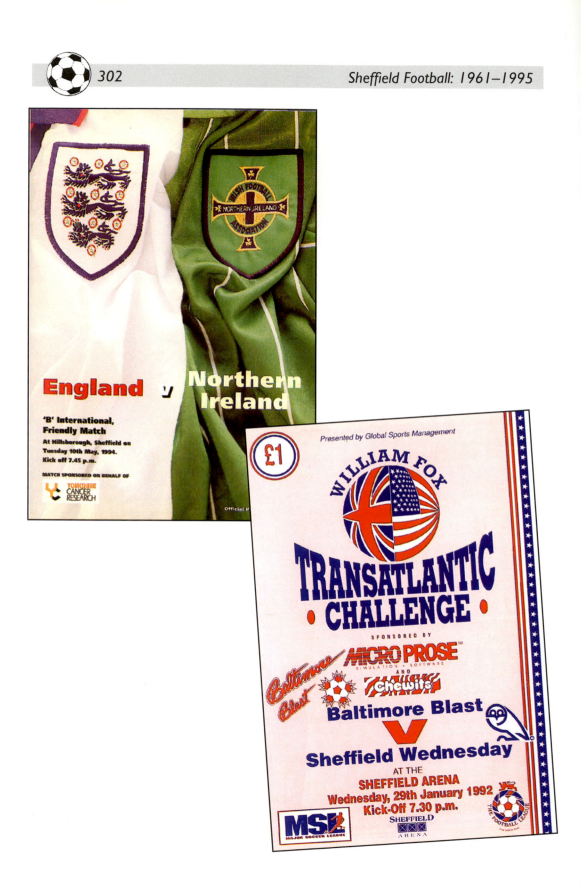

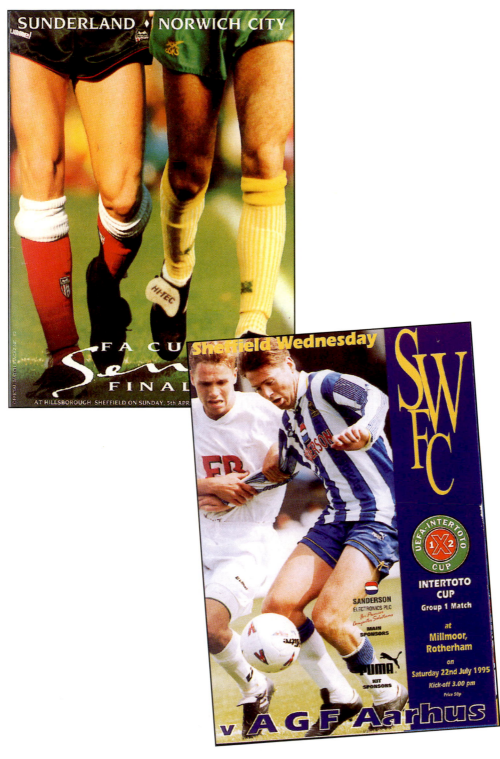